CW00742531

MY GRANDAD MY HERO

MY GRANDAD MY HERO

Paul Burchell

Riverside Publishing Solutions

ISBN (Hardback): 978-1-913012-47-2
ISBN (Paperback): 978-1-913012-48-9
ISBN (ePub): 978-1-913012-49-6

The moral right of Paul Burchell to be identified as the author of this work has been asserted in accordance with the Copyright, Designs and Patents Act 1988.

Published in association with Riverside Publishing Solutions, Salisbury, UK

www.riversidepublishingsolutions.com

Printed and bound in the UK.

CONTENTS

Acknowledgements xi

Foreword xv

Preface xvii

Introduction xix

Chapter 1 1

The birth and childhood of Ernest Burchell 1

The national and international context 7

Ernest's early life 14

The onset of World War 1 18

Chapter 2 21

Ernest's decision to enlist in the Royal Wiltshire Yeomanry 21

Ernest's initial army training 25

Training based at Winchester College and other locations 28

Events in the first months of the war 39

The continuing war, 1914 40

Training in 1915, including in trench warfare 42

The war in the first half of 1915 46

The war on the sea and the bombing of London 48

The Yeomans in the summer of 1915 49

The war in the autumn of 1915 50

Training in the art of bombing and mass military warfare manoeuvres 52

The war in early 1916 57

Chapter 3 59

Ernest is sent to the war 59

The Yeomans' initial routine in Belgium and France 62

CONTENTS

The war at sea	63
Ernest's squadron lays communication cables	66
The work of The Royal Engineer Signal Service	67
The Battle of the Somme, July 1916	68
Life for the Yeomans in the Somme area	71
The Mle Hotchkiss machine gun	73
Ernest becomes a dispatch rider	75
The use of pigeons for communication	79
Vital supplies during wartime	82
Further developments in the war from August 1916	83
The Yeomans' support for front-line regiments	86
Ernest at the end of the Battle of the Somme	88
The national and wider political situation	91
The war on the Eastern Front	93
Chapter 4	**95**
The winter of 1916–17	95
B Squadron in January 1917	97
The War in the Spring of 1917	98
Civil unrest in Russia	100
The USA joins the War	101
The Battle of Arras	103
The beginning of life at the front line for the Yeomans	105
The problems of the French Army	107
The Third Battles of Ypres (Passchendaele).	109
The Yeomans in Dunkirk	111
The Battles of Ypres and Passchendaele continue	113
Disbandment of the Yeomanry Regiment and time off in Rouen	118
Bad weather conditions hamper fighting	120
Ernest begins to serve in the trenches	121
Routine in the trenches	126
Continuing life in the trenches	130
My own commemoration of Passchendaele	131
The outcome of the Battle of Passchendaele	132

Chapter 5   135

The Battle of Cambrai   135

Further logistical problems with the advance.   137

The Wiltshires' training exercises   139

The Lewis machine gun   141

Artillery fire   145

My Grandad in the trenches again   151

The prospect of another winter at war   153

The New Year 1918   154

The role of the Padre   154

Work and rest   157

The use of gas   158

The War in January and February, 1918   160

German planning for the major offensive   164

Chapter 6   167

Preparations for conflict   168

Ernest in March 1918   170

Musketry practice   173

The German enemy   175

New improved German tactics   179

The first day of fighting, March 1918   179

The evaluation of Days one and two   182

Day three   186

The army behind the front   188

Prisoners of War   188

Retreat   189

Ernest survives a second retreat   190

The 6th Wiltshires are withdrawn from the front line   191

The German advance but to their cost   193

Chapter 7   197

The struggle continues   197

The wounded   199

CONTENTS

Field Marshal Haig reacts to a desperate situation   201

The Spanbroekmolen crater   202

Ernest's supreme act of bravery   209

The Red Baron   211

Counting the cost   213

The end of May and back to the trenches   216

Shell Shock   221

Chapter 8   225

Ernest is treated for the effects of combat   225

The war rages on   227

Ernest is awarded the Distinguished Conduct Medal   229

Allied success   232

The Spanish Flu   234

The Second Battle of the Marne   235

The role of the sniper   238

The Battle of Amiens   243

Chapter 9   249

The Wiltshires' position on 3rd of September 1918   249

The German opponents and Kurt Schlüter   250

Action begins   257

An initial lack of response from the Germans   260

The British advance   261

The Germans continue to hold their ground   263

Ernest is wounded   265

Kurt surrenders   267

Ernest's stretcher is carried by the German Prisoners of War   269

Ernest's injuries   270

The outcome of the battle   270

Chapter 10   273

Ernest's treatment   273

Marie Curie   278

Blood transfusions   281

A bullet is removed   282

Recovery   284

Return to England is necessary for Ernest   285

Arrival at Southampton and recuperation in West Yorkshire   287

Changes in English society   289

Recovery and the Citation in the London Gazette   292

Meanwhile in the trenches   294

News of impending victory reaches West Yorkshire   296

The last battle and victory   297

Press reactions in Leeds   298

Chapter 11   301

The meaning of victory   301

Rebellion from the Chinese Labour Corps   301

The surviving soldiers return home   302

Ernest moves to a convalescent home, is discharged and demobbed   303

Ernest returns to civilian life   306

The state of the nations at the turn of the year 1918–1919   307

A happy ending   309

Epilogue   313

Bibliography   321

ACKNOWLEDGEMENTS

I am so grateful to my wife, April Burchell, for her help, encouragement and support in writing this book. She has tolerated many days alone whilst I have been in my study writing.

I'd like to give my sincere thanks to Ernest's two surviving daughters and their husbands, namely my Aunt Olive Richards and her husband Jim, and my Aunt Margaret Yates and her husband Peter. They have provided me with historical documents relating to Ernest's war records. They have also given me access to photographs and family tree details, together with a chronology of events from Ernest's childhood to when he married my Grandmother, Elizabeth Leese.

I also thank my cousin Peter Richards for providing photos of the bullet that was extracted from Ernest's chest, and allowing me to photograph his war medals.

My thanks to Professor Geoff Eley of the University of Michigan, Ann Arbor, America, who is my second cousin. He gave me useful advice for my research on German history.

Thanks also to my other second cousins Ruth Eley, and Janet Mellor, who provided family history on Grandma Elizabeth's background, together with photographs. Janet has kindly edited the text. I am particularly indebted to Janet, for her patience and teaching skills, she spent hours with me reviewing the text, the presentation and lay out of this book is down to her.

I'd like to thank my brother Jonathan Burchell for the kind loan of Ernest's medal certificate.

I am indebted to a family friend, John Black BMBS, BAC (Hons), MRCA, PGA, an eminent surgical and transplant surgeon of Leicester

General Hospital, for sharing his medical knowledge on historical medical techniques and surgical procedures.

In addition, I would like to offer special thanks to:

- the Archivist Suzanne Foster of Winchester College. She kindly provided historical photos of the Wiltshire Yeomans encamped at the College in 1914.
- Jack and Molly Smith and the late Nigel Woodrow, local historians in Wiltshire, who kindly provided photos of the soldiers billeted at Forest Row near Ashdown Forest.
- Ann Crowne Lloyds Register Foundation for providing photos of SS Rossetti.
- The Commonwealth War Graves Commission for allowing me to use their map of the Battle of Lys 1918.
- Steve Cosslett of Electrostatic Document Analysis for his work on the postcards from Rouen.
- Tony Noble, a specialist in antique firearms.
- Michael Woods, an ex-colleague and military historian, who guided me through the archives at Kew, and recommended several very good reference books. He also assisted with the final proofread.
- Phil Franks, an ex-colleague and friend, who helped me to design the book cover, and compile the QR code tribute to the 'fallen' of the Wiltshire Regiments.
- the organisers of the Centenary Commemoration of the Battle of Passchendaele, funded by the BBC in 2017, who invited 5,000 relatives to attend.
- Great war digital.com – Linesman Trench Maps who kindly gave permission for the trench maps in this book.
- Thanks to my neighbour Sue Broughton who drew the Trench scene in Chapter 9.
- Chris Elwell of Genus graphics, who constructed early PDF files of this book.

- Chris Jackson and his staff of Leicester Police Reprographics department who compiled the finalised digital version of this book.
- Sam Thomas who was the Trumpet soloist for the QR code tribute to the fallen men of the Wiltshire Regiments.

Thanks also to the staff of a number of museums, libraries and archives who have provided valuable information. They are listed in the bibliography.

FOREWORD

A grandson's heartfelt tribute to a courageous and very decent man who honourably volunteered to serve his nation throughout World War 1, experiencing privation, hardship and loss while fighting on the Western Front as a cavalryman, dispatch rider and infantry soldier. Ernest Burchell was awarded the Distinguished Conduct Medal, was gravely wounded and calmly tackled all sorts of challenges. Paul's book about Ernest's war-time training and subsequent military actions is a very intimate, poignant testament about his grandfather whose experiences will strike a chord with any reader.

Brigadier Ian McGill CBE

PREFACE

The purpose of writing this book was to study the early life of my Grandfather, Ernest Burchell, and to see what kind of Britain he grew up in. What were the events that led to the World War 1, and of course what part did Ernest play?

I have tried my best to put myself in his position, standing on the duck boards in the bottom of the trenches, knee deep in mud in Belgium and France. What experiences did he have? I had very few accounts from Ernest as he was reluctant to talk about the subject. He broke down in tears on several occasions.

The few accounts he did give me are recorded verbatim in this book. Naturally they can't be precise, as my recollection of what he told me dates back to when I had tea with Ernest in the 1970's.

I've tried to approach the task of writing this book in a similar way to conducting a police investigation. I have researched the information from several different sources, and where possible applied provenance as to the accuracy of the data. Having done this, I constructed a timeline of events in a chronological order. The story follows two paths, the first being what Ernest was doing, in parallel with the second, namely events of the conflict as they took place.

I've tried not to overburden the reader with too many facts and figures, as there are abundant reference books which do this job a lot better than I could ever do. My book is not meant to be a reference book, but it tries to give insight into how individuals like Ernest coped with the horrors of trench warfare, in other words I've tried to see events from a human point of view.

I hope you all enjoy reading this book. It will be my legacy for future generations of the Burchell family, so that they may appreciate the contribution of what one of their forefathers did in this terrible conflict.

INTRODUCTION

The year was 1975, and a young impressionable teenage schoolboy walked past the village church, as it chimed four times. He continued his journey down the lane to his grandfather's farm in Hartshorne, South Derbyshire.

With his school satchel hanging over his shoulder, Paul entered the old farmhouse and walked into his grandfather's kitchen. The table had already been set, a whole loaf was on the bread board, waiting to be sliced. There was a selection of preserves on the table, including Paul's favourite, cherry jam. The tea pot and cups had been made ready.

This had become a normal routine for Paul, who had formed a close relationship with his grandfather, Ernest Burchell. In his late years Ernest had poor eyesight and relied on Paul to slice the bread and help with the tea.

Ernest was now nearly 87 years old, a remarkable man who had been a farmer for over 55 years. He and his wife Elizabeth had raised five children. Sadly, Elizabeth, who Ernest affectionately called 'Bessy', had just passed away. He would never get over this sad loss.

Paul glanced through the kitchen window and saw Ernest slowly walking up the garden path. The basket under his arm contained freshly laid eggs. He had just returned from feeding his chickens in the bottom paddock. The front door opened and then closed, and an old man walked into the kitchen. He was out of breath. Years of heavy work had taken its toll. His hands were still covered in the wet chicken mash feed as he walked to the kitchen sink. He greeted Paul and asked if he'd had a good day at school.

'When are you going to ask this April Brooks for tea? I should love to see her,' Ernest asked, Paul blushed. This was a frequently asked question.

Paul had innocently declared his undying love for April, and as a result, Ernest had great fun goading his grandson.

For the next hour Ernest would have a captive audience. Paul loved to listen to the old stories and Ernest's opinions on life in general.

On this particular day Paul had bought some homework back with him in his satchel. He was doing a project on World War 2. Clearly this subject was still on his mind as he tentatively asked Ernest about his part in the Great War.

Today was different. His grandad was in an unusually good mood. On previous attempts Paul had been rebuked for bringing up the subject. On this day Paul managed to prise another story from his grandad who shuffled awkwardly in his chair as he relayed the account of when he won his Distinguished Conduct Medal (DCM) at Messines Ridge in 1918.

Paul sat fascinated and in awe of his grandad. The conversation was going well and Paul probed Ernest for more detail, but then Paul's next question killed the conversation 'How many Germans did you kill with the Lewis gun, Grandad?' For a brief moment Ernest was back in that trench with his ten comrades, and Paul's last question jarred Ernest back to reality.

His whole mood changed; his breathing became shallower. Ernest looked across the kitchen table at Paul, and tears began to fall down his cheeks. The colour had drained from his face. 'I don't want to talk about it anymore!' came the stern reply. A strange silence followed, and Paul knew the conversation was now over. Ernest went and sat in his old armchair and slipped into a deep sleep, as he often did.

Paul sat watching the old man opposite. He had a mixture of feelings. Paul was too young to appreciate the full horrors of war, but he loved his grandad dearly, and could not begin to understand his modesty. Ernest Burchell was going to be by far the biggest influence on this young boy's life. Paul would grow up with his grandad's values.

Ernest Burchell died a year later in 1976, the year of the drought. Paul had his first job at a nearby farm and was inconsolable at the news of his grandad's death. He chose not to attend the funeral.

I write this book in dedication to you, Grandad Burchell. I will always love you. I'll never forget those afternoons in the old farmhouse and the love and guidance you gave me.

I want to find out for myself why you got so emotional when we talked about the Great War. It is for this reason that I write this book which I dedicate to you, and to all the soldiers you fought with.

Chapter 1

The birth and childhood of Ernest Burchell

My story starts in a little thatched cottage at number 20 The Marsh, Calne. This was a hamlet on the northern edge of the town of Calne in Wiltshire.

It is Thursday the 4th of October 1888. The Burchell household awakes to the sound of a newborn baby boy crying. The mother, Ann Burchell, takes a sigh of relief as she cradled the infant in her arms. Standing next to her is her proud husband Alan Burchell. This new baby was their 6th, who was named Ernest Burchell.

Alan Burchell was employed as a ploughman and general farm labourer for a local farm in Calne. He was 37 years old when Ernest was born. Alan and his wife Ann had been married for 16 years.

It was no easy task raising babies in the late 1800's. Infant mortality was still high. A lot of mothers died giving birth. There was no National Health Service or family support from the state, only the 'Poor House.'

When Alan Burchell grew up, it was common for children living in rural villages in Britain to do casual work on nearby farms. This naturally had to fit in with school work. Children often as young as seven years of age were employed scaring crows and other birds from the newly planted crops, and emerging corn and vegetables.

As Alan grew older, he is likely to have progressed to 'stable boy'. As the name suggests, he would have fed and cleaned the many farm horses. It was not unusual for a boy of eight or nine years to start ploughing the fields, so when Ernest was born, his father Alan, had probably been ploughing fields for over 25 years.

Alan and Ann Burchell outside 20 The Marsh, Calne

By now Alan Burchell had a reputation of being a very good ploughman. He took pride in his work, ploughing was a skilled occupation.

'My Dad was a very good ploughman. It was a recognised skill at the time. He used to enter local ploughing matches and won a few of these. He worked two heavy draught horses which pulled a single *furrow plough. He was lucky if he managed to plough an acre per day. He must have walked miles ploughing during the autumn and spring. When I was a little boy, mother and I used to meet him in the field and he used to put me on one of the horse's backs, so I could ride home to the farmyard. This is when I first developed my love for horses.'*

Ernest's father was the breadwinner and the family had to manage on his farm labourer's wage which would have been about 12 shillings a week. Just to give you an idea of their family budget:

A typical weekly rent would be 5 shillings and 6 pence
A hundredweight of coal (50kg) would have cost 1 shilling and 6 pence
A loaf of bread was about 5 pence
Butter was about 1 shilling per pound

Farm wages were by no means the highest paid employment at the time and Alan and Ann, like so many families, would have had to be thrifty and careful with their money. Farm work was physically very hard. Many of the farms in the area would have employed several workers per farm.

With the birth of Ernest, his mother Ann had to look after all six children. She had four other sons, William aged 14, Frank aged 10, Frederick aged 4 and Walter aged 2. She had two daughters Ellen aged 8 and Edith aged 2. Therefore, there would not have been much space in that thatched cottage. The children would have had to share beds.

Thatched cottages were common during this period. One of the benefits was that they were a lot warmer in the winter than slate roofed houses. It is also likely the Burchell's would have had a similar fireplace to the one featured in the picture.

I can only speculate as to the contents of the Burchells' cottage, because it was demolished sometime in the 1950's and 1960's. The area is now an industrial estate.

A typical lead grate fireplace

Ann Burchell would have had to use her fireplace for many functions, such as drying clothes, heating up water for washing clothes, cooking food, and heating irons to iron clothes. This fireplace would probably be the only heat source in the house. Ann would have even used the ashes to put in a copper bedpan to warm the beds in extremely cold weather. The children would have taken it in turns to wash in a zinc bath in front of the fire.

The electric light bulb had been invented by Thomas Edison in 1879 but electrical power was not available in general households until well into the next century. The Burchell's would have to make do with oil burning lamps and candles for lighting.

The Burchell's, like so many similar families in rural Britain, had a modest income, and they could certainly afford the basics like bread and dripping, tea and sugar, but they would not have been able to have meat more than once a week.

As far as schooling was concerned, Ernest was lucky enough to have been born during a period of significant change in the education system. In 1870 elementary education was made free. This would indeed seem fortunate but the 1880 Education Act made it compulsory for all children to attend school up to the age of 10 years. This had a significant impact on very poor families, as young children were no longer allowed to go out to work and thus bring much needed income to poor families.

Ernest is likely to have attended a state sponsored school in Calne, possibly John Bentley's School, but this has not been confirmed. He would have been taught the three basic 'R's, namely reading, writing and arithmetic. The pupils had to write with the right hand. Pupils started with slate boards and wrote with chalk. They would copy a sentence written on the black board at the front of the class. As they developed, the pupils would then write using writing quills, dipping the nibs into ink wells on their tables. This was the age of beautiful handwriting. Sadly, with the advent of computers in our modern day, this skill is in decline.

There were a number of sayings which were popular at the time, for example
'Cleanliness is next to Godliness'.
'Children should be seen and not heard'.

The child would have to stand up in class and wait for permission to speak. There was also a strong religious theme in their education. Strict discipline was maintained in the class. Any child caught with dirty hands would have twenty lashings.

What was it like for young Ernest growing up as a child? I suppose he had plenty of siblings to play with, but none of the mod cons that today's children take for granted. The first radio entertainment programme was not aired until 1922. Television was not invented until 1927. Children learnt to play outside, birds' nesting, tick, hide and seek, hopscotch, playing with rudimentary spinning tops, skipping, football, cricket, marbles, hoop rolling and swings in the wood. When the weather was

*The above picture shows young Ernest wearing his 'Sunday best' with his sisters
Edith and Nelly. He is very well turned out! At a guess Ernest was about 8–9
years old when this picture was taken, making it about 1896/1897.*

bad Ernest would play with his brothers and sisters inside the cottage
at snakes and ladders, draughts, cards, dominoes, and ludo. I played
draughts and whist with Grandad when I was a young boy. He never lost
his appetite for these pastimes.

Our generation is familiar with these leisure activities but with the
passage of time young people now spend less and less time outdoors.
A personal comment, and perhaps I am old fashioned, but I think this
is sad, especially with the problems of obesity which now prevail in our
modern society.

Children were not allowed to play on a Sunday. They had to attend Sunday School, sometimes twice on a Sunday. Grandad and his family were Methodists and he and his family would have no doubt attended the local Chapel in the area. Going to Chapel later on in his life had a significant effect on his future destiny.

The national and international context

Ernest and his brothers and sisters were bought up in Victorian England. 1888, the year of Grandad's birth, was the 50th year of Queen Victoria's reign. She was now 69 years old. Her husband, Albert, the Prince Consort, had been dead for 26 years. She reigned over a population of Britain of around 39 million people. Her Empire was vast, by far the biggest in the world at the time.

Queen Victoria had nine children. She was not the best of mothers, refusing to breast feed any of them, in fact she employed a wet nurse to breast feed her newborn children. She never recovered from the grief after the death of Albert. She became very reclusive and controlling of her children, even into their adulthood.

For a period of over 20 years since her husband's death, Queen Victoria carefully chose spouses for her children. She believed in the importance of dynastic marital alliances. It was her and Albert's wish to have a peaceful and stable Europe, with no wars. In order to achieve this, she set about making marriage alliances with the kingdoms of Germany, Russia, Denmark, Norway, Spain, Greece and Romania.

Queen Victoria herself was 'half' German. Her husband Albert, was also her cousin. He was of complete German descent from the Royal House of Saxe-Coburg-Gotha. In private Queen Victoria preferred to speak German.

The big concern for the royal households of Europe at the time was a growing threat of revolution. The British royal family prior to Victoria, had become unpopular with the public. This had concerned both Albert and Victoria who tried to improve their image. They tried to appear to the public as a loving family with strict family values. To some extent they were successful, and their popularity grew.

The last major conflict involving Britain had been the first Boer War which ended in 1881. This brief 10-week conflict had resulted in a humiliating defeat of the British Army. It had come about because of Britain's desire to control trades routes in southern Africa, the race to acquire even more territory than rival colonial powers such as France and Germany, and the discovery of vast mineral wealth in the region. The British had grossly underestimated the fighting prowess of the Dutch speaking settlers who were better known as Boers. The then Prime Minster, William Gladstone, knowing that he could not afford another costly colonial conflict had decided to call an armistice under unfavourable terms for the British.

I was curious to know what major events took place in 1888, the year of Ernest's birth. Queen Victoria's government at the time was the Conservative party headed by the Prime Minister, the Marquis of Salisbury, Robert Cecil.

I was surprised to find out that the year was very eventful. This was the year of the Whitechapel prostitute murders, which were too become known as the infamous 'Jack the Ripper' murders. The first victim on 7th of August 1888 was Martha Tebram. There was much speculation at the time about the perpetrator, and even one of Queen Victoria's grandchildren, Albert Victor, was rumoured to be responsible. However, a visit to the Museum of New Scotland Yard (Room 101) would be very worthwhile for anyone seeking more information about the likely suspect.

In this same year George Eastman designed a camera and subsequently registered the trademark Kodak, receiving a patent. This technology would pave the way for another invention, that of motion pictures.

Louis le Prince filmed the first motion picture in October of 1888. The following year in 1889 heralded the birth of Charles Spencer Chaplin. With this new invention of moving pictures, he would become a famous comic actor, an icon of the silent film era.

A further patent of the year was the Scotsman John Boyde Dunlop's pneumatic bicycle tyre. This invention was a significant step forward. The tyre could absorb shock loads, and cushion the load, important on the uneven roads and tracks of the time. A solid tyre reacts to every bump and hollow. This same technology was used for motor vehicles and commercial lorries. Pneumatic tyres also gave greater traction in poor conditions.

With the advent of better standards of living for the working and middle classes, more leisure time was becoming available. Sporting activities became more popular. William McGregor called a meeting this year to discuss the forming of the Football League. In the same year the Lawn Tennis Association was formed.

The Victorian Age was a period of vast improvements in living conditions for the poor. Working conditions slowly improved. The working week slowly became shorter, and the working man and his family started to be able to save money for leisure activities. With the development of the rail network all over Britain, travel became cheaper for the masses. Victorian seaside towns began to sprout up and flourish.

The country's wealth grew substantially, as did the population. Infant mortality was slowly reduced, and people started to live longer. A major factor was the building of underground sewers, improving health conditions. These were first built in Liverpool, and then progressed to London, and eventually to all the major cities. Drinking water became cleaner as the wells were no longer contaminated by raw sewage. Fewer people died of cholera and typhoid. Diet improved as people had more money to spend on a better food.

Food preservation techniques also had a significant effect on the quality of people's diets as well as impacting on the cost of food. Canned food had surprisingly been available for about 80 years by 1888. This method of food preservation had been pioneered by a British entrepreneur Bryan Donkin. At the request of the British Royal Navy, he successfully invented a process to preserve food in sealed tins. This took place not long after the Napoleonic Wars. I mention this now because whilst the invention was around 80 years old, the canning process had been improved further. In 1810 Peter Durand patented tin coated iron cans. The new sterilisation techniques meant fewer products were contaminated. The public's confidence had grown with this product, as food could be preserved at a more affordable price to the poor.

On a global front there was a 'new' wave of imperialism between 1850 and 1910. European nations occupied vast swathes of the continent of Africa and China and the Middle East. This was largely for prestige and economic advantage. In Africa, Britain had by far the biggest land concessions at 30%, followed by France at 15%, and Portugal 9%. The other nations included Germany, Belgium, and Italy, Netherlands, and Denmark. This race for territory led to friction and envy. Each of the nations, buoyed by their increasing wealth, started to strengthen their armies and navies.

In this period coal was still king. The energy it produced was used to drive the wheels of industry and fuel the Industrial Revolution. The textile factories in Lancashire eventually produced a third of the cotton goods in the world. The forward-thinking factory owners improved living conditions for their workers, even creating the first municipal park for the public to use in Salford. Many towns and cities followed suit.

Meanwhile, and over this same period, there took place the unification of the German states following the Franco-Prussian war in 1871, which was a resounding victory for Prussia. At the Hall of Mirrors in Versailles a new German super state would emerge. The German Emperor, Frederick, was the husband of Queen Victoria's eldest daughter Victoria, the Princess Royal.

In 1888 Frederick lll passed away after a reign of only three months, and his son, Wilhelm, became the new Emperor, Kaiser Wilhelm II. Shortly after becoming Emperor, he dismissed his Chancellor Otto von Bismarck, and embarked on a period of rapid expansion. He instigated a massive build-up of his navy and army, much to the concern of the other European superpowers.

Wilhelm craved acceptance from his grandmother Queen Victoria and the rest of his cousins. To a large extent he was tolerated, but also disliked for his arrogance and outspoken public speeches, which eventually made him more and more alienated. Possibly this fuelled his ambition and determination to be respected.

Massive changes took place in this new Germany. There were massive coal reserves in the Ruhr area at the turn of the century. One in every four tons of coal produced in the world came from Germany. The industrialization of this new country expanded at a rapid pace. Germany emerged as a new superpower to be reckoned with. German products rapidly gained an excellent reputation, and in particular German engineering skills were highly regarded.

It was no accident that this came about due to the rapid growth and development of the German education system. At the time of unification in 1871, Germany had nineteen universities to Britain's five, so over the period leading up to World War 1 the German nation was well placed to face the challenges of the 20th Century. It is true the other nations would catch up, but Germany had a head start.

The German nation had become a clever, resourceful and ambitious. This did not escape the attention of the other imperial superpowers who naturally started to become concerned, if not alarmed.

At the turn of the century Britain was involved on the international scene in two conflicts. The Boxer rebellion in northern China, supposedly a rebellion by the peasants and supported by the Empress Dowager's court, was eventually suppressed by the Western Powers, supported by Japan. China paid a price for this conflict with vast swathes of its territory remaining occupied by the European powers and Japan for years to come.

Then there was the 2nd Boer War in South Africa which began in October 1899. In February 1900 Britain sent 20,000 troops to invade the Orange Free State. Tension had erupted again between the British and the Boer farmers who were ruling an area of the Transvaal which had recently been found to contain the world's largest deposits of gold-bearing ore. This second conflict lasted over 2 and a half years. Lessons had been learnt from the previous conflict. The British soldiers now wore the khaki uniform and gone were the red jackets and white helmets.

This war was costly, but it was finally won by the British, as a result the Boers surrendered on the 31st of May 1902.

Significantly it was during this second conflict that a new invention was used to treat wounded soldiers. The X-ray machine led to a great improvement in the treatment and consequently the recovery rates of injured soldiers.

The discovery of X-rays was made by a German scientist, Wilhelm Conrad Röntgen. He experimented using a 'Crookes tube' which essentially was the discharge of a large electrical current through a vacuum in the sealed glass container. When the current contacted the diode inside, it emitted cathode rays, and one day, by pure chance, he held his hand between his Crookes tube and a piece of barium cyanide platinum coated paper, and was surprised to see the image of his hand, showing all the bones on the paper. This was the very first picture of what was later to be called an X-ray.

The significance of this discovery was not at first appreciated, but scientists eventually saw the true value in that it could be used before operations. The surgeons were able to examine the casualty for the precise location of bullets and shrapnel, and broken bones. The benefits of this new invention were immeasurable. A number of wounded British soldiers during conflicts now had a much better chance of survival.

On the theme of medical science, in this same year an Austrian biologist, Karl Landsteiner, was working at the University of Vienna. During the year 1900 and the following year, he worked as an assistant doctor, carrying out autopsies on patients. He discovered that on some occasions when different patients' blood came into contact, the fluid started to 'clump together' (thicken). This strange phenomenon prompted him to take samples from twenty-five different people. He experimented using a centrifuge and started to mix the twenty-five different donor blood samples. He discovered some of the mixed bloods 'clumped' and some did not. He concluded those that did not clump were compatible, in other words the same blood type. Following further research, he discovered three different blood types which were compatible, naming them blood groups A, B, and C. Later C was changed to O. Suspecting that there were even more blood types, he performed the same experiments on a larger number of donors (about 100 in total). These further experiments led to the discovery of one further blood group, AB.

This pioneering work led to more success with blood transfusions. Chief beneficiaries were mothers who had just given birth and who had haemorrhaged, and casualties and patients during operations, who could now be operated upon and have a transfusion during the process.

The discovery of these different blood groups meant that patients who received transfusions where more likely to recover, as their bodies would not reject the blood because it was compatible with their own.

Other events in 1900 included the formation of the British Labour Party. The working class now had a political voice, and this new force in British politics aimed for social equality. In April, the first Daily Express newspaper was sold to the public. A further development for children was the prohibition through the Mines Act for those under the age of 13 years from working down the mines.

Every generation has individuals who make a significant impact on events in history. Such a person was Winston Churchill, an up-and-coming aristocrat, who in December 1900 was elected MP for Oldham. He had made his name as a war correspondent during the Boer War, and like his father Randolph Churchill, embarked on a career in politics.

Not far into the new century brought the sad death of Queen Victoria at the age of 81. She had ruled for just under 64 years. She passed away at Osborne House, her palace on the Isle of Wight. I have tried to explore the suggestion that she died in the arms of Kaiser Wilhelm. The evidence is inconclusive. All of her family were present at the time of her death, including her surviving children and a number of her grandchildren, of which there were forty-two. When the doctor certified death, Queen Victoria's body was placed into her coffin by her son Albert, and two of her grandsons, Kaiser Wilhelm and Arthur, Duke of Connaught. At her request they placed a plaster cast hand of her beloved Albert, his dressing gown, and a selection of photos inside the coffin.

In summary, there were many events that took place in the years of Ernest's early childhood. None of them would have had any real impact on young Ernest's life at the time. They are mentioned because they would affect him in years to come and probably save his life.

Ernest's early life

The town of Calne is located between the chalkland of the western edge of the Marlborough Downs in North Wiltshire. In the 1880's the town had a population of just over 5,100 people. Calne was a significant hub for the woollen industry. The town's woollen trade can be traced back as far as medieval times. It has rich and fertile land ideal for growing arable crops and rearing livestock. The River Marden runs through the town. With the advent of railways in the 1870's, the town flourished. There would have been a plentiful number of jobs and employment in the area.

A famous family in Calne was the Harris family. Brother Charles and Tom amalgamated their businesses to form CT Harris Ltd, purveyors of pork products. Their success was helped by the very good canal and rail network, and their business rapidly expanded. The Harris brothers made the town of Calne synonymous with quality pork products. There was a distinctive smell in the air when pies were being baked. Locals have told me that on days when they slaughtered the pigs, the roadside drains would be overloaded, and pedestrians could often see blood running down the gutters.

The turn of the century saw young Ernest leave school at the ripe old age of 12. In this same year he had his first employment as an apprentice baker and delivery boy for one of the bakers in Calne. Grandad once said to me:

'It was whilst I worked at the baker's that I learnt my trade. We perfected the recipe for lardy cake which was very popular. I couldn't understand when I moved to Derbyshire that no one had heard of it.'

There were several bakers in Calne at this time, and it has not been possible to find out which one Ernest worked at. Needless to say, within a very short time, Ernest would know every street in the town like the back of his hand. I can say from personal experience that Ernest baked very good bread, and of course very good lardy cake.

Ernest remained in employment at the bakers for several years. Having mastered the skill of baking, he and his older brother Walter and older sister Ellen ('Nelly') left Wiltshire and bought a bakery business in Church Street, Hartshorne, South Derbyshire. They shared this address with Joseph and Mary Yeomans and their two children, Lesley and Sidney. It is possible that this family ran a milk round from the same address. It could be that the Yeomans helped with the running costs of the business by paying the Burchell's rent.

This must have been a bold move on the part of Ernest, Walter and Ellen, to leave the family home in Wiltshire and set up in business 125 miles away in South Derbyshire. The three Burchell's are shown on the 1911 voters list as living in Church Street, Hartshorne. At this time Walter was 25 years old, Ellen 31 and Ernest 23.

The move to Hartshorne would prove to have a significant impact on Grandad's life, as it was in this village that he met his one true love, Elizabeth Leese, whom he fondly referred to as 'Bessy.'

Elizabeth Leese was the daughter of a miller family who originated from north Staffordshire. The Leese family had been prominent millers in that area for over 100 years. They ran the first mill on the River Trent at Knypersley, a village near Biddulph. Elizabeth was born some four years after Ernest in 1892. Her parents Daniel and Mary had ten children. 'Bessy' had three sisters, Selina Mary and Lydia, and six brothers, James, George, Arthur, Albert, John, and Daniel. It was a big family, but typical in those days.

The Leese family moved from Knypersley to Little Aston near Sutton Coldfield for a brief period, and then moved to Greysich Farm in Bretby, South Derbyshire. This must have been sometime between 1897 to 1899, as Elizabeth attended the primary school at Bretby before moving to a high school in Burton upon Trent.

The Leese family photo.
Elizabeth is sitting on the grass in front of her father.

During this period, the Leese family were active members of Hartshorne Methodist Chapel. My Grandma Elizabeth became the piano player and organist. But by far her greatest gift was that of singing. Naturally, she sang in the choir. Her reputation as a fine contralto singer was well known throughout the area.

Greysich was a 200-acre farm located in a beautiful area of South Derbyshire, nestling between the picturesque undulating hills of Repton Bottoms and the ancient Viking settlement of Repton. In the 1911 census, the Leese family is listed as living at Greysich Farm. Elizabeth Leese was employed as a milkmaid. She would spend many hours sitting on a milking stool, hand milking the cows, collecting the milk in a bucket.

I must confess to the reader that I am not a very religious person. However, such was the influence of my Grandad Ernest Burchell, that I was made to attend Sunday School at this chapel from the age of 4 to 10. I resented this because I was a little boy full of energy, who just wanted to play on his grandfather's farm. However, clearly the chapel in Hartshorne

My Grandma Elizabeth Leese, around the time that Ernest met her

was very significant for Grandad, as it was here that he met and fell in love with his future wife Bessy. He spoke to me about her.

'*Your Grandma had a beautiful voice. I first set eyes on her at Hartshorne Chapel where she sang in the choir, she had a low voice for a woman, it sounded so lovely*'.

It must have been love at first sight, but Grandad never spoke of his romance with Bessy. His generation were very discrete about these things. His comments about her beautiful contralto voice have been substantiated locally.

On Wednesday the 13th of March 1912 there was a fund-raising event at Burton Town Hall in aid of The National Society for the Prevention of Cruelty to Children. I have the privilege of owning a copy of a programme where Grandma is listed as one of the soloists, singing 'How changed the vision' by Handel in part 1, and 'Sunshine and rain' by Blumenthal.

For some reason, unknown to me, Grandad and his brother and sister moved back to Wiltshire between 1911 and 1914. They purchased a greengrocer's business at 3 The Parade, Marlborough.

A number of questions occur to me. Why did he leave Hartshorne? Was it his intention to establish the greengrocery business in Marlborough, then get engaged to Elizabeth and bring her to Wiltshire? I will never know the answer to these questions but tragically world events were to take over Ernest Burchell's destiny.

The onset of World War 1

Further afield during this period, King Edward VII, the successor of Queen Victoria, died in 1910, and George V succeeded the throne. The new King witnessed increasing tension in the Balkan states, which unbeknown to him were to have far reaching consequences in the coming years. Over several centuries the area had been a hotbed of conflict. Serbia in particular had been occupied by so many different empires, including the Byzantines, Ottomans, Slavs, Venetians, and Bulgarians. The whole area was subject to many conflicts and land disputes, the boundaries forever changing. It was a 'ticking time bomb'.

On the morning of 28th of June 1914 Archduke Franz Ferdinand of Austria, heir presumptive to the Austro–Hungarian throne, was travelling on a state visit with his wife Sophia, Duchess of Hohenberg, in a convoy of cars in Sarajevo, Bosnia. Their intention was to visit members of their party in hospital who had earlier been victims of a terrorist bomb attack.

They took a wrong turn on the journey and the chauffeur stopped the car on the side of the road in order to seek new directions.

Standing on the pavement next to the car was a member of 'The Young Bosnian Secret Society'. His name was Gavrilo Princip. This young student reached into his pocket and pulled out a revolver, shooting into the royal car and immediately killing Sophia. He then aimed at Ferdinand and fired his gun. Ferdinand died shortly afterwards.

The news of the assassination travelled rapidly throughout Europe. The suspected terrorists were all rounded up. Over the period that followed a total of over 5,000 men were arrested. Gavrilo Princip escaped execution because he was 27 days too young. Not having reached the age of 21 he was spared the hangman's noose. Many of the 5,000 suspected terrorists are not so lucky.

The irony is that the Austrian royal couple were not very popular, but even more ironic was the fact that Archduke Franz Ferdinand of Austria was opposed to any future conflict with Russia. His ambition was for a tripartite state with Austria, Hungary and the Balkan States. He never lived to see this ambition fulfilled. However, the death of the royal couple had massive immediate and longer-term consequences for the lives of many people throughout the world.

Young Ernest

Young Lizzie

Chapter 2

Ernest's decision to enlist in the Royal Wiltshire Yeomanry

Between 1913 and 1914 Walter, Ernest and their sister Nelly moved back to Wiltshire, purchasing a greengrocer's business at 3 The Parade, in Marlborough, Wiltshire, currently an ironmonger's shop.

As we all know, world events took a turn for the worst in 1914. A lot of major powers were looking towards the colonial achievements of the British Empire which presided over 23% of the world population at the time. I mention this figure because in the coming years this massive pool of human resources would be advantageous to Britain, her empire and her allies. In the coming years there would be a huge demand for men and resources.

There was one particular power, Germany, headed by Kaiser Wilhelm II, that aimed to gain extra territory in order to compete with his two cousins, Tsar Nicholas II of Russia and King George V of Britain. The German military leaders exploited the Kaiser's ambition, and he allowed them to expand the army, navy, and air force rapidly.

Over the period prior to World War 1 the major powers had set up alliances with each other in the hope that this would prevent a major war. Ironically, these alliances would eventually compel the major powers to be dragged into a world war.

The circumstances leading up to World War 1 are well documented, but what really amazed me was the public's response to Lord Kitchener's call to arms, which was made three days after Britain declared war on Germany on the 7th of August 1914.

The world has changed significantly in the last 106 years. Back in 1914 the population of Britain was about 42 million people. Its people had become accustomed to the successes of the British Empire and the wealth it brought. The broad section of the British public, in comparison to today, was far more patriotic, yet there remained a huge disparity in living standards between the working classes and the ruling elite.

The word 'patriotism' was a popular word. However, a lot of soldiers chose to enlist as they saw the war as an opportunity to travel overseas. In their eyes the war would be an 'adventure', and in any case it would be over by Christmas!

Let us not forget the poor families and the poverty that was still rife in Britain. Many families had small incomes and a lot of mouths to feed. Men who enlisted from these back grounds were clearly malnourished. I suggest that it was not patriotism alone in their minds, but it was rather an opportunity to earn a wage and have three meals a day. They filled out and put on weight. In a relatively short space of time in the army, it was noticed that they went from skinny adolescents to well-formed men. Many young men grew an inch taller and put on a stone in weight within six months. However, there clearly was an overpowering sense of duty and loyalty to King and Country. Ernest and the young men of Calne were no exception.

The influence of the press would no doubt have also made a considerable impact on young men's decisions to enlist. The Germans were labelled the aggressors. How dare they demand free and unhindered passage through Belgium in order that their armies could invade France? It was a time of rapid expansion for the newspapers, as the public were desperate for news. Ernest would no doubt have read the 'Wiltshire Times', dated the 8th August 1914. The headlines read:

'Great Britain stands by France against Germany's aggression. The insolent and bullying actions of Germany caused Great Britain to enter the arena of war which is feared will devastate Europe.'

A lengthy article follows which goes into detail about the attempts made by the then Home Secretary, Sir Edward Grey, to avoid war.

'Sir Edward read out to Parliament the telegram from the King of the Belgians making a 'supreme appeal' to King George to safeguard the integrity of Belgium.'

There were other articles offering assurances to the reader, including that of Irish Nationalist John Redmond. As the Wiltshire Herald reported

'The whole of Ireland would stand by Britain'.

There were also reassurances from New Yorkers, yet on the 8th of August 1914 America declared itself to be a neutral nation. The then President Woodrow Wilson was against the colonialist policies of the European superpowers and continued to supply food to Germany for the early part of the war. Other headlines read:

'Support from Overseas Dominions' and 'Superior strength of the British Royal Navy'.

All of this would have been reassuring to the reader. The young naive minds of these raw recruits would be brainwashed into thinking that Britain and her allies could not possibly lose this war.

The Wiltshire Times also goes into detail about the success of the Belgium Army to halt or slow down the German advance and inflict heavy losses on them. The newspaper included a 'Call to Arms' and advice for householders to avoid waste, with reassurances that there would be plenty of food. These carefully worded articles were designed to stir the emotions of young adventurous men, who would have been 'chomping at the bit' to join up.

On the morning of Wednesday the 5th of August 1914 Ernest Burchell went to the recruiting office, and together with a number of other men from Marlborough enlisted in the Royal Wiltshire Yeomanry. This was a mounted cavalry regiment, which, at the time, was the oldest Yeomanry Regiment in the country.

Ernest at the start of his army service. Note the moustache. The British Army rule was that if you could grow a moustache, it was compulsory.

Ernest was to receive the grand sum of 7 shillings per week. However, there would be deductions, in total 1 shilling and 6 pence for insurance, food and clothing. He enlisted as Private 971 Burchell.

B Squadron 1/1st Royal Wiltshire Yeomanry
Photo with the kind permission of the Swindon Archives

Ernest's initial army training

Ernest was to become part of 'B' Squadron which itself was divided into four troops. His sergeants were Sgt. Palmer, Sgt. Drewett, their immediate supervisor was 2nd Lt. Irwin. Number 1 section comprised of Pvt. Maisey, Pvt. A. Mace, Pvt. H. Mace, Pvt. Palmer, Pvt. Hillier, Pvt. Langfear and Pvt. Burchell.

I have been able to obtain these details from the squadron's diary kept by Squadron Major Charles Selwyn Awdry. This list was taken from the diary entry dated the 13th of October 1916.

The squadron naturally had HQ officers together with a transport troop and other attached officers. The total of 'B' Squadron as of the 13th of October 1916 was 136 men. The list changes numerous times over the period that follows.

The squadron had been made up of volunteers from the Wiltshire towns of Devizes, Marlborough, Lavington and Urchfont. In September alone over 5,000 men volunteered in Devizes. Amongst the squadron there were, however, soldiers who had pervious military experience.

I have no doubt it would have taken some time before Ernest and his squadron were fully equipped. His kit would have been similar to that of an infantryman.

Essentially from top to bottom the kit was:

1. Cloth cap, oil impregnated, to include the badge of the Wiltshires on the front. This would be replaced by the 'Brody' steel helmet at the end of 1915.
2. Vest
3. Blue/grey standard issue shirt
4. Khaki trousers – supplied with belt and braces
5. Socks
6. 'Putty' – this was a cloth rolled around the leg up to the knee
7. Brown leather ammunition boots/riding spurs
8. Khaki tunic together with four large pockets
9. Army great coat
10. Waterproof cape
11. Body bandola, capable of carrying 150 rounds of .303 bullets
12. Haversack – to contain food/rations, field dressing bandages etc
13. Water bottle
14. Rifle to be stored in holster attached to horse
15. Cavalry sabre

In addition, there would be the usual riding harness for his horse and grooming and feeding equipment. Following initial training, it would be Ernest's responsibility to account for and maintain all of this equipment.

Ernest's training was in two parts:

1. Individual training – this would take place over a period of about four months.
2. Collective training – this would take place over a period of eight months.

The initial course would cover a number of subjects which included 'the development of discipline and soldiering spirit'.

- When at the barracks individual duties would be, for example, sentry duties and defence of the barracks, upkeep of equipment, tidiness, minimum standards of uniform and appearance.
- Physical Training – Generally the soldiers would not be allowed to ride their horses until they had successfully completed a period of 12 weeks physical training.
- Horsemanship – Understanding the different methods of control techniques, the capabilities of the horse, health and welfare, use and maintenance, cleaning of the tackle and how to fit and adjust it to the horse.
- Best use of ground cover – The use of the naturally topography of the land for example the cover from wooded areas, high hedges, and undulations in the land to conceal cavalry formations from the enemy.
- Elementary night operations – The ability to harass the enemy, carry out reconnaissance and capture small units of enemy for integration.
- Map reading – The ability to understand the layout of a map, where the natural obstacles are located, and natural features present to assist with navigation, and the location of enemy positions.
- Musketry instruction – The use and adjustment of the Lee Enfield rifle, understanding its limitations, and rapid fire. The payment of a full wage depended on the ability to fire at a minimum rate of 15 rounds per minute.
- Semaphore signalling – This method was used by both sides to communicate in a battle situation and involved the use of different coloured flags and the flashing of lights in darkness.
- The use of the sword and lance – This involved charging on horseback at a dummy stuffed with straw. The really skilled cavalrymen would eventually perfect the skill of 'tent pegging'. This involved cantering towards a small tent peg on the ground, and at a precise moment

dropping the sabre or lance, piercing the tent peg, and lifting it up off the ground in one swift movement, without stopping the horse.

Ernest had also to learn key cavalry commands, key words and instructions. A few examples are *forward, advance, walk, trot, gallop, annul, troops half right, troops left wheel, form line*. In addition, there was the requisite understanding of the meaning of trumpet and bugle calls, and their significance in battle scenarios.

All of these skills, techniques and understandings were difficult enough in a classroom and a lecture situation, but trying to apply them during the noise and chaos of battle was another matter. During the weeks and months that followed the recruitment, the men and horses had to be introduced also to the sounds of war, in other words, to exploding shells and rapid rifle fire.

There was much to learn and absorb, and it would certainly have seemed daunting to those young soldiers. For sure, there were many potential occasions for my Grandad to fall off the horse.

Training based at Winchester College and other locations

On the 10th of August 1914, the squadron was moved by train to temporary billeting at Winchester College in West Sussex. My visit to the College has enabled me to appreciate its vast history.

Founded following the 'Black Death' in England in 1348, the College was built in 1382 by the then Bishop of Winchester, William Wykeham, who had previously been Lord Chancellor to both Edward lll and Richard ll. It was an all boys' school, and the scholars, who were known as 'Wykehamists' were taught Latin and Religion.

Ernest's squadron was not the first cavalry unit to have been billeted at the College. During the English Civil War, part of the Round Head Cavalry had billeted in its cloisters.

Reference is made to the arrival of Yeomanry Cavalry in the 'Wykehamist' Magazine dated October 1914. It reads:

'On Monday the 10th of August the Wiltshire Yeomanry under Colonel Palmer began to arrive, their stay lasted until the afternoon

of Saturday the 22nd of August. The Yeomanry made a regular encampment here and the early sign of their coming was a piece of raw beef thawing in the sunshine outside Mr Carter's classroom. On the 12th of August there were 471 soldiers sleeping in the classroom and gymnasium'.

The Yeomanry in the grounds of Winchester College

Major Awdry, together with two of his relatives, had been Wykehamists. Perhaps it was therefore no coincidence that the squadron chose to stay at the College. The Awdrys would have known that the College brewed its own beer within the grounds. The question is whether the squadron was allowed to drink any.

Over the period of the World War 1 over 500 Wykehamists enlisted. By the end of the War, they had been almost all wiped out, and the Headmaster was devastated.

On leaving the College the farrier sergeant left a horseshoe embedded in the mortar of the brickwork as a memento of their stay, and this can still be seen today.

On Saturday the 22nd August the squadron moved to Worth Park, a 40-acre Victorian park, located in the borough of Crawley, West Sussex. This was Ernest's first experience of a long march. By car, the distance is 82 miles, but cross country it would have been a shorter distance. In any event it took them five days. They are likely to have stayed overnight in

*Above: the plaque commemorating the billeting
of the Yeomans at Winchester College*

*Right: the horseshoe set in the
mortar by the farrier sergeant*

military bell tents which slept six to eight soldiers. From evidence of photos at Winchester College, clearly there were horses, but it is not possible to ascertain if the whole squadron was mounted. It might be that most of the officers had horses as well as some of the non-commissioned officers.

I suspect that Grandad was either very 'saddle sore', or in the event of having to journey on foot, he would have had blisters on top of blisters on arrival at Worth Park. It is now about six weeks since Ernest had been provided with a pair of army boots. They were strong boots, but the leather was very stiff, and this in itself would cause blisters. Some soldiers would resort to urinating in their boots to soften the leather. A more subtle treatment would be to apply dubbin wax.

There would have been hundreds of army bell tents erected in the area of Worth Park. The regiment stayed at this location for 26 days, with training continuing for the whole of this period. It is likely to have been drill, theory and physical education.

At that time the army referred to rifle target practice as 'musketry training', a term which evidently continued to be used, despite the fact that muskets had been long since replaced. Instruction would be given into the component parts of the Lee Enfield rifle, and its maintenance and adjustment.

At this early-stage Ernest would have had to learn 'rifle drill', in other words how to hold the gun when marching. During basic drill, he would have to follow a sequence of commands in synchronisation with his section. He would develop muscle groups in his arms and listening skills.

The principal rifle used by the British Army was the Lee Enfield, generally thought to be the best rifle of World War 1. It could hold two magazines each containing 5 x .303 bullets. In the hands of a skilled soldier, it could fire at least 15 to 20 rounds per minute. The record set was 31 rounds per minute. It was said that concentrated fire from 30 of these rifles had the same effect as a machine gun. It had an effective firing range of 2441 ft (550 yds). That is the equivalent of four times the length of a football pitch.

I have held a Lee Enfield rifle at Aldershot Military Museum, and it felt quite heavy, the total weight being 4kg (8.8lbs). This would have been even heavier when the bayonet was fixed.

Author holding a Lee Enfield rifle at Aldershot Military Museum

The German 98 Gewehr was a good rifle in its own right, but it had a slower firing rate of about ten rounds per minute. More significantly, the two rifle designs were different, in that the German soldier, when working the bolt action of his rifle, had to take his eye away from the sight to avoid the sliding bolt hitting his cheek. This would have been a hindrance during rapid fire in a battle situation. The British soldier was able to keep his eyes on the sight during constant fire, only taking his eyes off the sight for reloading.

This simple difference in design is significant. British units on the front often fooled the Germans into thinking they were facing a machine gun emplacement, when in fact they were being subjected to rapid fire from Lee Enfield's.

I am sure that part of Ernest's training would have been to accustom his horse to the extreme noises of battle which would have been terrifying for some of the animals. Some simply did not make the grade and were auctioned off before they even arrived in France. They were the lucky ones.

The horses were requisitioned from all over Britain. One example is the Bass Brewery located in Burton upon Trent, the town of South Staffordshire near to my home. They had a total of 300 heavy draught beautiful shire horses. The mighty shires would be used in teams to pull heavy artillery pieces, for instance. Large numbers of these animals went to France. Fewer than 1 in 10 returned and they were subsequently of little use, because, just like human beings, they suffered from shell shock and the after-effects of being exposed to gas and other injuries. At the beginning of the war, no horse under 15 hands was deemed suitable for army use. A large proportion of horses were shipped over from North and South America.

It might be a good time to mention briefly the mule. This was a marvellous creature, known for its strength and stamina. It was the result of mating a 'jack' (male) donkey with a female horse (mare). The mule did not stand as tall as the army horse but did vital work in carrying shells and supplies in places where motorised transport could not reach. The strange aspect for me is that mules cannot mate and produce offspring.

Grandad was extremely impressed with this animal; I remember him telling me:

'I never ceased to be amazed by the sheer stamina and strength of those poor mules. They could get to places that the horse couldn't reach. They would often be seen carrying artillery shells, four shells each side. They would work all day. At night they would be given a nose bag full of oats and bran. Their handlers would take off the harnesses so that the mule could have a good roll on the ground. This behaviour seamed to invigorate them, and afterwards they would be good to go again.'

Army mules. Note the mud on the coat. Clearly this poor animal had previously been up to its belly in mud. Many had to be pulled out of mud filled shell craters, by whatever means. Many drowned.

There were a number of depots set up in the South of England in order to process the huge numbers of horses. One such location was Romsey in Hampshire, which was ideal, because of its close proximity to the docks in Southampton.

The Romsey remount depot processed over 120,000 horses. These poor creatures were semi-wild and had to be broken in by a team of 2,000 men. It must have been a spectacle for the villagers as the horses were led through the village to the Swaythling depot, ready for shipment to France.

I have read old newspaper articles relating how army horses, that had not made the grade, were sold off in Sussex. The average price at auction was about 25 Guineas. They would have been much sought after as many of the 'draught' horse and riding horses in Britain had been requisitioned, leading to a shortage for the home front. There is more about our trusted friends later on in this book.

Over one million horses and mules from Britain were transported to France during World War 1, and very few returned. It is estimated that over 8 million horses from all the armies were killed. The extra duties of the cavalry soldier, in addition to those of the infantryman, were tending his horse, and feeding the animal three times per day. He would also have to clean and maintain the harness and monitor the health and wellbeing of the horse. All of that was in addition to the maintenance and cleaning of his own equipment and weapons, which were the basic duties of the infantryman.

I cannot imagine Ernest having a lot of spare time on his hands. I am sure that he would have found time to write to his mother Ann, and perhaps to his brother Walter and sister Nelly who were running the greengrocer's shop in Marlborough, and of course to his beloved Elizabeth.

Ernest was a strong man but even he would have to train very hard in improving his fitness. Over the months that followed he would have to participate in long marches not always on horseback. It should be remembered that he would be carrying all of his kit together with his

Ernest mounted on his horse. Note that its tail has been cropped.
Each of the horses was given a unique number.

Typical accommodation at Forest Row

rifle. He would have to develop the muscle groups in his legs, arms and wrists, in order to strengthen his grip. He would have to learn to control the horse with one hand, exerting pressure with his knees and ankles to assist with changing direction.

On 16th of September 1914 the Yeomans moved to Tyes Cross, East Grinstead, occupying the billets on Forest Row. It was during this period that the Wiltshire Yeomanry amalgamated with the Hampshire Carbineers, the North Somerset's, Duke of Lancaster's Own, the First Signal Corps ASC, and the 1st Field Mounted Ambulance, to become the South West Mounted Brigade.

During this period Ernest would no doubt have received his horse. By now his head would be full of cavalry commands procedures and drill. There would now be a new dimension in his training. He now had to learn the drill of the brigade. There were brigade formations to learn, in other words, moving forward on the open heathlands of the South Downs in a set formation. It could be said that this appears to have been a waste of time, given the stalemate on the Western Front and the advent of trench warfare. However, neither side thought this stalemate would last forever. One day there would be a breakthrough and, as a consequence, large amounts of troops and cavalry would need to advance or retreat in an effective coordinated orderly fashion.

Grandad and his comrades had to learn how to erect the army bell tents to army regulations. He slept in these until the construction of the hutted camp was completed. These tents were erected in Kidbrooke Park. Whilst visiting the 100 years commemoration at Passchendaele in 2017, I had chance to examine one of the bell tents that were on display. There was little space inside and it must have been cramped for Ernest and his fellow soldiers. I am sure that it would have been a huge relief for Ernest to move from the bell tents to a wooden hut as autumn was approaching. The huts would have been luxurious by comparison. He certainly would not have this luxury in France although he would not have known this at the time.

Whilst living in these huts Ernest had his 26th birthday. I wonder if he had chance to celebrate it. No doubt he would have had parcels and cards from his family. He was no big drinker. Perhaps he had a tot of rum with his mates.

Little remains of the original site of Kidbrooke Park. The golf course still exists, which was where the firing range was located. Sycamore Cottage was the site of the headquarters, where wooden stables were erected to house 500 horses. The area today is full of shops and residential houses.

In true army tradition, life in these wooden huts was no holiday for Ernest. Each hut would be subject to regular inspections by officers. Beds had to be made in a certain way, with the army blankets folded in the regulatory manner. Certain items of equipment had to be stored and made ready for inspection. Any losses had to be accounted for.

Other huts were allocated as canteens, grocery bars and coffee bars. Alcoholic beverages were available (whilst off duty) at subsidised prices. The recreation hut would have had facilities including a billiard table, bagatelle, and dominoes. Some huts were used as theatres. All these facilities, including a library hut, would help to relieve Ernest's boredom, if indeed that was a problem. Other huts would also be adapted as lecture rooms for theory training.

The army camps encouraged sporting activities, the main one being football, but cricket came a close second. Inter-regimental competitions were encouraged, the obvious benefits of which were team building and maintaining fitness. Ernest would not have known this at the time, but in the months and years to come, his physical resilience would be tested to his limits and beyond.

Sadly, it was whilst in billets in Forest Row that Ernest received the sad news of the death of his father Alan Burchell, who died at the age of 67 years on the 21st of November 1914. In general, soldiers in the army during the Great War were allowed leave every 15 months. Ernest had only been a soldier for two months, but whether he was given compassionate leave to attend his father's funeral, I don't know. It was never discussed with me. I suspect it was unlikely.

Ernest would have been comforted by the fact that his mother was not on her own. She would surely have received help from her other sons and daughters, and possibly from the greengrocer's shop in Marlborough. Widows did not receive State Benefit until the Benefits Act was passed in 1925 when she would have received 10 shillings per week. In any event, November 1914 would have been a sad time for Ernest.

That same year the Yeomanry received further musket training in Ashdown Forest. This was not what its name suggests. It was an area of about 6,000 acres which consisted of some woodland, but also large areas of open heathland, ideal for cavalry training.

The forest area had been planted since Norman times, and as a consequence was well established. It was located in the High Weald area of the South Downs. Grandad's musket training was carried out at 'The Old Lodge' which is now private property. There was also training at Broadstone. The army dug a lot of trenches in the forest to practise trench warfare. The North West Mounted Brigade remained at Forest Row until March 1915.

I have already mentioned the aspect of army drill training. I had some experience of this when at Police Training College. I did wonder at first why we were engaged in this, and it was then explained to us. For a unit of officers to be effective, they need to work as a team and be able to respond rapidly to changes in circumstances in a coordinated way, by listening to orders from supervisors and responding promptly even under stress.

In a situation of chaos, for example in my case, a public order situation or riot, or in Ernest's case, the middle of a battle, teamwork and keeping one's nerve, however difficult, would often save the day and make the difference between success or failure, survival or death. It is easy for me to say, I was not present on the battlefields.

The unit needs good leadership and ideally, for that unit to survive during the chaos, someone would have to step up to the challenge and take over. Ernest was one of these officers. It will be seen later in the book how he had his chance to demonstrate this ability.

Events in the first months of the war

Meanwhile events on the Western Front were gathering momentum. As part of the 'Schlieffen' plan, the Germans were marching through Belgium avoiding the bulk of the French army in the south. The plan was thought up as early as 1905 by Alfred Von Schlieffen, who had been the Chief of the Imperial German Staff 1891 to 1906. The success of the plan relied on speed to encircle Paris and drive the French army to the south. They boasted that they would be in Paris within six weeks. The Germans were convinced that if Paris fell then the French would capitulate.

The British Expeditionary Force (BEF) of 82,000 men were professional soldiers who were very well equipped and trained. Fighting at their side were 120,000 Belgian soldiers. They faced a German army of 840,000 strong, most of whom were conscripts.

As the Germans advanced, they met stiff opposition. The advance slowed as the French and Belgians ripped up railway tracks and blew up bridges. This seriously hindered the Germans who had problems reinforcing the front-line troops. These reinforcements were not so well equipped or trained, so the huge numerical advantage became less of an advantage to the Germans. The siege of Liège, which was an important town for its rail network, lasted two weeks instead of the two days which the Germans had planned for.

It was at the bridge and canal network at Mons that the first Victoria Cross medals were awarded on the 23rd of August 1914. These were won by Lieutenant Dees and Private Goddly who were in the machine gun section defending one of the bridges. The sheer weight of German numbers eventually forced the Allies to retreat from Mons. They retreated 200 miles, fighting fiercely all the way.

By the end of October 1914, there was a major breakthrough by the Allies in that they stopped the German advance on Paris at the Battle of Marne. The cavalry was put to good use in that they slowed the German advance. This was a rare moment on the Western Front. The Allies not only halted the German advance, but on part of the front the Germans were ordered to retreat to prevent being outflanked by the French. Both sides received heavy casualties. Nearly half a million soldiers were killed or wounded. This was not going to be a quick victory that the Germans boasted of. This would be a prolonged war of attrition.

The continuing war, 1914

The war on the Western Front continued. Following the Battle of Marne saw the Battle of Aisne, which was the attack by the Allies on the right German flank. Many of them were named after the river systems in the area, the river Aisne being no exception.

The Germans made a very important tactical decision at the time. They deployed themselves on the high ground in the area using the natural features in the countryside to give themselves maximum advantage, not only for concealment of their artillery, which during this battle was far superior to that of the Allies, they also made sure that their machine guns had a maximum arc of fire.

The Allies sustained heavy casualties. It could be argued that the Germans were quicker to adapt to trench warfare than the Allies who at the time of this battle had no spades and pickaxes in order to dig adequate trenches to protect their infantry. The Germans exploited this weakness with the effective use of trench mortars and rifle grenades and superior calibre artillery pieces. The situation soon became a stalemate and head on frontal attacks were halted. The cream of the British Expeditionary Force (BEF) was slowly being wiped out.

There then followed a race to the northern coast of Belgium, the Germans being anxious to seize the important Belgian ports to prevent reinforcements and supplies being landed.

The first Battle of Ypres took place during this race to the Belgian coast. Each of the opposing armies tried to outflank each other to reach the coast first. By November both armies were exhausted, and some units refused to fight any further. Troop reinforcements, supplies, and ammunition were all running low.

At the Battle of Yser the Belgians, the BEF and the French managed to prevent the Germans from reaching the coast by flooding the lowlands between their coastal town of Niewpoort and Diksmuide, making the flooded plains and the banks of the River Yser a natural barrier to the Germans. This was an important result and moral boost for the Belgian Army in that they retained 5% of their territory, and this gave them the will to fight on. King Albert l of Belgium was hailed a hero and the Belgians continued the fight alongside their British and French comrades. However, the civilian population of occupied Belgium suffered terrible deprivations during the following four years of the war, many being forced into labour gangs for the Germans.

A stalemate had now been reached on the Western Front culminating in a system of trenches spreading from the Belgian coast at Niewpoort and south to the Swiss border town of Belfort. This was over 400 miles of trenches. Just to put this into perspective, it is equivalent to digging a 'zig zag' trench system about 10ft deep from London to Glasgow. Most of these trench systems had three trenches running parallel to each other. This system of warfare would eventually render the use of cavalry as ineffective.

Ernest Burchell and his horse would be used in a totally different role than he was expecting or being trained for. There were calls for the cavalry regiments to be disbanded and some indeed were, but General Haig, who would eventually become BEF commander was reluctant to do this, so many of the regiments including Grandad's continued to be held in reserve. Their training continued.

At this time the public were being told that we had the strongest most powerful Navy in the world, which would protect our shores, but on the 16th of December 1914, tragedy struck the north east coast of England when six German cruisers shelled the coastal area killing 137 civilians. There would soon be a new menace off the coast of Britain the 'Unterseeboot', which was be more commonly known as the German U-Boats.

The winter months of 1914 and the beginning of 1915 was a period of relative inactivity. The superpowers were taking stock of the situation, and the bad weather hampered the movement of troops and supplies. They were also counting the cost, which was escalating.

One country which emerged out of all this mess and carnage to grow rapidly and become the superpower we know, was the United States of America. In the coming years Britain was lending billions of pounds to the French and Italian governments. In turn Britain borrowed billions of dollars from the American treasury. It took Britain until the 21st Century to pay off this debt.

Training in 1915, including in trench warfare

For the first three months of 1915 Ernest and the rest of the South West Mounted Brigade continued training. They carried out manoeuvres on the South Downs in West Sussex. Ernest was developing his riding skills, jumping over various obstacles, engaging in further weapon training and cavalry battle tactics.

During October 1915 Ernest's squadron trained also at Wrotham in Kent. The training involved the construction of trenches and trench warfare. Trenches were beginning to be dug in France as early as September 1914 during the Battle of Marne. Lessons were being learnt in France and Belgium as to how best to construct these trenches. This was naturally passed on to the training camps in England.

In general, the average depth of the trench was ten feet. Sandbags on either side were stacked three to four layers deep above ground level to give extra protection. This sometimes gave the trench about four metres in depth. The soldiers were taught to dig these trenches in a 'zig zag' stepped pattern. The idea of this was to minimise the impact of a shell burst. At any one time a soldier would only be able to see about ten metres either side of him along the trench.

The front of the trench where the soldier leant against was known as the 'parapet'. The rear bank and lip of the trench was referred to as the 'parados'. The lip had extra layers of sandbags stacked above ground level to protect the soldier from the effects of shell bursts to the rear. Each section of the trench had a 'fire bay' where the soldier stood on a ledge to fire his weapon. In front of the soldier was a small gap between the sandbags to enable him to look out into no man's land towards the enemy trenches. Sometimes there was a steel plate ('loop hole') with an aperture for the soldiers to look through. The German snipers used armour piercing bullets to penetrate this plate with disastrous consequences for the poor 'Tommy'.

The sides of the trenches were supported by wooden frames and posts between which were placed zinc sheets, or sandbags, or woven thin tree branches. The bottom of the trench had a wooden slatted board referred to as a 'duck board'. This was a vain attempt to keep the soldiers' feet dry and away from the water below.

In the race to the Belgian coast, the Germans tried to choose high ground where possible to locate their trench systems. This would prove to have big advantages, namely that they could often dig their trenches deeper as the level of the water table would not be so restrictive.

Sadly, for the British Army this would be a major factor at the Battle of the Somme in 1916.

With the constant artillery bombardments on the Western Front, it was not long before the drainage systems in France and Belgium were rendered useless. Large parts of Belgium have heavy clay soils which do not drain easily, and in low lying areas the water table was as shallow as one metre below ground level. So, if a trench was dug ten feet deep in these areas it would rapidly fill up with water. This in turn would be churned into seas of mud which the poor soldiers had to stand in, sometimes waste deep.

It could be said that surely these trenches would have already been dug by the time Ernest arrived in France and Belgium. However, the sad fact was that in the aftermath of heavy artillery attacks, the trench systems sometimes were unrecognisable. Therefore, the trenches had to be dug out again and repaired. Ernest would have had no idea just how much shovelling he would end up having to do. The army guidelines dictated that a group of 450 men should be able to dig 250 metres of trench at night in six hours.

Ernest would have been taught the system of trenches, namely that the trench nearest to the enemy was referred to as the 'Fire Trench', and in general there would be two further trenches running parallel to the rear of the 'Fire Trench'. These two other trenches would be linked by communication trenches. It would be through these trenches that all the reinforcements and supplies would pass.

In front of the 'Fire Trench' would be what was known as 'Saps', these being trenches dug out towards the enemy lines beyond the protection of the barbed wire. These in effect were listening posts where two sentries were deployed for two-hour intervals at any one time.

It is obvious that Ernest had a lot to learn. He would no doubt have had to dig part of a trench using his pickaxe and spade. He would be becoming quite a fit man by now. It should be remembered that when a soldier was advancing towards the enemy and pinned down by overwhelming firepower, his only protection would be to find cover or rapidly dig a small hole. A mound of earth, behind which he could lie, could mean the difference between life and death.

I will talk about snipers in more detail later, but the Allies were slow to appreciate their effectiveness for the first part of the war. The British lagged behind in this field of warfare, but the risk of sniper fire was by now an integral part of training.

Ernest was also taught night-time training exercises, the use of trench periscopes, the use of wire cutters, repairing telephone lines, gathering intelligence, and sentry duties. However, above all Ernest must have learnt not to fall asleep whilst on sentry duty, as this would mean death by firing squad.

I can imagine by now that Ernest and his mates were becoming a bit impatient. They had joined to fight the Germans and not to play war games in the Ashdown Forest. The sensible soldiers amongst them would have been more patient. The fact was, they were still alive in contrast to the hundreds of thousands of soldiers who had been slaughtered by the end of 1914. Most of the BEF had been wiped out. It should be remembered that these were our crack professional troops. Britain would have to recruit and train a new army from the civilian population.

Because of the mass slaughter of this conflict, the policy on reserved occupations was nowhere near as strict as the policies of World War 2. My father, Peter Burchell (Ernest's second eldest son), was prevented from joining the Tank Corps in World War 2 because he was a farmer's son.

In World War 1 people from all professions enlisted, from ploughmen, farm labourers, and skilled manual labourers, to barristers and lower management in the middle classes. I was surprised to find out the Chief Constable of Wiltshire enlisted together with at least one local Member of Parliament.

Managers from the middle classes eventually became the junior officers in the ranks as these were being wiped out at alarming rate. It should be borne in mind that when the whistles blew and the men climbed up the ladders and out of the trenches to charge the enemy, the junior officers were leading the attacks, carrying Webley and Scott revolvers, and wearing riding breaches. They stood out as priority targets for German machine gunners and snipers.

The war in the first half of 1915

The beginning of March 1915 saw the start of the Battle of Neuve Chapelle. This was the Allied Spring Offensive on the Western Front. This was the first coordinated attack on the German trenches and would become the template for future battles. Time had been spent on planning this attack with the use of aerial reconnaissance which led to the production of detailed maps. This assisted the artillery and the infantry to work together in a coordinated effort to break through the German lines.

The first stage of this planning was for the artillery to bombard the German barbed wire in order to make a breach allowing the troops through. The artillery would then raise its aim beyond the front line and target the second two German lines in an attempt to destroy the reinforcements or severely hinder their deployment.

At 7.30am on Wednesday the 7th of March 1915 the Allied artillery opened up and carried out a 30-minute bombardment of the German line. Following this the troops attacked, many were Bengali Troops. They had mixed success. They were supported by reinforcements, but chaos ensued, and communication broke down.

It must be appreciated that by now, most of the professional British soldiers had been wiped out. The Allies relied on many other troops from the Colonies. The Indian Corps provided over one million troops in this war, and over 200,000 were deployed on the Western Front. Had it not been for these and other colonial regiments (including the Gurkhas), it is unlikely that the British lines would have withstood the numerically superior numbers of the Germans and Central Powers.

After three days of this battle, the Germans counter attacked but were decimated by the Allied artillery. The offensive petered out after the Allies ran out of shells. Over 40,000 Allied troops were killed or wounded, and sadly, the result was that the Germans were only pushed back one mile. Lessons were learnt from this battle. The Allies needed to increase significantly the production of artillery shells in order to sustain future major offences. It was estimated that after the first half hour of artillery bombardment, more shells had been fired than during the whole period of the Boer War in Africa.

This serious miscalculation led to the downfall of the British Liberal government of Prime Minister Asquith. A coalition Government emerged.

One of the main problems on the British side was the production of enough artillery shells to keep up with the demand. Ironically, Britain used to import cordite from Germany prior to the outbreak of war, so naturally this stopped abruptly in 1914. A crisis emerged which called on typical British ingenuity. The labourers in the armament's factories worked flat out to find an alternate process to produce acetate, which they solved using the fermentation processes for brewing beer, and incredibly an extract from pulped up horse chestnuts. Saltpetre (potassium nitrate) was also extracted from high grade lard by boiling the left-over carcases or bones of animals slaughtered for meat. The armament factories in Canada and North America also started making shells in ever increasing numbers. They had to learn this new skill. During this learning process, a proportion of their shells failed to explode on use.

On the 22nd of April 1915 the Second Battle of Ypres commenced. The salient which was the result of the first battle, gave the Germans an advantage in that the 'bulge' in the front line occupied by the Germans, favoured their artillery which was now able nearly in range of the town of Ypres. A further push forward enabled them to shell the town and port beyond.

At 17.00 hours on that evening of the Germans had unleashed their new deadly weapon. They were waiting for favourable weather conditions, namely wind direction blowing from their lines towards the Allies. They then let off 168 tons of chlorine gas. The wind caused the gas to drift to the Allied trenches. The gas itself was heavier than air so when it reached the Allied trenches, it descended into their trenches. When this gas comes into contact with water or watery solutions like the mucus from the inside of the nose, or respiratory tracts, and around the eyes, it turns to acid. The effects were horrific, within a short time thousands of Allied soldiers were incapacitated or died. Those that could move, instinctively jumped out of the trenches only to be targeted by German machine units and snipers.

The initial success of this attack took both the Allies and the Germans by surprise. The casualties caused a huge gap in the Allied lines but the Germans failed to push home their advantage as they had not amassed sufficient reinforcements quickly enough, and the lateness of the attack meant it was soon dark. The Canadian regiments saved the day, and under immense pressure and foul conditions eventually managed to push the Germans back and plug most of the holes.

A desperate situation had called for desperate measures. It was discovered that by soaking a cloth or bandage, or handkerchief or sock with urine, the soldiers gained some protection against the gas. It was even better if the urine was stale. The ammonium in the urine neutralised the chlorine in the gas.

Again, the losses were horrific, the allies losing 69,000 dead or wounded, and the Germans 35,000 dead or wounded. The numerical advantage was no doubt down to the use of the chlorine gas. The Germans gained in that the salient had been made deeper. This meant that their artillery could now reach the town of Ypres, and the famous Cloth Hall was subsequently reduced to rubble.

I visited Ypres in 2016 and discovered that famous Cloth Hall had been rebuilt back to its former glory. It is now a museum dedicated to those who fell in the Great War.

The war on the sea and the bombing of London

On the 7th of May 1915 German U-Boat U-20 sank the RMS Lusitania off the coast of Ireland. Of the 1959 passengers and crew only 761 survived. Of those drowned 128 were American citizens.

Up until this period the German U-boat campaign had been gathering momentum causing large losses with Allied shipping. This bought the

Americans to the brink of war with Germany who responded by significantly curtailing their U-Boat campaign easing the pressure on the Allies.

At this point the Germans started their bombing of London, thereby increasing hostilities. Naturally, this action galvanised public opinion against the Germans which worked wonders for the recruiting campaign. Women from all over the country rallied to the call and started working in the armament and munition factories, but for much lower wages. The social structure of Britain would change for good.

The Yeomans in the summer of 1915

In June and July 1915 Grandad's brigade carried out exercises crossing the River Ouse near Lewes in Sussex. There was friendly competition between the regiments to gain the best time for the crossings. Eye witnesses stated that the horses appeared to have enjoyed the experience. The brigade also continued training on the South Downs. I have of course referred to military training manuals covering the technique. The horse can swim naturally. It is a herd animal, and amongst the herd are leaders and those that are followers.

Before the crossing could be made, everyone including Ernest would have had to learn to swim. Common sense dictated that the strong swimmers in the squadron would teach the others to swim. The crossing point, where possible, would be chosen so the bank opposite would be easy for the horses to climb out of the water. The horses would swim four abreast at 10 yard intervals. They would have all their harnesses taken off leaving just the bridle and reins attached. The reins would be knotted with a handful of mane pulled through the knot to prevent the rein from becoming tangled in the horse front feet as it swam forward.

The rider would strip off to his underpants and swim alongside the horse downstream side, holding the offside rein to try and steer the horse to the bank opposite. Care would be taken to leave a few horses on the opposite bank so that the following swimming horse could steer towards them. The men and equipment and clothing would follow on boats and rafts.

I can appreciate the sense in this training because in the first 12 months of the war the Belgian and French armies destroyed a lot of the bridges in order to hinder the advancing Germans. Should the Cavalry be deployed at some time in the future, it would be important that they could cross rivers in Belgium and France.

Ernest would have had to develop further his basic skills of horse riding. As each week progressed there would be additions and more challenges along the way, for example the Cavalry would sometimes have to stop and deploy on foot in order to engage the enemy. This made their numbers less effective because a lot of the soldiers had the job of looking after the horses who were tethered up in what was referred to in Cavalry terms as a 'picket'. Some would be agitated and nervous at the sound of the rifle fire.

The art of jumping obstacles in the field would also be a challenge. This would have been under fire and therefore training involved getting the horses used to the noises on the battlefield. In addition to the riders, the horse was carrying all their equipment as well.

Care had to be taken when choosing cover. The Yeomans would have been encouraged to use the natural 'lay of the land' and features around when setting up camp and or deploying units on foot. Natural cover, for example woodland, high hedges, ridges and undulations would be used. The purpose of this would be to make it difficult for the enemy artillery spotters, who were on the lookout for large troop and cavalry concentrations, with the use of field glasses and binoculars. Ernest would find out soon enough the devastating effect of enemy artillery fire on concentrated groups of troops and cavalry.

The war in the autumn of 1915

The next major conflict on the Western Front was the Battle of Loose.

In September of this year, 1915, the Allies were concerned about the successes of the German Army fighting the Russians in the East. If the Russians collapsed, then this would release significant numbers of German soldiers to move to the Western Front. As a consequence, the Allies launched their Autumn offensive, The British attacked at Loose, the French attacked to the south.

This was the first time that the British used chlorine gas. They released 150 tons of gas from canisters which drifted across to the Germans. It is estimated that the gas killed 600 Germans. The British were able to advance rapidly past Loose and beyond.

Tragically this success was short lived as the British faced 84 German machine gun teams which were deployed facing down reverse slopes towards which the attacking British advanced. The whole of the battle front was covered by the German machine guns' arc of fire. They opened fire on the advancing British troops to devastating effect. The first waves of infantry were slaughtered, over 8,000 out of the original 10,000 soldiers were killed or wounded within the first four hours. Over the 18 days of this battle the British army suffered over 48,000 dead or wounded. If there was ever any doubt about the effective use of the machine guns in warfare, then this battle proved the point.

General Haig had previously been quoted as saying '*The machine gun is a much-overrated weapon*', *two machine guns per battalion are more than sufficient*.' How wrong he was. The superpowers went on to make over one million machine guns during this war. Some of the Anzac units eventually had one Lewis machine gun per 10 soldiers.

It is fact that during part of this battle, the Germans ceased fire out of pity for the mass of dead and dying bodies in front of them. I have read accounts that state that the Germans even assisted with their stretcher bearers to carry the bodies away. The Germans in the aftermath referred to the battlefield of Loos as "The Field of Corpses."

After the guns stopped firing eyewitnesses reported hearing a strange humming noise from 'no man's land'. This was the sound of hundreds of wounded soldiers, many of whom would be calling out for their mothers. That sound would no doubt haunt so many survivors of the war, probably for the rest of their lives.

There is also a moving account of a British Army chaplain who went around the battlefield under the cover of darkness. Soldiers from both sides saw him bury the dead, giving them their last rights and praying. This must have been such a sad and pitiful sight. This has surprised me given some of the atrocities that the Germans carried out. At the risk of being controversial, the Prussian divisions appear to have been the most brutal. There was clearly ill feeling between them and some of the Bavarian divisions.

Training in the art of bombing and mass military warfare manoeuvres

For the period between July and the 17th of November 1915, the Yeomans continued training and moved to the North Downs and into the county of Kent. They practised in the art of 'bombing'. Today the phrase conjures up a totally different image, that of mass formations of planes dropping tons of bombs over industrial cities, but not so in 1915. This was the practice of throwing the Mills bombs at the enemy positions. We now refer to these bombs as grenades. Very little has changed in their design since they were first invented by William Mills who drew his inspiration from the Belgian Roland grenade.

William Mills was born in Sunderland and as a young adult qualified to become a marine engineer. In 1915 Mills set up his factory in Birmingham. The output of the factory was rapidly increased in 1916 until the Mills bombs were mass produced. Once the pin was pulled on the grenade it released the steel spoon which in turn released the plunger down into the body of the grenade. When it struck the bottom, the detonator was ignited, causing the ignition of the high explosive. This caused the metal body of the bomb to break up into many fragments, which flew through the air causing horrific injuries and death.

It was estimated that the average soldier could throw the bomb up to 15 yards with a degree of accuracy, but in any event up to a maximum distance of 30 yards. The defensive bomb was designed to be thrown by the soldier from cover and immediately after throwing the bomb, the soldier would dive down to avoid the flying metal fragments. Having been thrown 30 yards, the damage area of this fragment bomb could be as much as 100 yards.

This is a picture of a practice Mills bomb on display at Aldershot Military museum, note the white paint signifying it to be a dud. The soldiers referred to them as 'Pineapples'.

The other type of bomb was an offensive bomb, which instead of fragmenting on explosion would cause a major shock wave effect on the intended victim(s) numbing their senses to enable the attacker to gain advantage.

The bomb was originally designed to have a seven second delay before exploding. In the theatre of battle this was found to be too slow. The enemy had too long to react and in some cases the enemy had time to throw the grenades back. As a consequence, the delay was reduced to four seconds.

The bomb was later modified to have a steal rod attached so that it could be used as a rifle grenade fired by a Lee Enfield rifle. In the chaos of a major battle these distances would soon be forgotten by many a desperate soldier.

Grandad told me about Mills bombs whilst I was having tea with him:

when we were off duty resting behind the lines, some of us used to creep to nearby fishponds and throw a Mills grenade into the water, when it exploded it had the effect of stunning the fish causing them to float to the top of the pond, we then scooped them up and had them for supper, we were in deep trouble if we got caught!

Ernest would have trained with 'dummy' bombs which were not armed. I have seen the practice bombs at Aldershot Museum. They have a white band of paint around the middle signifying they are 'duds'. The armed grenades had red crosses.

It was said that cricket bowlers had a definite advantage because of their accuracy throwing the bomb which was not much different in size and weight to that of a cricket ball. Sadly, there would not have been enough of these men for the task ahead. However, Major Awdry of Ernest's squadron would not have been able to resist having a go in front of his troops, as he had been a successful cricketer, having played at Lords before the outbreak of war.

Ernest's training involved dismantling the component parts and then reassembling them. He had to throw the bombs with accuracy to the required standard. He had to understand the circumstances of when best to use this weapon, and how to prime it ready for use. Lessons would have been learnt at the front which would have filtered back to the training grounds where training methods would be modified and improved.

In consulting books from both sides of the war, I consider that it is evident that each side learnt from the other. If an effective technique was discovered by one side, it would be copied by the other.

Timing would have been of the essence. Imagine a scenario where a group of 50 enemy soldiers is coming towards your position. You throw your bomb which because of the delay fails to explode until after the enemy soldiers have long since passed it. I guess many bombs would have been thrown under these circumstances out of shear panic and adrenalin rush, also out of fear of being overrun. In other situation's soldiers would find that a weapon jammed or they ran out of ammunition. The grenade was sometimes thrown as a last resort. The list of possible circumstances is endless.

I see the real advantage of this weapon in a situation where the attacking troops are approaching the enemy trenches. They throw the bomb in to the trench, causing maximum effect especially if the defenders are clustered together. This method would have been particularly effective during a creeping barrage. The enemy troops would be taking cover anyway, with their heads down, few of them would see the grenades coming.

Another use would be when approaching a concrete German pill box. The attacker would throw the Mills bomb into the slots or apertures of the pill box to devastating effect. Another priority target would be the German maxim machine gun crews who would be despised by our troops. A well-placed grenade would often take out a six-man machine gun team. A pioneer of the creeping barrage was General Sir Herbert Plumer who was in charge of Ernest's army group during the Third Battle of Ypres covered later in this book.

Having reached the enemy trench some of the defenders refused to come out of their dugouts. Sadly, both sides would throw bombs inside the dugouts with horrific results.

On the 17th of November 1915 the South West Mounted Brigade moved to the Military Barracks at Aldershot in Hampshire. It was here that Ernest and his fellow Yeomans practised the art of Mass Military Warfare manoeuvres in conjunction with large bodies of advancing infantry, aircraft support and artillery covering fire. The war was getting nearer for Ernest. The next stop would be a troop ship at Southampton Docks.

In December 1915 General Haig succeeded the French commander and become overall commander of the BEF. In January He was promoted to Field Marshal.

Aldershot Military Barracks is located in Hampshire and was established in 1854. In the years that followed a 'Military Town 'grew and is still such

Bell tents at Aldershot
This photo was kindly donated to me by the Curator of the Aldershot Military Museum

in present day. Over the period of the Great War, the garrison rapidly grew and by 1917 there were over 300,000 soldiers camped in the area. It is interesting to imagine how many bell tents were erected in the area.

The South West Mounted Brigade practised the art of Mass Military Warfare manoeuvres with other units of the Army and the Flying Corps. It was here that they joined the 41st Division.

Field Marshal Haig always clung onto the hope that there would be a decisive breakthrough by the Army on the Western Front and that he would then be able to use his 'beloved' cavalry to charge through the breach, attack the retreating enemy, and that there would then be a 'decisive final victory.'

I guess the highlight of the time spent at Aldershot would have been the King's visit to the barracks on the 26th of April 1916. Probably Ernest did not have much of a view of the King and his dignitaries. He never mentioned the visit to me.

SALAMANCA INFANTRY BARRACKS
ALDERSHOT.

Ernest has sent a letter to Elizabeth ('Bessy') which is dated the 13th of January 1916, he is clearly on leave in London at the time of writing the letter, he mentions having spent an evening at the Opera, he is shortly returning to Aldershot barracks where he is attending a course at the Salamanca Barracks, the above Post Card shows a military band performing outside the barracks.

There were concerns nearer to home in April of 1916. There was civil unrest in Ireland and soldiers were dispatched there, including at least one Battalion of Wiltshire regiment, but it did not affect Ernest who remained at Aldershot.

The volunteers of the previous year were not enlisting fast enough to keep up with demand, and as a consequence Parliament passed the Military Service Act making conscription compulsory for single men between the age of 18 to 41 years.

The war in early 1916

The new year on the Western Front saw a major offensive commence at Verdun which commenced on the 21st of February 1916. The plan by the

German High Command was to engage the French army and through attrition, bleed it dry of its men and resources. This city and surrounding area was territory that had been disputed over between the Germans and French for 100 years.

Germany took the view that France would fight to the last man over this territory. The area had 20 major forts and 40 smaller forts. However General Joffre deliberately depleted the garrisons of men as he saw the main threat coming from further north. The Germans seized on this opportunity and attacked in force. Initially they had a superior number of heavy artillery which was a significant factor at the beginning of the battle.

The Germans used every modern weapon and tactic that was available to them, including phosgene poisonous gas, flame throwers and German 'shock' Storm Troopers. Initially the Germans made good progress but over the weeks and months that followed, the French slowly redressed the balance in artillery. To improve morale four fifths of the French army would rotate and spend a proportion of the time in Verdun. The Germans did not do this, and they continually faced fresh French troops.

This was the longest battle in World War 1, lasting over 300 days. The French claimed victory in the end, but if anything, it was a moral victory restoring national pride, as the French were determined to keep fighting! Over 370,000 French troops were wounded or missing or killed against a total of 337,000 German losses. The stalemate continued and Generals were replaced on both sides. This was to become the year of mass slaughter. It was the turn of the new Kitchener's Army to take pressure off their French allies.

Chapter 3

Ernest is sent to the war

After months of training and some frustration, on the morning of Friday the 5th of May 1916, the Wiltshire Yeomanry travelled by train from Aldershot to the port at Southampton. The train arrived at the docks between 6.20 hours and 7.50 hours. They started loading the squadron on to steamship SS Rossetti at 09.00 hours. This was no mean feat, and it took until 17.00 hours that afternoon for the task to be completed. I have checked the weather for that day. It was blowing a north-easterly wind and there was heavy rain, and isolated thunderstorms. Certainly not the best of conditions for Ernest's maiden voyage.

The SS Rossetti, some years after World War 1. She's not looking her best, but the ship no doubt provided vital means to convey troops and supplies during World War 1.

Can you imagine the horses having to be winched onto the ship by crane, some would have panicked. I am sure a safe distance was kept from their legs thrashing about especially when they were placed on deck. All of the supply wagons and equipment would have been loaded in a similar fashion.

The SS Rossetti was a 6,508-ton cargo ship. It had been previously doing mail and parcel trips to South America under the management of the Lambert and Holt Line. The ship had a full speed of 15 knots. The journey from Southampton to Le Havre is about 130 miles.

This would have been Ernest's first trip on the sea. Judging by the weather forecast, the sea would have been rough. I am trying to picture him standing on the deck of the ship looking back towards the fading lights of Southampton Docks on the horizon. Many of the troops would have been placed on the upper deck. Ernest would have sat there with his comrades with his riding cape over his shoulders to protect him against the wind and rain. Soldiers all around would have been suffering from seasickness, as he sat on the deck shivering. What would have gone through his mind? Would this be the last time he saw England? Would he ever see his family and his beloved Elizabeth again? What was it really going to be like in Belgium and France? The soldiers had heard so many stories and rumours. Soon he would find out for real.

The ship probably sailed deliberately at 17.00 hours because of the U-Boat threat off the French coast. The ship would arrive at 02.30 hours under the cover of darkness. This cannot be confirmed but it is highly likely that the Rossetti would have had a naval escort to counter the threat of a U-Boat attack. Ernest would not have known this, but the U-Boat threat was ever present in the English Channel. The officers of the Rossetti and of the escort ships would have been constantly scanning the surface of the sea with their binoculars to try to detect any periscopes protruding from the surface.

On that very evening of Ernest's voyage to Le Havre, some 225 miles to the west of Southampton a lone German U-Boat, SM U-20, was patrolling. This predator was lurking in the depths of the sea off Lizard Point,

Dearest Elizabeth. Ernest would have had a similar photo to this in his inside pocket.

Cornwall. The captain sighted the sailing masts of a Swedish schooner, the 'Herald' in the cross hairs of his periscope. He ordered the torpedo to be fired. A short while later the 'Herald' took a direct hit and sank.

I mention this U-Boat because it was this U-Boat that torpedoed and sank the British ocean liner, the Lusitania, just over a year previously on the 7th of May 1915.

Ernest's first sea voyage passed without incident and the SS Rossetti docked in Le Havre harbour in the early hours of Saturday the 6th of May 1916. I can only imagine the scene in Le Havre docks, troop and supply ships being unloaded, a mass of soldiers and dockers going about their work. I wonder if Ernest saw any of the wounded soldiers waiting to be loaded onto the ships from the hospital trains. He never mentioned this to me so I can only speculate. It would have been a very sobering sight, had he seen these pitiful men.

The Yeomans' initial routine in Belgium and France

On Monday the 8th of May Ernest's squadron travelled via train north-east to billets in the village of Merris, which is located south of Ypres. For the remainder of the month various patrols were sent out to reconnoitre the front line in the area, generally around the town of Baillieu. The squadron used this period to acclimatise to the area.

The typical daily routine for the Yeomans was as follows:

07.00 hours Reveille – Wake up call. This word comes from the French who bugled their troops in the morning to wake them up.

07.30 hours Stables – Wherever the horses were stabled, it was the duty of each Yeoman to feed and water his horse and clean up the 'mess' they had made overnight. Once in France there would be no stables, and the horses would be tethered in picket lines.

08.30 hours Breakfast – The soldiers had various meats for breakfast, including bacon, steaks and liver, with eggs, coffee or tea.

08.45 hours Parade – The squadron would parade in drill order without arms.

11.30 hours Stables – Feed, clean and water the horses.

13.00 hours Dinner – The dinners would vary from day to day. The meals included baked meats, normally beef or mutton, brown curry rice and potatoes. The soldiers would have fish once a week, and also Irish stew. To accompany dinner, they had plum puddings, and apple tarts.

16.30 hours Stables – Feed, water and clean the horse.

17.30 hours Tea – Bread and jam, bread and dripping, coffee or tea.

21.00 hours Lights out.

This routine would vary as the role of the Yeomanry changed.

Between 1914 and 1918 an estimated three and a quarter million tons of food was shipped to and consumed by the British Army on the Western front.

On the 31st of May the Squadron marched to billets in the Champagne area of France, south-east of Amiens. The purpose being to train with the Second Cavalry Division.

During this period Ernest would have settled down to the routine of life on the Western Front. When not training, a lot of his time would be spent looking after his horse. He would have to water the horse regularly. By now it was summer in France. A horse can drink 20-22 gallons of water per day in hot weather, and half this amount in the winter. He would also have to feed his horse with oats, bran, and hay. The easiest way to feed the horse would be to use a nose bag that fitted over the horse's head. The recommendation for a heavy horse was about 14lbs of grain, 15lbs of dried hay and one ounce of salt per day. Due to the successes of the German U-Boat campaign the following year in 1917, these rations were considerably reduced. Both men and horses suffered malnourishment.

The war at sea

This same year, 1916, the Germans blockaded the port of Le Havre with their submarines, sinking three Norwegian merchant ships, the Baus, Kannick and Salliust. The Saliust was sunk by U-Boat SMUB-18 in the English Channel on the 9th of March that year. The other two Norwegian merchant ships were sunk by the same U-Boat under similar circumstances, the Kannick on the 23rd of March and the Baus on the 5th of April. Many other ships suffered a similar fate over this period. There is an article in the 'Dundee Evening Telegraph' dated the 19th of May 1916, where it is reported that the Norwegians wrote to the German authorities in protest. The Germans responded by saying that the ships were in a war zone.

The end of May saw a major sea battle between the German Imperial Navy and British Royal Navy. It took place at Jutland in the North Sea.

It had been decided between France and Britain, that the French Navy would patrol the Mediterranean theatre of war, leaving the north coast of France and Belgium to the responsibility of the British Royal Navy. Britain had enjoyed naval supremacy for several years prior to World War 1, but the German Navy was catching up. The ratio of war ships had been reduced to just over two to one in favour of the British Royal Navy at the outbreak of war.

In 1906 saw the launch of the first British dreadnought class battleship. This was a fast ship with large calibre guns. HMS Dreadnought could fire 10 x 12inch guns over long distances and had steam turbines which could propel the ship at 22 knots. This sparked a race between the superpowers to try to catch up with this ship design. By the end of the war Britain had 29 Dreadnought battleships, Germany had 17, yet there can be no doubt about the design and engineering skills of the German people. They built their ships to an extremely high quality, and significantly the armament of their ships, in particular the deck armour, was superior in strength and thickness. They also designed better watertight compartments below deck. These would become significant factors in battle.

The British Fleet was commanded by Admiral Sir John Jellicoe, and the German Imperial Navy by Reinhard Scheer. The battle commenced on the 31st of May 1916. The German plan was to lure part of the British Royal Navy into pursuing a small part of their fleet. Once committed, the British ships would be confronted by the whole of the German Imperial fleet and be destroyed. The Germans were confident because they believed that the bulk of the British fleet was in dock at Scarpa Flow in north-east Scotland. What the Germans failed to realise was that the British Intelligence operatives (room 40), some of whom were code breakers, had decoded the German fleet's wireless signals and had set sail with plans to spring a trap of their own.

At the commencement of the battle there followed a series of manoeuvres by both navies, each of the ships exchanging salvos. It soon became apparent that some of the British older ships were taking a battering. A number of them, which had German shells explode on deck, were completely destroyed.

This had been caused by bad practice and design on the part of the British Royal Navy who for some time had stacked their powder charges in quantity near to their guns in order to speed up their rate of fire during battle. When a German shell exploded, this in turn caused the powder charges to ignite, which also caused the ship's magazines to explode below deck.

The initial advantage which the British fleet had in numerical supremacy was lost during the course of the battle due to inaccurate signals between the command ships. Poor visibility at times was made even worse when night fell. Many ships did not have adequate search lights so that during darkness the German fleet was able to slip past the British fleet, which saw their ships but did not fire on them for fear they were British ships. The German fleet escaped, sailing on to their port at Wilhelmshaven.

The German Kaiser was quick to claim victory stating, 'The spell of Trafalgar is broken!' He was confident because the Germans had lost fewer ships. The British Royal Navy had lost 6,094 sailors to Germany's 2,551. The British had lost 14 ships to Germany's 11. The debate as to who won still goes on today, but it can be said that this was a tactical victory for the British in that the British were able to continue to blockade the German ports depriving Germany of vital resources for their war machine.

Over the years that followed Germany would slowly be starved to death. By the end of the war, it was estimated that in excess of 800,000 German and Austrian civilians died through malnutrition and starvation. The German soldiers' food ration was reduced from over 3,500 calories per day, to less than a half of that amount by the end of the war. Some of the harvests in Germany during the war were poor, part of the reason being that the British naval blockade of their ports meant that fertilizers could not be imported into the country.

After the battle the German Admiral Scheer wrote to the Kaiser stating, 'Real victory can only be achieved by sending U-Boats to sink British merchant ships!' For the rest of the war the German fleet did not engage the British fleet in strength. Britannia still ruled the waves!

However, it was not all one-sided. Ignoring the risk of bringing the Americans into the war, the Germans stepped up their U-Boat campaign again. Their vessels sank nearly 13 million tons of allied shipping before the end of the war. It should be remembered that Britain still partly relied on food imports to feed its civilian population and soldiers. At the outbreak of war 25-30% of the food consumed was imported.

The vital work of the code breakers in this battle should not be forgotten. Had it not been for their tireless dedication, this battle and the outcome of the war could have been so different.

Ernest's squadron lays communication cables

Ernest's squadron remained in the Champagne region until the 21st of June when it marched to La Niepe, and then the following day to Schaeren. They spent the remainder of the month digging trenches during the night to lay communications cable in the Mount Kemmel area of Belgium. This work is likely to have been carried out with the Engineer Signals. The Yeomans would have to assist in unrolling the cables which were coated in steel lead or brass. Animals, including dogs, mules and horses would have been used to carry the cables. The soldiers would be instructed to dig trenches to bury the cables to a minimum depth of six feet. By the end of the war there were over 120,000 soldiers deployed in this type of work. It would have been physically demanding. The shovel and pick work which the Yeomans had learnt in the Ashdown Forest the previous year was now being put into practice.

Trench digging and laying cables was laborious work for some members of the squadron who considered trench digging as not work for the cavalry. It was a question of swallowing their pride and 'getting on with it'. No doubt much of the digging was done during the night because of the threat of hostile fire from the Germans, in particular their snipers. This was necessary work as maintaining communications was of vital importance. Exploding artillery shells broke these cables rendering the system useless until repaired. Some of the heavy shells used by the Germans left craters ten feet deep. In any event the soldiers were kept busy and maintained their fitness. The Yeomans dug trenches for cables laid along the third trench, known as the Reserve Trench.

After this work was completed, the squadron spent the daytime in the grounds of the Château du Mont Noir, probably in bell tents, with the officers likely accommodated in the château itself.

The work of The Royal Engineer Signal Service

A tribute should be paid to the work of the Engineers. New recruits with telecommunication, wireless and engineering skills were shortlisted to join the Engineer and Signals Regiment. The Engineers were also attached to various other frontline regiments in a support role.

The Royal Engineer Signal Service was formed in 1912, but communications systems by today's standards were still crude. The main types in use were flags, lamps and lights, as well as heliographs, together with the worded messages carried by dispatch riders, many of whom provided their own motorbikes. Dogs also became an effective carrier of messages. Some breeds were so good that back in Britain conscription was introduced for those breeds. The dog had a canister attached to his neck similar to those attached to pigeons, but larger. Dogs proved their worth during the battle of Verdun.

The flags used by the Engineers were normally blue or white. A competent operator could signal about twelve words per minute. Ernest and his fellow Yeoman would have been taught this procedure back in England. In 1915 signalling was also done by lights with disc cutters from a cover which could be read from long distance with the use of a field periscope. This method succeeded the outdated Begbie lamp.

Trials were also being carried out with wireless sets, which worked on the long wave frequency. The wirelesses were heavy and cumbersome. It took three men to carry them and six men to carry the batteries. Better results were being obtained with the wireless sets made by Marconi which were installed in the planes of the Royal Flying Corps. The co-pilot would operate the set, but the early sets were also heavy and took up a lot of space. This innovation proved very useful during offensives. The co-pilots in the planes could tap Morse code to the receivers on the ground, leading to better and more accurate coordination with the artillery during battle.

However, problems occurred using this method during the Somme offensive because of poor aerial visibility. To try to overcome this problem, the allied planes would descend to about 900 feet and then activate a claxon on the underside of the fuselage. This audible alarm would alert the infantry below to set off a red flare. Once this flare was seen by the pilots, they could then report back via Morse code to HQ as to the position of the infantry amongst the smoke and mist of battle.

Sad news came on the 5th of June 1916 with the sinking of HMS Hampshire by a mine. This ship was on its way to Russia when disaster struck. There were heavy casualties, including Lord Kitchener and his staff. It is a tragedy that he survived many historic battles only to drown in the North Sea off Scarpa Flow, aged 65. Lord Kitchener had been a Royal Engineer in his early days.

The Battle of the Somme, July 1916

There was a massive military build-up on the Western Front during June, leading to another major conflict, the Battle of the Somme, which began the following month. As has been seen, the French Army was under terrific pressure at Verdun. The purpose of the Somme offensive was to create another front, thus drawing some of German forces away from Verdun and relieving pressure on the French Army. Field Marshal Haig was convinced that he could break through the German lines and gain a decisive victory. It was to become known as the 'Big Push.'

The battle commenced on Saturday, the 1st of July 1916. Prior to this there had been a week of continuous artillery fire from 1,400 allied guns which fired a total of over 1.6 million shells. Haig's plan was to wipe out the German trenches along a 25-mile front spanning an area near to the River Somme. The artillery would also destroy large sections of German barbed wire defences, paving the way for the infantry to advance. During this advance the British artillery would then target the second and third line of German trenches. Timing was of the essence.

Sadly, of the 1,400 artillery pieces, there were not nearly enough guns of a heavy calibre to do the job properly. It has been estimated that as much as one in five shells failed to detonate. Some of the shells that had delayed fuses failed to explode at the right time in order to destroy the barbed wire. Not nearly enough of the right type of shells were used for this purpose. The timed fuses used at the beginning of the battle often sank into the earth before exploding, having no effect on the barbed wire at ground level.

Towards the end of the Battle of the Somme the British experimented with the wire cutting 106-mark ll fuse. This was fired from a standard 18-Pounder field artillery gun. The 106-mark ll was the first instantaneous percussion artillery fuse. In layman's terms, this means that the shell exploded instantaneously the moment it made contact with an object, which in this case would be the surface of ground on top of which was located the barbed wire defences. If only enough of these shells had been fired during the pre-battle bombardment, then the outcome may have been different. But this war was full of 'ifs and buts.'

The area of trenches chosen for this attack had previously been a quiet area, enabling the Germans to build substantial defences. Their trenches were up to ten metres deep in places and many of them were able to withstand the artillery bombardment. They also had time to dig deeper trenches to bury the wireless cable to their command posts, and, as a consequence, they had much better comms with their artillery.

German accounts of this battle show clearly that they were aware of the approach of the attack, but that they did not expect the attack to extend as far south as it did. When the artillery barrage started, the Germans simply went into their dugouts with their weapons, and waited. By now the British were becoming predictable. The Germans referred to the artillery barrage as the 'drum roll' and they knew that as soon as it stopped, the attack would begin. In some areas there was a delay of as much as thirty minutes before the Tommie's blew their whistles and came over the top, giving them ample time to prepare and deploy their deadly Maxim machine gun units.

The British had dug nineteen tunnels under key German positions, and between 07.20 hours and 07.28 hours on the morning of the 1st of July the underground mines were detonated. The mines had mixed success, because the Germans were aware of some of the mine positions and had simply withdrawn backwards from their original position. Consequently, when some mines exploded, they had no effect, whereas other mines were more effective destroying whole units.

When the artillery bombardment ceased and the mines detonated, the Germans climbed out of their dugouts. Some had to dig themselves out with spades as the entrances had been blocked by soil and debris. They carried their Maxim machine guns to the top of the trench and commenced firing at the advancing British and French soldiers. These machine guns were capable of firing over 600 rounds per minute. They were water cooled to prevent them from overheating. Even so the fire was so rapid and continuous that some of the gunners' skin from their fingers stuck to the firing controls. In places it was a massacre. The British and Commonwealth troops in some areas had to cluster together in order to penetrate the small gaps in the barbed wire defences.

Timing and coordination between the artillery units and the advancing infantry was critical. However, allowances were not made in the planning stage for any delays the infantry might incur during their attack, and there were delays.

The communication systems failed miserably. The British Command in the northern sector did not receive the results of the initial attack for hours and in some cases days, the artillery lost its coordination with the attacking infantry. As a consequence, the German soldiers in the front line' fire trench' were not pinned down long enough, and they were ready and waiting with their machine guns. This was because the artillery, working to a strict timetable, finished targeting the German front trenches and extended its aim to target the second and third German trenches too soon. In this modern day and age, it is difficult to conceive how crude the communications were.

There was however more success in the southern sector where the British and French armies fought together. They had been supported by heavier French artillery pieces which were more effective. Most of their objectives had been reached on the first day.

At the end of the first day of the battle the total number of casualties was horrendous. The British lost over 57,000 dead, missing or wounded, the French 7,000 and the Germans 12,000. Clearly these losses were not going to be sustainable. Field Marshal Haig, who would become known as 'Butcher Haig', was not deterred. He continued to send his troops 'over the top' to be slaughtered for another four months until bad weather in November stopped the battle. Historians have debated Haig's reputation and since the 1960's many have defended him, insisting that towards the end of this battle, Haig made every effort to try and minimise the losses, including insisting on adequate Tank support, and differing tactics during night-time attacks. I don't want to get involved in this debate; however, I would like to point out that when he died on the 29th of January 1928, over 300,00 World War 1 veterans lined the route of his funeral procession. I doubt Lloyd George was afforded this amount of respect.

The Battle of the Somme continued into August. The Yeomans were deployed in working parties in the Fricourt area. Ernest would have had his work cut out, over these next three months. The casualties in men and horses rose significantly. It would seem highly likely that it was during this first three-month period of the Somme offensive that Ernest lost his two horses.

Life for the Yeomans in the Somme area

Some of Ernest's Yeomanry were deployed in the area of the Somme in July. On the first day of the battle many Yeomans were deployed on Mounted Police duties, others were deployed in working parties. Later in the month there were casualties in Mametz Wood where some of the Yeomans were used as ammunition carriers, and shells exploded amongst them. During this same period, the Yeomans were billeted at a village called Ribemont near Saint Quentin, south-east of the battlefield.

They had two periods of supply duties in Mametz Wood, as well as continuing Mounted Police duties.

It is over this period that Major Charles Awdry in charge of B Squadron was made temporary Second in Charge of the IX Cavalry Corps. His brother R.W Awdry replaced him as the new Major of B Squadron.

Army discipline was very strict. If caught drunk whilst on duty, the soldier would receive a 28-day punishment. Offenders would have to parade each day in full pack, which could weigh up to 100lbs. The offender would be ordered to march where directed. At the beginning and end of each day, the offender would be bound by wrists and ankles and spread across a large wheel of an artillery piece for everyone to see. This punishment could happen on a cold winter's day, adding to the suffering and making the scene reminiscent of the Napoleonic Wars. In addition, the soldier would have his pay stopped, affecting any allowances that his wife may have received back in Britain. It was a terrifying aspect of life as a Yeoman.

Furthermore, if an officer were caught asleep whilst on duty, the punishment would be more severe. It could result in a Court Martial and, if found guilty, death by firing squad. Some of these executions took place in the nearby city of Poperinge, where there were over 300 executions carried out by the Allies during World War 1, traditionally at dawn.

For nurses one of the saddest jobs was to care for those soldiers who were facing a court martial and had attempted suicide. In some of these cases, they would have to restore the soldier to a level of fitness to be able to face a Court Martial and the firing squad. The suicide rate increased as the war progressed, affecting soldiers and officers serving on the front.

Major Awdry mentions a couple of separate incidents of misconduct in his diary. One such incident involves a Yeoman being caught trying to cook a rabbit whilst in the trench. Another Yeoman is caught 'cadging' a lift on the back of a supply truck. The punishment seems to have been extra guard duties. Ernest was punished for a misdemeanour, referred to later in this book.

The Mle Hotchkiss machine gun

For the remainder of July 1916, the rest of the squadron carried out training in the use of the Mle Hotchkiss machine gun.

This machine gun was the main stay of the French Army, and it was used by the British Army too. It was known for its reliability and robust design. It was quite a heavy weapon weighing 52lbs with a barrel length of 30 inches. It could be loaded with a strip of ammunition, or it had an articulated metal belt of cartridges containing 249 rounds. It fired 8mm bullets. When in transit these guns would be carried on the supply wagons or on specially designed harnesses for horses to carry. Part of the training would be the drill in unloading these weapons at speed and deploying them with concealment in mind. Emphasis would be put on the right location of their deployment, preferably a wooded area and where any other cover was available. Another factor would be to ensure that the arc of fire covered the desired area. The main function of this weapon was to provide effective covering fire for advancing infantry and cavalry charges.

The Hotchkiss machine gun had a fire rate of 450-600 rounds per minute and was gas activated. The expanding gas created by the bullet when it ignited together with the recoil, was a combined effect operating the firing mechanism for the next round. So as long as the trigger is pressed and there is ammunition attached to the magazine, the gun will fire continually. This weapon, when set up correctly, claimed many German lives. The Yeomans were taught the system of enfilade fire, commonly used when a machine gun is deployed in a flanking position where the maximum arc of fire can be aimed at a large group of infantry crossing in front of the machine gun's position.

The machine gun was most effective when part of a four to six-man team. Essentially number one would help position the gun on the tripod and fire the weapon, number two would help number one do this, he would also act as a range finder and observer whilst the gun was in action but crouch a short distance away in hear shot, he would also help feed the ammunition into the chamber. Numbers three and four, five and six would do relays in carrying the ammunition to the emplacement and open the ammunition boxes ready for use. The group would be instructed not to cluster together, so that they did not draw attention to themselves by enemy spotters or snipers.

There were three types of fire:

Range fire – bursts of 10-20 rounds to determine if the gun was hitting the target(s)

Rapid fire – bursts of 30 rounds with short intervals for a correctly aligned target

Traverse fire – bursts of fire designed to cover a wide area, of sufficient volume to ensure maximum effect.

The men would have to act as a team, adjusting to the change in circumstances, in case one of the team was shot or wounded. In this case another member of the team would have to take over that person's role.

In the heat of a battle, when the defenders were faced with masses of attacking infantry, an effective team would make the difference between driving the attackers back and containing them or being overrun and killed.

Attacking infantry would make it their priority to take out the machine gun emplacements. The skill of the gunner was critical in this situation, at a fire rate of 500-600 rounds per minute. A gunner could get through a massive amount of ammunition, and sometimes the supply team would not be able to keep up with demand, especially in the case of team members having been killed or injured.

The maintenance and care of the weapon was also vital. Dirt and mud would cause problems with the firing mechanism, sometimes causing it to jam. The severe frosty weather, unbeknown to Ernest, was on its way later that year also played havoc with the firing mechanisms, unless they were properly lubricated and cleaned. Sometimes bullet cases would split open causing the mechanism to jam. Many units would have a spare weapon in case this happened.

There were a number of machine guns used by the British army, some of which were referred to as heavy machine guns, for example the Maxim and Vickers. A popular light machine gun was the Lewis light machine gun. The Americans appeared to be world leaders in this concept and design. They must have made a fortune prior to and during the war in supplying arms to the different nations.

Ernest becomes a dispatch rider

July 1916 would have been about the time Ernest was seconded to the Engineer and Signals as a dispatch rider.

The Yeoman machine gun section was disbanded shortly after arriving in France. One can only speculate as to why, though it could have been because they were only a support unit, and their weapons were badly needed by other active units on the front. However, the training Ernest received during this period proved vital later in the war. I suspect that he would not have had as much training as some of the other Yeomans because of his dispatch duties, but nonetheless he would have had a certain amount.

Sometime in the summer of 1916, brother Walter Burchell was eventually called up and sent to the Machine Gun Corps as he was a very good shot. He had been a keen shot prior to the war, shooting game and vermin in Wiltshire.

Later, in August 1916, some of the Yeomans were transferred to Mounted Police units. One of their main tasks was to escort German prisoners and search them prior to their incarceration in Prisoner of War camps. Sometimes vital intelligence could be obtained in the course of questioning, especially if the prisoner was an officer. Some of the captured officers were found carrying important documents, for example trench maps. In one such case an officer was found in possession of his trench map including the location of all the German machine gun emplacements. This information was evaluated by the Army Intelligence Department and subsequently fed to the artillery units.

When referring to the Yeomanry Diary for this period, it is clear they were being held in a reserve and support roll. A number of officers were sent to other divisions to carry out various duties, which included secondments to escort duties and intelligence gathering. It is highly likely that Ernest and his horse were seconded to the Signals and Engineers sections. The precise date that Ernest was transferred is not easy to define as several references are made in the diary. Over several weeks, soldiers were temporarily transferred as dispatch riders. I will therefore continue to refer to the Yeomanry Diary to explain the other tasks and duties which they carried out.

The soldier chosen for dispatch duties would be a man of resourcefulness, capable of finding his way across country under extreme conditions, sometimes under fire and in difficult weather conditions, and in darkness. Grandad had been handpicked for this task, which leads me to believe that he had built up a certain amount of respect by his supervising officers for his competence, and he would prove them right.

When Grandad became a dispatch rider, he used his horse regularly. His primary aim was to deliver urgent orders and messages between Head Quarters and military units on the front line. The dispatch rider soon became a target for snipers and artillery spotters. As if proof of the danger were needed, two of Ernest's mounts were killed from shell bursts.

'I often rode during the night to minimise the risk of being spotted. Even so they must have heard the horse's hooves on the cobbled street I was riding along. A shell burst nearby and shrapnel hit my horse in the chest. The poor beast slowed to a halt and collapsed underneath me. This happened to me twice and eventually I was given a motorcycle. It was belt drive. I used to get annoyed because the belt would often come off or slip'.

All of the motorbikes began to suffer with breakdowns in increasing frequency. As one of the main problems was the lack of spare parts, dispatch riders managed by cannibalising old bikes, and salvaging parts from bikes that were shell damaged wrecks.

This is possibly the type of bike Ernest would have used, it was a belt driven Douglas motor bike. Other manufacturers made Army bikes for the same purpose, these included; Triumph, Norton, BSÁ, Matchless and Ariel. I came across this bike during my trip in 2017 to the Passchendaele exhibition. The Douglas motor bike was 2.75 horse power and capable of speeds around 25 m.p.h.

A lot of the dispatch riding would be carried out during the hours of darkness. These early motorbikes did not have the best of headlights, as the carbide substance in the generators became less effective with constant use. In any event Ernest was not allowed to use his headlights if he was driving in the area between Divisional HQ and the front line. He was only allowed to put his lights on if he was driving rearwards in the opposite direction away from the front-line trenches, towards Divisional HQ. He probably lost count of how many times he fell off his motor bike.

Can you imagine a cold wet night, it's raining, you're heading towards the front lines with a dispatch, you're travelling in complete darkness except for the glow of distant exploding artillery shells on the horizon, you get a puncture, you stop at the roadside? You get out your repair kit, your hands are cold, the adhesive will not stick properly because of the wet and mud, you continue to fumble in the darkness, you're running late. What a nightmare situation this must have been for poor Ernest and other dispatch riders! Some nights they would be blessed with a full moon which would have made conditions slightly better.

Having delivered dispatches, Ernest would obtain a signed receipt and then would often have to wait for a reply. Then he would return from whence he came with further orders. The dispatch rider would have regular such runs each day. After a while Ernest would slip into a routine. Having become familiar with the routes, he would have to try to pick out distinctive features in the daytime and put these to memory for his night-time runs. He would have to deliver divisional orders daily and ensure that every unit of the Division received these orders. There would be regular runs between Division and Corps HQs and also Army Group HQs. Another job would be to deliver Brigade Post. He would also have to make regular trips to the supply column.

The Second Army Group HQ were located in the little village of Cassel, located between Saint Omer and Poperinge. This was where Second Army Group General Herbert Plumer was based.

Many dispatch riders were killed or seriously wounded. Their importance and vital role in the thick of a battle cannot be overestimated in my view. Not enough of these riders would receive medals for their bravery. Some routes became high risk for artillery attacks, 'Hell Fire Corner' being one such location, a junction between the Menin Road to the city of Ypres railway crossroad. Another location was called 'Hell's Avenue'. This was a track between Brielen leading to Essex Farm near Passchendaele.

The German artillery spotters over a period of time began to use distinct features to gain their correct coordinates. An example could be the ruins of a church or a road junction. Using their maps and eight-digit coordinates they called up an artillery unit and instructed them to fire. Following a period of trial and error, and making minor adjustments to the sites of the guns, the shells began to drop with a degree of accuracy.

So, you can imagine the scene. A German spotter identifies a lone horse and rider or the dim headlights of a motorcycle travelling towards the known coordinates of a road junction. The German spotter calls up the artillery unit. Experience would tell him to allow for the seconds it took for the shell to land and explode, against the time it would take the dispatch rider to reach that junction. This sequence of events happened twice to poor Ernest and his horses with tragic results.

During this time there are numerous references in the Yeoman's diary to horse fatalities. Each horse had a unique identification number. It is difficult to believe Grandad's luck at not being wounded or killed, or seriously injured when his horse collapsed beneath him.

The dispatch riders, upon approaching these dangerous locations had the choice of watching and waiting for the pauses between shell bursts for the artillery crew to reload, and making a dash, or to pull the throttle open full and hope for the best. It was a hard choice. The role of the dispatch rider was to become vital during a battle or major campaign, even more so when other communication methods broke down and became ineffective.

During battle there were also runners. These brave men received an urgent message from the front-line commander, and had to run to the nearest dispatch rider, handing the message over to him. This would then be delivered to Divisional HQ. If communication cables were broken, the message had to be delivered even further back behind the lines. The work during a major battle would be exhausting.

The use of pigeons for communication

The role of pigeons in World War 1 is well known and Ernest would sometimes have to take homing pigeons back with him to the front. I must admit to being rather sceptical about the use of homing pigeons. They are for me a crude technique of communication, especially in twentieth century warfare, but there was an element of tradition. The method had been used as far back as Egyptian times. However, with my research completed, I have to concede that the system did work successfully.

The use of pigeons relied on the fact that given two to three months of time to settle at one location, the pigeons would treat this mobile coop as home. They had shelter, protection from predators and were fed here. Above all else their mates would remain in the coop awaiting their

A Mobile Army pigeon coop

return. It worked best with the cock birds who would be taken from the coop by the signallers and handed to the Dispatch riders, who in turn would take the pigeons to the front in cages. Grandad would have fitted the cage at the back of his seat, or strapped to the rider's back.

Having arrived at the front, Ernest would hand over the pigeons. Microfilm messages or hand-written notes were then placed in a small canister attached to the pigeon's leg.

The pigeon would then be released to fly back to the coop located behind the lines. Sometimes the pigeons would circle a short while before setting off on their homeward bound journey. This is when they would be vulnerable to enemy fire. The Germans also used hawks to attack the birds. It was often practice for more than one bird to be released with the same message to improve the odds of one of them returning safely back to the coop.

Once airborne the pigeon has an in-built homing mechanism sometimes referred to as 'magnetoreception'. The pigeon is a fast bird which can fly at an average speed of 60mph. Some modern-day racing pigeons have been recorded as flying at 100mph when the wind was in their favour.

A pigeon basket strapped to the back of the dispatch rider
Photo courtesy of the Royal Signals

Upon arrival at the coop, the pigeon would set of a bell or a buzzer, notifying the Signal Corps of its arrival. This officer would carefully remove the canister and send the contents of the message by telegraph, field phone or personal messenger to Divisional HQ.

There are numerous references to the successful and valuable missions these pigeons carried out. They did vital work at Verdun, and during numerous other battles. During the battles near Paris, pigeons were sent from the capital to London maintaining vital communication with Britain. Over 100,000 pigeons were used on the Western Front during World War 1. Their work was deemed so valuable that the Government passed legislation in Parliament which made it an offence punishable with six months in prison or £100 fine for anyone caught shooting a homing pigeon. A reward of £5 was offered for information leading to the arrest of an offender or offenders. An amazing number of thirty-two pigeons received the 'Dicken' medal for outstanding work.

A pigeon with the small canister attached to its leg

I have deliberately included some detail about the use of pigeons because in the Yeoman Diary reference is made to pigeon training sessions, and it is highly likely that Ernest would have taken part.

Vital supplies during wartime

At this point acknowledgement needs to be paid to the vital role that the British Army Veterinary Corps (BAVC) played in the war. Their work had a significant link to food production.

Very little is said about this group of professionals. They had been formed before the Napoleonic Wars in 1796. The army had dispatched 122 officers and 797 other ranks with the British Expeditionary Force. They treated over 725,000 horses on the Western Front during the war. Of those treated, 80% returned to duty.

It could well be asked why this is significant. Britain's food production was beginning to suffer in 1916, partly because there was a shortage of heavy horses to do the field work. Had it not been for the success of the vets, in returning 80% of the horses back to the front, then even more horses would have had to be transported to France from Britain, horses which were already in short supply.

The food supply became even worse the following year in 1917, as the U-Boat campaign stepped up a gear. The new mechanised agricultural tractors were not arriving in Britain in large enough numbers from Canada and America to have a significant impact. Had the BAVC not been so competent, Britain may have run out of horses and mules.

Further developments in the war from August 1916

On the wider scene, August 1916 saw Romania declare war on Austria and Bulgaria. Prior to the outbreak of war in 1914, Romania had supplied Germany with petroleum and food. Romania had the biggest oil fields in Europe. Initially the Allies feared that the Romanians would side with the Germans, but following King Carol's death on the 10th of October 1914, his son, the new King Ferdinand, favoured the Allies, and the petroleum and food supplies to the Germans eventually ceased. In the period between King Ferdinand taking over the throne in 1914 and Romania's declaration of War in 1916, promises were made by the Russians and French to supply modern arms and men to Romania, the motive being to encourage the Romanians to invade Bulgaria and Austria, and to disrupt rail connections between Germany and Turkey.

At the news of Romania declaring war on its Allies, Germany responded by declaring war on Romania the following day.

The advantages of an extra ally would be short lived, as German and Austrian armies swept into Romania in the autumn of 1916, and the capital city Bucharest fell. The Armistice of Focsani was signed in December 1916. Large swathes of Romania, including the prized oil fields, were occupied by the central powers. However, the unoccupied part of Romania was steadfast in continuing the fight.

The Italians, who were allies of Romania also declared war on Germany in August 1916. Italy had a reasonably sized navy, and this was deployed in the Adriatic Sea against any threat from the Austrian navy.

It was able to inhibit supply routes to the central powers via the Adriatic Sea. Amongst other ships, they possessed six dreadnought battleships which were put to good use. The Italian army was also deployed along their northern border, but it was poorly equipped, and the Austrians enjoyed the advantage of occupying the higher ground. After early Italian successes along the Insonzo river front, the situation rapidly became a stalemate.

By the end of August 1916, now two months into the Battle of the Somme and six months into the Battle of Verdun, horrific casualties had been sustained by both sides. The cream of the German soldiers of the Western Front were being killed and wounded at an alarming rate. This clearly concerned the German High Command. If this fighting continued the Germans would have to consider retreating from the Somme battlefield to a stronger line of defence. It was at this time that they started to construct the Hindenburg Line of defences.

The Hindenburg Line was the idea of General Eric von Ludendorff, who was Hindenburg's subordinate. Ludendorff was the architect of these plans.

Because of the heavy losses in the Somme and Verdun offences, by the end of 1916 the Germans were outnumbered on the Western Front by almost two to one. This superiority would only increase in 1917. The Germans must have felt they had no choice given the disparity of troop numbers in favour of the Allies. Over the next few months, under complete secrecy, the Germans planned to retreat ten miles back towards the Belgian border with Germany, along a 70-mile front between the towns of Arras to the north and St Quentin to the south-east.

This was to be a carefully designed system of trenches, the idea being to lure the attacking allies into a killing zone, which would then have a devastating effect. The previous line of defence in the area had a number of salients (bends and bulges), and by constructing a straight line ten miles back, the width of the front line would be considerably shortened in this area, freeing up a number of German divisions to be deployed elsewhere.

The first defence would be a three-metre deep by four-metre wide trench designed to be impassable by tanks. Then there was a line of thick barbed wire craftily designed at intervals to be weak, thus encouraging the advancing infantry to cut through the thinner wire and funnel through these areas. Behind the barbed wire would be purpose-built concrete and steel bunkers, spaced out in a 'zig-zag' pattern along the front. These bunkers were to contain heavy machine guns set up to do enfilade fire concentrated at the massing infantry which was pouring through the gaps in the barbed wire. The bunkers were designed to enable the occupants to withdraw quickly to the fire trenches located one mile behind. Between the fire trench and the second supply trench would be a distance of one further mile. The gap would have heavy artillery emplaced.

The third German trench would be even further back, between two and three miles, where the reserves would be located. This was a deliberate tactic making the reserves in trench three out of range from the allied artillery. Where possible the German artillery would be located on reverse slopes making it difficult for the Allies to target and destroy with their artillery because they were out of sight from forces on the ground and needed to rely of air surveillance to be able to target the German artillery. All of these defences would be constructed by 370,000 workers who would consist of army reserves, civilians, and Russian prisoners of war.

In September 1916, with the Somme offensive continuing, the Yeomans were based in the Ribemont area, where they were deployed as observers in the Bernafay Wood, Ligny, and Tilloy areas. Ernest was one of nine dispatch riders seconded to the Engineer and Signals units. Towards the end of the month some of the other mounted Yeomans were deployed with the 19th Lancers (Indian regiment) south of the village of Gueudecourt, where they engaged enemy machine gun positions, eventually being relieved by the infantry.

On the 15th of September tanks were first used in the Battle of the Somme. The prototype, the British Mark 1 tank, came in at just over 27 tons with a crew of eight operators. It was a British invention and made by Fosters in England. The first models had two large steel wheels located at the rear to assist with steering. The tank had a fabricated dome roof above the main roof which was sloping, so that German stick grenades would not stay on the roof but would slide off. Winston Churchill saw the potential of this invention and put his full backing behind what would be called the 'Land Battleship Project. '

A total of 49 Tanks were used on the 15th of September, only nine succeeding in their objectives at the end of the day. Many broke down, got stuck or were destroyed by German artillery. However, the weapon did have a psychological effect on the Germans, some of whom were horrified to see the tanks approaching them.

Several years ago, I had the experience of sitting in a World War 1 tank at Bovington Tank Museum. I was surprised to learn that most of the fatalities with tank crews were from carbon monoxide poisoning from the exhaust fumes. I imagined being one of the tank crew. It must have been a nightmare as the interiors were not padded. There would be bruises and broken bones as the tanks went over the rough terrain and trenches. There certainly was no thought about health and safety issues for those crew members.

The Yeomans' support for front-line regiments

The month of October 1916 saw the Yeomanry continuing in their support roles for the front-line regiments. In their diary it is noted that the Squadron HQ is located at the town of Becordel to the south-east of Albert. This was one of many locations where there were guard duties. The mobile field ambulance stations nearby held wounded German soldiers, and these tents were guarded by the Yeomans.

On the 7th of October, the Squadron moved to Fricourt. For the rest of the month they were deployed on police duties, ammunition supply and intelligence gathering. Some of this work was carried out in purpose-built models of shell damaged tree trunks, and also suspended from hot air balloons. The purpose of these observation posts (OPs) was to report on enemy positions, troop and cavalry movements,

An observation post disguised as a shell torn tree

and the location of artillery. The observers normally worked in pairs. They would have binoculars and field glasses to assist them to view the enemy from a distance. Ground OPs would be on the lookout for machine gun emplacements and snipers.

Experience would teach them to look for the 'muzzle flash', and rising smoke when the weapons fired, which in turn would lead to pinpointing their location. The intelligence gatherers used powerful field binoculars and periscopes. They would be on the lookout for identifying badges on the German helmets which signified the regiment. Something as simple as the digging of soil and the colour of the soil or subsoil deposited on the trench bank and surrounding area might reveal the possibility of German tunnels being dug under the allied lines, and the consequent obvious risks of mines being planted in these tunnels. The findings would all be recorded in daily logs and submitted to the intelligence units for dissemination.

The hot air balloon OPs were deployed by both sides. The balloon skin was made of canvas, and was filled with hydrogen. The balloon was attached to a steel cable on a reel which would slowly uncoil allowing the balloon to rise to heights between 1,000 and 1,500 metres. There would also be a length of telephone cable extending down from the balloon to a receiver on the ground so that the operators in the balloon could inform the ground crew of their observations. The two observers in the balloon basket would each have a parachute in the event of being attacked by enemy aircraft. They were able to jump out and parachute down to the ground.

Observation balloons were targets for enemy planes and hundreds were shot down. The observers did not always survive these attacks, many would die. Reference is made in the Yeoman diaries to Sgt Bullock of Ernest's troop who was deployed in one of these observation balloons. He was subsequently commended for his work.

At the end of October, the squadron moved to billets in the village of Flessells. The squadron then appears to be on the move frequently in November. Ernest's B Squadron eventually joined the 9th Army Corps on the 21st of November. They continued to train in the use of the Hotchkiss machine guns and musketry.

Ernest at the end of the Battle of the Somme

The Battle of the Somme came to an end on the 18th of November. Over the following winter months each side counted the horrific cost of this offensive. British casualties amounted to over 430,000 killed, missing or wounded, the French had 200,000 losses, and the Germans 450,000.

The British losses on the first day of the Somme would go down in military history as Britain's darkest day. Over 19,000 British soldiers died and were buried in France. They never returned home to their loved ones.

What was gained out of all of this, I ask? The sad truth was that with all this sacrifice, the Allies only managed to push the Germans back ten miles. However, this campaign arguably did relieve some of the pressure on the French army at Verdun, but slaughter would continue.

This battle had a significant impact on the Germans also. The new German recruits used to replace these losses were very young men with no experience and even less pre-battle training than the veterans they replaced.

Ernest would now have completed two to three months as a dispatch rider. He would have experienced some horrific sights, those summer months being very different from the peaceful countryside of north-west Wiltshire, with the rolling fields of ripened barley, wheat and oats, the sweet-scented rose blossoms in those lovely country cottages of Calne, the smell of freshly baking everywhere, the smell of the wild honeysuckle growing in the hedgerows, and the fragrant smell of hay being made in the meadows. He would miss his home comforts, clean and fresh smelling bedsheets, fresh water and his mother's home cooking.

Ernest had now experienced the environment of the trenches, with the putrid smells of the latrines intermingled with the rotting corpses of men and horses. Many men took up smoking purely to disguise these horrid smells, and then there were the dust and flies, which settled on Ernest and the other Yeomans, these flies had previously been feeding and laying eggs on the rotten corpses. Ernest understood what it was like not to wash properly for several days, and to live in lice infested clothes. He would be offended by his own smell. His soft bed of previous years had now been replaced by straw.

Whilst riding his motorbike along the roads and tracks of Belgium and France, Ernest had a view of scenery which had been transformed. There had once been meadows full of wild flowers, fields of ripening corn, and avenues of poplar trees lining the roadside. All of this had now been destroyed by the senseless relentless artillery barrages from both sides, and with the gain of a few miles at most. However, as Ernest travelled further away from the front, he would notice that the land was beautiful. There were wooded cops with streams running through, farmsteads, country cottages, farmyard animals and birds singing.

Ernest would have no comprehension of what a lunar landscape looked like, but this is how the battlefield appeared for the next two years and beyond. His heart must have sank seeing these sights, a profusion of shell holes all around, partially filled with stagnant water, some with bloated bodies of horses and mules partially submerged, maggot infested human body parts, discarded broken weapons and broken lumber wagons.

Where there were once woods and spinneys, now all that remained were torn remnants of tree stumps. There was mile upon mile of barbed wire defences, some with empty food tins attached containing pebbles, the purpose being to alert the defenders during darkness of the presence of raiding parties approaching. The ruins of the churches and abandoned cottages reduced to piles of rubble, starving stray dogs and cats with pitiful looks on their faces. These are just a few of the sights that Ernest would become accustomed to on his daily trips backwards and forwards to the front.

Travelling along the dusty roads, pock marked with shell holes, which were constantly being refilled and repaired by the labour gangs, Ernest would see a constant stream of supply wagons, as well as the upturned carcasses of supply wagons hit by the artillery fire. Dead horses would still be attached, covered in greedy bluebottle flies. He would see the columns of clean clothed fresh-faced reinforcements travelling on their way to the front, the looks of nervous apprehension on their faces. The bedraggled formations of the walking wounded travelling in the opposite direction. Some of the soldiers marched in lines each man touching the shoulder of the man in front. This was done because of their visual impairment from the recent gas attacks they had endured. Some of the soldiers were heavily bandaged from the effects of the mustard gas. What pitiful sights they must have been to Ernest as he rode past on his motorbike.

No human being could ever be immune to the horrific sights. They came back to haunt Ernest for the rest of his life. I now understand why he refused to talk to me about what he had witnessed. This was total war. Ernest would not be going home this Christmas or the next Christmas, and the question on everybody's lips was 'when will it all end?'

When Ernest arrived with his dispatches at the various HQs behind the lines, he would see the senior officers in their 'swagger' with their shiny riding boots, pristine uniforms, and with their Public School 'patter'. Knowing Ernest as I did, he would have been angry at the comparative luxury of the 'Ruling Officer' class. I too am annoyed, just looking at the black and white film footage of them all, posing for the cameras.

The Yeomens saw out the remainder of the year 1916 training, resting and reorganising. However, they were about to face a massive trial, the coldest winter of the war on the Western Front.

The national and wider political situation

The end of 1916 saw the downfall of the Asquith coalition Government, which was blamed for failing to bring about an early end to the war. The failures of the Somme offensive, the Gallipoli Campaign, the Easter rising in Ireland and the onset of conscription were all factors which bought about Asquith's downfall.

The new Prime Minister was Lloyd George. As he was a seasoned politician who had been Chancellor until 1915 and Secretary of State for War until 1916. Most historians would say this was a good move. He would be no pushover to Field Marshal Haig and would keep him under close scrutiny. He would not be writing him any blank cheques. Only time would tell as to how this relationship would develop.

The British way of life was changing for good. The role of women in the work place was expanding. More and more women were being employed in jobs which had traditionally been for men only. One of the most important industries which saw these changes was munitions.

Vast numbers of women were doing 12-hour shifts in these factories, and for half pay. There was a large factory in the Wembley area of London, again employing large numbers of women in the production of poisonous gas. Britain out-produced Germany during the course of the war, producing twice as much of this deadly substance as the Germans.

Women were also being employed in business and commerce, and heavy industries. The Suffragette movement was gaining support and women would have the vote by the end of the war. Women accepted the challenge of filling in where men had been conscripted, and with vigour and enthusiasm. This was their contribution to bringing down the 'evil German' war machine. The shells, bullets and weapons which they were producing were regarded as protecting their husbands, sons, fathers and friends who were fighting the Germans.

The Empire of the Realm Act passed during the beginning of the war had additions during the course of the war. The State would have an ever-increasing control on people's lives and industrial practices and development. State censorship controlled the press. The public would only read what the censors had approved prior to the papers going to press. The British public would not learn about the true horrors of the war in the trenches until the soldiers came back in 1918. Even then many would be reluctant to believe the soldiers' accounts.

All of the letters Ernest wrote home were, as a matter of course, read by a ranking officer before they were dispatched. During the war over two million letters per week were sent to the front, taking two days to arrive. Back in Britain over 2,000 state censors would check letters and parcels going to the Western Front. It was possible to pay extra for 'express censorship' which would mean that the letter or parcel would arrive with your loved one more quickly than normally. However, the price was an extra shilling and six pence for this privilege, and to afford this meant some affluence.

The population of Britain was about 42 million at the outbreak of war, about one million men were employed in the mining industry.

Coal was by far the most important source of power, far more so than petroleum at that time. The miners in Wales had gone on strike the previous year in 1915 over pay and conditions, and Lloyd George had reacted by increasing the pay to the miners. However, the Trade Union movement continued to grow as did civil unrest and complaints about working conditions and pay. There were hundreds of unofficial strikes. These strikes and civil unrest were a concern for the British Government which had one eye on the events in Russia. This would be a major factor the longer this war continued.

The end of the year saw the superpowers counting the cost of the war, in both men and materials. In the new year of 1917 the Germans stepped up their U-Boat campaign. Their own country was being starved of raw materials and food, and to make matters worse, the German harvest failed through lack of fertilizer. They would play Britain at their own game. If the British naval blockade was starving the Germans of food and vital resources, then the Germans U-Boats would continue to sink ships which were supplying Britain with food and resources.

The war on the Eastern Front

The Germans slowly saw the error of their ways in fighting a war on two fronts. Soon the strategy took root to free up their soldiers on the Eastern Front.

The growing communist movement in Russia, known as Bolshevism, was of grave concern to the royal dynasties and ruling classes of the European powers, because the aim was to overthrow governments and capitalist economic systems and replace them with a proletariat socialist regime.

The German strategy was to fan the flames of revolution in the hope that it would destabilise the Russian political system and ultimately bring down the Tsar. To do this they colluded with and supported the activities of the Bolshevik activist Vladimir Lenin and his followers. Whilst in exile in Switzerland, Lenin promoted and printed his Bolshevik theories in outlawed newspapers and literature. These in turn would be smuggled into Russia. The German treasury financed this propaganda campaign to the tune of two million marks.

Prior to the war in 1900 Lenin had spent time in Munich with his girlfriend and fellow revolutionary Nadezhda Krupskaya. He could speak fluent German. He would sit it out in exile and patiently wait for the right time to return to his mother country Russia. This time was rapidly approaching.

This is a sad picture of the bloated carcases of dead horses lying next to their handlers, from their uniforms they appear to be French soldiers, it is estimated that over 8 million horses were killed during this conflict (over 256,000 on the western front alone).

Chapter 4

The winter of 1916–17

The winter of December 1916 to March 1917 was the coldest on record in Belgium and northern France. There were six weeks of continual frost, to add to the misery of life in the trenches. From reading some of the letters which the soldiers sent home to their families and loved ones, it is clear that there was a constant demand for warm socks, gloves, scarves, woollen balaclavas, and warm underwear. The importance of the mail parcel deliveries would be vital to maintain the fragile morale of the soldiers. Many British charities were set up to make and donate cold weather clothing to the troops. Some of these charities were even allowed to send clothing to British prisoners of war held by the Germans.

One of the few benefits which Ernest would have had as a dispatch rider, was the opportunity to call at village stores when working behind the lines. The prices were rising rapidly, but he would have had the chance to buy basic foods in small quantities as well as festive beverages, enough to save for a decent Christmas dinner. This, together with parcels from home, would have enabled Grandad to have a Christmas feast with his fellow Yeomans.

Having spent a large time working on Ernest's farm in my youth, I can appreciate how miserable it would have been for him, being out in the open during those cold winter months. The soldiers had enough to contend with trying to avoid 'trench foot' besides the added discomfort of frost bite. The small blessing of the frost would mean that the mud would freeze, but the mud in the bottom of the trenches would not freeze unless it was a severe frost. Fires were difficult for the front-line troops

This is a well-known picture taken by the War Ministry photographer Ernest Brooks. It gives you an idea just how cold it was, at times so cold that the boots froze onto the soldier's feet, making it almost impossible to take off their boots. It was common to see soldiers wearing goat skin coats which were quite warm.

because they had to mask the smoke so as not to give away their position to the enemy. On a freezing cold day, it was not possible to light a fire with scrap wood and warm yourself next to it. Can you imagine on a cold winter's night being on sentry duty, not only were you freezing cold, but you couldn't walk about to keep your circulation going? You had to remain still and alert.

In addition, there were problems with weapons as mechanisms would jam in the severe frosty conditions. All the weapons had to be checked and greased to ensure they were fit for firing. There were problems too with army vehicles, whose radiators would rupture if the coolant froze solid.

In comparison, the situation for Ernest and the Yeomans would have been slightly better, as they were not on the front line, but some distance to the rear. The opportunities for a hot meal would have been better for them. There would have been opportunities to sleep on straw mattresses in the army bell tents, but there is no denying that it must have been very cold during the nights. Being a Yeoman had its disadvantages, because of the attention which every soldier needed to give to looking after his horse. During the freezing weather the Yeomans would have been constantly breaking through frozen ice to provide water for their horses.

Trench maintenance and digging were a nightmare in frosty conditions. The first six to ten inches of topsoil would be frozen solid, making digging without mechanical aids a lot harder.

B Squadron in January 1917

January 1917 saw B Squadron of the Yeomans in billets in Chipilly in north France, where they carried out traffic control duties under the supervision of the Army Provost Marshal (APM). This was no easy task. The roads leading to the front would have been full of supply trucks, troops, cavalry, horse drawn artillery, and prisoner of war columns. Any soldiers doing these duties would have to know the area and the key locations of army units, field hospitals, supply depots, army HQ's etc. They would have been constantly asked for directions by soldiers of all languages and accents. Chaos would have arisen, had wrong directions been given. The constant artillery bombardments would mean that the roads and bridges would often be blocked. It was vital to clear these routes and keep the traffic moving, especially during battles. This had to be achieved under the constant threat of exploding artillery shells.

I want to mention the work support units who were attached to the Yeomans, without whose work, the squadron would simply not have functioned. Attached to B Squadron were:

Five x Shoeing Smiths – these were kept very busy as there were over 120 horses in each squadron. The rough conditions of the roads meant that horses were constantly losing their shoes, and there would have been numerous hoof problems associated with walking knee deep in mud. The ground would be littered with shards of metal and shrapnel. The Germans deliberately secreted spiked boards under the surface of roads and paths leading to the front lines, which inevitably led to severe case of lameness for the unfortunate horses and mules who walked on them. There were inevitable injuries for foot soldiers too.

One x Sadler – the poor weather and constant use of the saddles and harnesses necessitated the need for regular repairs and replacements.

Three x Army Service Corps (ASC) attachments – it was the job of the ASC to provide the Yeomans with food, ammunition, equipment, horses and vehicles. Any wounded horses would have to be taken behind the lines to the Army Veterinary Corps for treatment. More and more horses came to be injured, especially in the months to come.

The cooks had to feed the Yeomans in difficult conditions. They took portable cooking stoves with them to France. They often cooked stews and curries. For the troops to have hot food in their stomachs on a freezing cold day was a massive comfort. The ASC sometimes had to carry hot food a considerable distance from their ovens to the soldiers in the trenches. They were often exposed to enemy fire, and many were killed. It is estimated that over 8,000 ASC personnel were killed during World War 1.

Eight x Transport Troops – the Yeomans did not need shells but they did need tons of oats, bran and hay, food and ammunition, clothing and supplies. This would all have to be collected from the supply depots and railheads, and the work was ceaseless. It would be made particularly risky as a lot of supplies would have to be moved in darkness to reduce the risk of losses from enemy artillery attacks. The Allies erected 15 ft screens along the roadside to try to foil the German artillery spotters.

The War in the Spring of 1917

In February 1917, the Germans started to retreat to the Hindenburg Line. The Allies were initially confused as to what was happening. Suddenly the

The portable cooking stoves in this picture were used at Winchester College in 1914, prior to the Yeomans sailing to France. These stoves travelled with the Yeomans and were used to make many a stew for the troops.

Germans started shelling their own trenches, and soon after this, clouds of smoke started to appear on the horizon. The Germans were on the move. In their wake they left total destruction, the idea being that they would leave nothing that would be of use to the Allies. Their trenches were destroyed together with their communication systems. Some of their command posts were 'booby trapped' with explosive devices. All water supplies including wells were destroyed or poisoned. Roads, rail networks and bridges were destroyed to hamper and slow down the Allies, who, once it was discovered that the Germans were retreating, followed and kept track of them, reporting their location and progress. Houses and commercial buildings were also bombed.

As the Allies continued to follow the retreating German armies, they travelled through Peronne located south of Bapaume. Here they came across a German signpost attached to a building which had recently been blown up. There was arrogance in what was written 'Nicht ärgern, nur wundern' which translates as 'Don't be angry, just be amazed!'

For the first two weeks of February 1917 the Yeomans carried out training exercises and signals work, assisting also with working parties in the construction of cages for German prisoners of war. The numbers of German POW's grew steadily as the war progressed, and by the end of the war there were in excess of one million. Some of these remained in France and Belgium and were made to do labour work as and when required. Some were shipped to Britain; however, these would not be allowed to carry out work in Britain because of opposition from the British trade unions.

Other Yeomans carried out working parties at the base of the 14th Royal Flying Corps at Plateau. This included work on perimeter defences and general maintenance. Those Yeomans trained in the use of the Hotchkiss machine guns were temporarily deployed in the protection of this airfield against enemy attacks from their air force.

During the second half of February part of the Yeoman squadron followed the German retreat, keeping in touch with their rear guard, doing constant reconnaissance tours and gathering intelligence. They were part of the XV Corps Cavalry Regiment. They also worked closely with the Royal Canadian Dragoons. The remainder of the regiment then spent the first half of March training and carrying out working parties.

On the 19th of March, the Yeomans carried out reconnaissance in the area north-east of Aizecourt-la-Haute. They engaged with the retreating Germans as they passed through the villages of Templeux-la-Fosse, Loneavesnes, Norlu, Sorrel and Heudicourt. The Cycle Corps and forward infantry units were not far behind the cavalry, securing this area until the rest of the infantry arrived and then handing it over to them.

In the area of Sorrel, the Yeomans came under heavy machine gun fire and sustained casualties. The total losses for the month included two men killed and 15 wounded, with 22 horses killed and 35 horses wounded.

Civil unrest in Russia

The month of March 1917 saw major events on the Eastern Front. The Russian Revolution started on the 12th of March, beginning with a peaceful protest from predominantly women who had been joined by Russian soldiers, deserters from the Eastern Front. The protests took place in St Petersburg, where there was outrage at the huge losses of their men folk, and at the devastating famine. These protests grew and eventually students and workers joined the crowds. The Army was deployed to disperse the crowd, but instead joined in the protest. On the 15th of March Tsar Nicholas abdicated, and a Provisional Moderate Soviet Government was set up, its leader being Alexander Kerenski. This government wanted to continue to support the war, and Kerenski went on with his Generals to plan for a further decisive offensive.

All of the superpowers were concerned about civil unrest at home, and Germany was no exception. The socialists, who for so long had supported their government, abandoned it and set up a movement called 'The Spartacus League'. This was Marxist and revolutionary in essence, grew rapidly and called for an immediate end to the war. It prompted a reaction from the German military who decided to go all out for a quick victory.

The USA joins the War

In order to facilitate rapid and significant gains over the British in particular, the Germans threw caution to the wind and stepped up their U-Boat campaign in the Atlantic. Using captured ports on the Belgium coast, the Germans launched over one hundred U-Boats to attack the shipping in the Atlantic. Any ship that supplied Britain, even if owned by a neutral country would be a target. The month of March saw the sinking of three American ships which outraged the American President Woodrow Wilson, but he needed to gain support from the public in order to join the Allies in the fight against Germany.

The Americans had a relatively small army of 125,000 men, only 15,000 of whom were properly trained marines. They had very little equipment. In charge was General John Pershing, who had been involved with his cavalry in fighting terrorist attacks across the border into Mexico. The American

President had for some time suspected that the Germans were funding the Mexicans in these terrorist activities, suspicions which were confirmed when Woodrow Wilson received a copy of a telegram intercepted by British intelligence. This telegram had been sent by the German Foreign Secretary, Arthur Zimmermann, to Heinrich von Eckardt, the German Ambassador to Mexico. The gist of this message was that if America declared war on Germany and Mexico took up the fight with the Americans, Germany would guarantee that the Mexicans would gain the territories of New Mexico, Texas, and Arizona, should Germany win the war.

The British were very shrewd in dealing with the Americans. They had been sitting on this information contained in the intercepted telegram since January 1917. The sinking of the three American merchant ships in March was the perfect time to inform the Americans of facts.

President Woodrow Wilson was also a shrewd man. He had promised the American voters, many of whom had German ancestry, that he would not involve America in the war. He was also acutely aware that the American press was against participation. Furthermore, America's industry and commerce had profited significantly during the first two years of the war in Europe.

Wilson saw his chance, however, for America to become a world superpower. He also knew that the French and British owed him two billion dollars and this sum was rising. If these two superpowers lost the war, they would not be in a position to pay back the loan. He also harnessed the American public's adoration for the French Republic, who had supported the Americans against the British during the American War of Independence.

It is for these reasons that Wilson was able to convince the American Congress into supporting him. The result was that on the 6th of April 1917 America declared war on Germany. However, before America could have an impact on the war, it needed to expand the army, equip it with modern weapons, and institute training for this new army, which could not go to France until the German U-Boat threat was neutralised, in the battle of the Atlantic. The protection of the convoys would have to be a priority.

The Battle of Arras

The fighting in March against the German machine gun units was the last time that the Yeomanry Cavalry was used in a combat role. At the beginning of April all of the Yeomans were given new numbers. Ernest's new army number became 320252. Some of the Yeomans were deployed in prisoner escort duties, the others were involved in regimental rides over the newly acquired ground that the Germans had abandoned during their retreat. This was in order to acquaint the officers with the Corps front and the general topography of the area.

The previous months' engagements had taken their toll on the horses who were exhausted. They were moved to the rear where stables were constructed in Moislains, south-east of Bapaume.

The next major offensive was known as the Battle of Arras, a beautiful ancient city, the pride of the Pas de Calais region of France. It was known for its Gothic style buildings, halls and churches. Artillery bombardments would destroy over 80% of these buildings. The purpose of this battle in April was to be a diversionary attack, engaging significant German resources to enable the French to prepare for their Nivelle offensive planned for the following month in May at Chemin des Dames located north-west of Reims.

This would be the first time that the British Army fought alongside the Dominion Armies. The Australian, New Zealand and Canadian armies would prove their worth significantly in the weeks to come. They all fought alongside the British 51st Highland Division, widely regarded as one of the best fighting divisions of the war. Such was their reputation that the Germans referred to them as 'Ladies from Hell' or 'Devils in Skirts'! This would also be the first time the Allies would test the defences of the Hindenburg line. This responsibility initially fell to four Canadian divisions at Vimy Ridge. Again, tanks were deployed to assist the advancing infantry.

For a six-month period prior to this battle the New Zealand soldiers had secretly excavated 13 miles of tunnels under the city of Arras, in order to house 25,000 of their soldiers, the idea being that when the battle commenced, they would all come to ground level and attack the Germans, who would be shocked by the sheer weight of numbers.

On the 4th of April, the battle started as usual with a heavy artillery barrage. The Allies were confident as they were now using the new 106 wire cutting fuses in their shells.

In many places the first days of the attack were successful. Smoke shells were being used by the allied artillery and the smoke screen helped to protect the advancing infantry. German machine gunners found it difficult to identify them as they approached. They were also being pinned down by the advancing 'creeping artillery barrage'. This type of barrage was carefully coordinated. By exploding shells 100-200 yards in front of the advancing allied infantry, the shells exploded in front of the advancing infantry at this same distance, which caused reduced visibility for the Germans, and had the effect of making them keep their heads down to avoid flying shrapnel. The advancing allied soldiers were then able to approach the German trenches with reduced losses.

For this creeping barrage to be effective, it was imperative that the allied artillery maintained contact and coordination with the infantry. When it worked, it was very effective. If communications broke down, or the infantry advance was delayed, disastrous consequences followed. We will never know just how many soldiers were killed from friendly artillery fire.

The artillery was using 'zone call artillery' tactics. In simple terms this was accurate concentrated artillery fire on identified German artillery emplacements and other enemy stronghold positions and fortifications. In many parts of the front both the first and second line German trenches were completely destroyed. Over 6,000 German soldiers were taken prisoner in the early days of the battle. The Yeomans were busy for the next two to three weeks escorting these German prisoners to the rear.

There was mixed success along the battle front overall. The Australians encountered heavily fortified German defences at Bullecourt and Lagnicourt. They had been promised 12 Mark 1 tanks to assist them in breaching the German barbed wire defences which were 30 yards deep in places, but only one tank arrived. Another problem was that the British artillery was failing to keep up with the advancing troops. The horses were having to pull heavy guns through previously held German territory. After the initial snow at the beginning of the battle, there followed a thaw causing the ground to turn into a deep muddy quagmire, and some of the poor horses sank so deep in the mud that they had to be put down.

Eventually the Germans counter attacked, and the Allies sustained heavy casualties. The Allies had managed to break into the Hindenburg line but had not been able to break through all three German lines.

Sadly, the Battle of Arras would be remembered for the highest daily casualty rate of all the battles of World War 1 with over 4,000 casualties per day. The battle lasted for 38 days ending on the 16th of May when the town of Bullecourt eventually fell to the Allies, who sustained over 159,000 casualties, and the Germans 130,000.

The allied soldiers had fought with bravery and distinction, but they had been let down by poor decisions and planning on the part of their Generals. They did however succeed in tying up a significant number of German troops which was one of the main objectives. In doing so, they allowed the French Army to prepare for their Nivelle Offensive. Many German divisions, who would otherwise have faced the French, had been moved north to counter the British at Arras.

Following the battle, the Allies had advanced into German held territory between 3 km and 9 km along a wide front.

The beginning of life at the front line for the Yeomans

The month of May saw the Yeomans continuing in their support roles, however their diary states that they began to deploy at the front some of their sections that were attached to battalions. In company with the front-line soldiers they carried out patrols, and were also deployed in listening posts and wiring parties. The strengthening and construction of barbed wire defences would have been fraught with danger, as the German snipers (see picture of sniper hide page 134) were on the constant look out for fresh targets. The Yeomans would by now begin to sense a change afoot. Rumours were rife that some of the cavalry regiments would be disbanded. These deployments on the front line would only serve to fuel this speculation. I suspect that it was over the period of May and June 1917 that Ernest would be returning to his squadron from his dispatch rider secondment.

There was one story Grandad told me about his time at the front. I cannot be precise about the exact date that this incident occurred, but it was definitely whilst Ernest still had his horse.

One evening I was near to the front-line trenches. My friends were sat around a 'make shift' stove. They were boiling water to make a brew of tea, they were laughing and joking together as I walked past them, one of them called out to me "are you stopping for a brew Ernie?" I replied, "I'll join you after I've fed my horse" Thinking no more of it, I continued to walk towards where the horses were tethered up, all of a sudden there was a huge explosion behind me which knocked me off my feet, after a moment I struggled to my feet and instinctively looked back to where my friends had been sat, I was shocked by the sight, there was a crater where my friends had been sat, as the smoke cleared, all I could see their body parts everywhere, and then the smell hit me, burnt flesh, mingled with the smell of cordite fumes, I'd seen so many dead bodies by now but the tears rolled down my face, but I couldn't cry. I'd been so lucky that day, the image will haunt me for as long as I live.

Like so many other soldiers, Ernest must have felt guilty that he had survived but his friends had not, but in farming there is a saying; 'Don't feed yourself until you've fed your animals first!' He could so easily have stopped and had that cup of much deserved tea, but he had chosen to tend his horse first. This decision had saved his life that day. Good for you Grandad!

The Yeoman squadron were now billeted at Villers Guislains and received further reinforcements. The soldiers trained in the use of machine guns continued to defend the airfield at Plateau, and the remainder carried out guard duties for the POWs captured during the previous Battle of Arras.

During the course of this war there were many arguments for and against the deployment of cavalry. Clearly, they were not effective in the cratered muddy landscapes of the front, but Haig and his Generals continued to save a lot of their cavalry squadrons in reserve, in the hope of making that 'decisive breakthrough' and sending the cavalry to 'rout' the retreating enemy. Field Marshal Haig would continue to resist the disbandment of his cavalry. He partially gave way to this argument over the period that followed, and the cavalry regiments were more than halved by the end of the war.

The statisticians would argue that with the continued U-Boat pressure on the convoys and the losses sustained, would mean that there was always competition for freight space. Horse fodder was bulkier than ammunition and armaments. For the period of the war, the tonnage of ammunition shipped to France totalled about 5.25 million tons. This was against just under 5.5 million tons of oats and hay for the horses, that being far less dense than ammunition, consequently taking up more space per ton.

The problems of the French Army

During the first half of 1917 the French generals perceived problems with their front-line soldiers. Many of these soldiers had not had leave granted for several months and during the ten-month Battle of Verdun, there had been no leave granted at all. Food rations had gradually become reduced and the quality was poor. They were very dissatisfied with their pay, morale was at an all-time low. As a result, the French soldiers gorged themselves on cheap wine, which in turn made them drunk and more outspoken and reckless in their behaviour. Some wrote anti-war songs and poems. They started to question the whole point of the conflict.

They wrote home to their loved ones, expressing their feelings openly and ignoring the risks of censorship.

It appeared to the soldiers that their generals thought that they were all dispensable, the huge losses necessary and acceptable, and that this situation would continue. There had been horrific losses during the Battle of Verdun. The promised decisive victory of the Nivelle Offensive had simply not materialised. Of the male population of France at the start of the war, numbering about 20 million, over one million French soldiers had been killed so far.

Stories were beginning to filter through from the Eastern Front. Russian soldiers who had come in contact with French soldiers spoke of a revolution that was growing in momentum, and that many Russian soldiers had deserted. By May 1917 it is thought that over two million Russian soldiers had abandoned the fighting. This news had a significant psychological impact amongst the French army and many soldiers refused to 'go over the top' when ordered, simply remaining in their trenches. This was a serious situation for the Allies. Over this period many French soldiers were court-martialled and found guilty.

Fortunately, the French high command responded in time. General Neville was replaced by General Pétain. The soldiers responded favourably to this move. During the Battle of Verdun, General Pétain had gained a reputation amongst his troops for being sympathetic towards their welfare and living conditions. He had become known as the 'Hero of Verdun'. The French soldiers were given a rise in pay, and food rations were rapidly improved. General Pétain made regular visits to his front-line troops in particular those regiments that had mutinied. Many troops were granted badly needed leave. It was decreed that a French soldier would receive seven days leave every four months. This was eventually increased to ten days.

Of the 400 or so French soldiers that had been court-martialled and sentenced to death, only 55 of these were executed, the rest being sent to labour camps. The mutiny 'fizzled' out by late August 1917. The French soldiers rallied and continued to fight, but France was reluctant commit itself to any more major offensives in 1917. The British now had to take the initiative.

The Allies and opposing Central Powers all knew that their domestic civil unrest could not be ignored. People were starving and the cost of the war was spiralling out of control with mounting debts. In this same year Germany and Austria had made peace overtures, but these had been rejected in the main because Germany wanted to keep the territory it had captured. All sides knew that this war could not go on for much longer, but each side carried on trying to devise a quick victory. Further battles would be planned, and the slaughter would continue.

Knowing that French morale was fragile, Field Marshal Haig and his general staff hatched up another plan, this time to retake the Belgium ports now being used as German U-Boat bases. There was still a concern that the U-Boats could seriously affect the allied war effort.

There would be another 'big push' on the Belgian town of Ypres and the German salient at Passchendaele would have to be taken. The Allied armies with the support of British naval guns planned an amphibian landing which would enable the Allies to retake the Belgian ports. This would ease the pressure which the U-Boats exerted on the Atlantic convoys, allowing more food and armaments to reach Britain and France. Above all this would allow the American army to come to France, and give the French army time to recover and reorganise.

The introduction of the convoy system began to have a positive effect in May. A convoy had sailed from Gibraltar and arrived in Britain without any losses. It had been escorted by a battle cruiser and six destroyers, together with armed merchant vessels. The tide would eventually turn against the U-Boats.

The Third Battles of Ypres (Passchendaele).

The British high command continued to put pressure on Parliament in London to allow them to attack the Germans at Ypres. Field Marshal Haig had done extensive research on the weather in Belgium dating back over

70 years. He had gleaned that the weather breaks in August with a degree of certainty. Heavy rains follow, and this was an obvious concern to him, as he knew it would hamper his advance in the inevitable sea of mud.

The Prime Minister Lloyd George and his War Council gave Field Marshal Haig permission to prepare for the offensive, but not to go ahead with it. This delay wasted valuable good dry weather, adding to Haig's frustration. A further condition was made that the War Council would not allow an amphibious landing to support the attack on Ypres until the docks at Roulers had been taken by the Allies.

It was decided that before the Battle of Passchendaele could commence, the high plateau to the south of Ypres would have to be taken from the Germans. This area was known as the Messines Ridge. General Hubert Plumer commanded the British Second Army in this area. He had been preparing for this assault for over 12 months. Miners and engineers who had built the London Underground had been drafted in to dig a series of tunnels which led from the British lines and under the Germans lines on the Messines Ridge.

I want to pay tribute to these miners and engineers who worked long shifts in very difficult and dangerous conditions. Not only did some of these tunnels collapse during their construction, but there were constant risks of methane gas. Sometimes the miners would come across German miners coming in the opposite direction and a fight would ensue. It is difficult to imagine the two teams of miners beating each other to death with pickaxes and shovels in the confined space of a dark tunnel.

To add to this, the miners were often 'goaded' by the soldiers who were no doubt jealous of their much deserved five shillings per day wage!

A total of 22 mine shafts were dug and they were packed with high explosives. Over this period the Germans discovered one of these tunnels, rendering it useless. However, the remaining 21 tunnels were undiscovered.

On the morning of the 7th of June 1917, just prior to zero hour, the mines were detonated. All but two exploded, causing heavy casualties amongst the German lines on the ridge. Tragically there were delays in some of the mines detonating, meaning that some of the Irish Regiments had already reached the German lines when the mines eventually detonated. As a consequence, many brave Irish soldiers were buried alive.

The battle was a resounding success for the Allies who gained the high ground on the Ridge. Had they known the chaos in the German lines, there could have been a decisive break through, but the high command being perhaps over cautious, called a halt once the Ridge had been taken.

I have visited the Messines Ridge, in particular the hamlet of Spanbroekmolen. The reason for my visit will become more evident later on in this book. There is a farm located near to one of the mine craters, the Pool of Peace, which is now a designated remembrance site. The farm is called Peckham Farm and featured on a TV program in the 1960's. One of the unexploded mines was set off by a thunderstorm. However, there remains one unexploded mine which is located underneath one of the farm buildings. Whilst at the farm, I also visited the graveyard where the Irish soldiers are commemorated, a truly sad experience.

The Allies were now ready for the main attack on the town of Ypres, but when would the politicians give the go-ahead? Towards the end of the month of June saw the arrival of the first American troops in France. There were only about 1,500 troops, but it was a morale boost all the same.

The Yeomans in Dunkirk

During the month of June, the Yeomans continued to be deployed on the front line. Other parts of the regiment carried out squadron and regimental exercises. They continued to receive reinforcements. On the 9th of June the Yeomans marched towards the port of Dunkirk where they were deployed in the defence of Mardick, a subsection area of Dunkirk, located inland between the ports of Dunkirk and Calais. The high command had for some time feared a German attack in the area. The French General Nivelle had written to the British high command as early as March 1917 expressing his concerns that the

Germans were likely to attack the ports of Dunkirk, Calais and Boulogne, as these were the main hubs for a large proportion of the supplies coming to France for the Western Front.

The Yeomans arrived at the town of Grand Synth on the 30th of June 1917. En route they had travelled through the towns of Méaulte, Beauval, Petit Bouret, Hernicourt, Sachin-les-Pernes, Steenbecque, Eecke, Wormhoudt and La Capelle. It was over this period that Ernest and some of his fellow Yeomans 'got into a bit of trouble'.

Major Awdry wrote in B Squadron orders, dated the 21st of June 1917.

'Punishment
Passes for Dunkirk for the undermentioned men are stopped, until further orders for being late off pass – 320106 Topliss, 320252 Burchell, 320661 Barwell, and 41826 Kitney'

I wonder what had distracted Ernest and his comrades that made them late returning to their squadron. Was it the good food and wine, or had there been other 'distractions'? It would have been great for them to escape from the battle front and breathe in that wonderful sea air. It must have been intoxicating for them after those putrid smells they had been forced to live with. Ernest commented to me:

'Our Major Awdry was a popular officer with his troops. He was firm but fair'.

One of the first things a soldier would do whilst on leave would be to fumigate his uniform. This would kill all the lice that had buried themselves into the seams of the clothing. How good would it have felt to have a good hot bath and put on clean fresh clothing, and to taste that wonderful freshly baked French bread, accompanying a good hot meal. His spirits would have been lifted by these ordinary pleasures which we all take for granted. British soldiers serving in France in World War 1 were paid in local currency, the French Franc. The demand for basic consumer goods, food and drink, rose sharply during the war, and many a shopkeeper made good money out of the huge demands for their products.

I visited Dunkirk in the summer of 2017 and stood on that famous beach with my back to the sea. I looked at the seafront cafés, some of which look as if they are from the period of World War 1. I tried to imagine the scenes back in 1917, with a multitude of troops of all nationalities intermingling with the local population. The fraternising between troops of different nationalities was discouraged by the powers that be, as in all towns and cities the Germans had spies deployed. Dunkirk would be no exception. The British did not want their troops talking to the French, especially regarding the talk of mutiny, for fear it would spread to the British troops.

Some of the cafés and bars had 'female' entertainment, and this was not just restricted to singing and dancing! The women were always in demand and it is not surprising that venereal decease was quite common. Outbreaks occurred during the period of the war. A young soldier could lose his innocence for a shilling, and many of them were pleased to part with their money, as there was an overriding fear that their next battle could be their last one.

In fact, the big German attack on Dunkirk and the other ports never materialised. The Germans did however bombard the city with heavy long-range artillery, and as a result there was extensive destruction. By the end of the war 2,370 homes had been damaged of which over 400 homes were destroyed. Over 1,500 soldiers lost their lives in the defence of Dunkirk.

The Yeomans were deployed in the Mardick area by Dunkirk for the best part of July and August 1917. They were engaged in the defence of the area with the Cycle Battalion.

The Battles of Ypres and Passchendaele continue

The month of July saw preparations for Haig's next 'big push.' There was a massive build-up of artillery pieces deployed in the area of the Ypres salient. By the end of July 1917 Haig amassed over 2,100 guns, requiring tons and tons of artillery shells. There was also a massive build-up of troops. The British Second and Fifth Armies would be fighting alongside Australian, Canadian and New Zealand Divisions. They would be opposed by the German Fourth Army. The allied soldiers were shown large, scaled models of the battle area, with the objectives clearly marked out for all to see. The Allies amassed 136 Mark IV tanks to assist the infantry advance across no man's land, breaching any remaining barbed wire defences.

Haig pondered over the choice of which General would have overall command of this next battle, eventually choosing General Gough over the older General Plumer. Most military historians would say that this was a mistake which cost lives.

The good weather of July would not last for ever and Haig continued to press the politicians in London to give the go-ahead to commence the battle. Precious time was wasted. In the meantime, the German Army used this time wisely. They strengthened their defences building many concrete pill boxes and heavily fortified strongholds, an example of which would be the Bremin Redoubt, which was constructed with reinforced concrete and deep tunnels housing over 100 soldiers.

The condition of the land and poor drainage would be a significant factor in the approaching battle. For three years now, the area around Ypres had been subjected to heavy artillery bombardments, and this had had the effect of destroying the drainage systems in the area. Prior to the war the area had a network of banked streams passing through the fields to keep the water table below ground level. The exploding shells from both sides had destroyed these embankments and consequently the streams overflowed into the surrounding land creating large areas of boggy ponds and swamps.

On a positive note the Royal Flying Corps had air superiority over the Germans for this battle. The quality of the airplanes had improved and the Allies had superior numbers. Improved training and the harmonised communications codes in the planes led to better coordination with the allied artillery. The Germans, however, had better extended views for their artillery spotters because they held the high ground. Where possible they had also deployed their artillery on reverse slopes making it difficult for the allied spotters, viewing from the ground, to locate. The effective use of aircraft to spot the German artillery proved invaluable during the coming battles, though this was hampered by mist and smoke on the battlefield.

Eventually Lloyd George gave Field Marshal Haig the go-ahead for the attack at the end of July 1917. The Battle of Passchendaele commenced on the 31st of July. The Allies attacked on a 25 km front, the French on the left with six divisions and the British on the right with nine divisions. There were ten divisions in the centre commanded by General Gough, and seventeen divisions in reserve. In all the Allies had just under half a million troops available. The German Fourth Army had twenty divisions opposing these forces.

Air cover was not provided on the first day due to mist and fog. The attack commenced with a creeping barrage. The infantry advanced across no man's land with the tanks, but because of the poor terrain and boggy conditions, the tanks fell behind the infantry, and as a consequence were not so effective as had been hoped. Of the 52 Tanks in Gough's Army, 22 broke down and 19 were put out of action.

There were however early successes with many German front line trenches completely destroyed. The Allies advanced four kilometres in places, but the troops were exhausted. Those carrying heavy equipment such as Lewis machine guns, sank waist deep in the mud. After day one of the attack, it started to rain again, and in the following month of August it rained every day, apart from three days. The month of August 1917 would go down as the wettest month in 75 years in Flanders. Haig had been right.

After four days of the battle the Allies sustained over 31, 850 casualties, the Germans slightly less at 31,000.

These early achievements would not have been possible but for the tireless work of the 'Labour Corps', who under very difficult conditions repaired roads and maintained supply lines, so that the artillery could keep in touch with the advancing infantry and maintain covering fire and the creeping barrage which was proving to be so effective. Very little credit is given to the Labour Corps who like any other branch of the army was not immune to hostile enemy fire. This group of men consisted of Chinese, native South Africans, and workers from the West Indies. Many of these men died in the Flanders fields never to return home to their loved ones.

By far the biggest group was the Chinese Labour Corps who numbered in excess of 140,000. They had been recruited from specially selected provinces in China where the men folk were larger and stronger than their average Chinese labourer. They were all made to sign three-year contracts and paid one French Franc per day. The Empress Dowager in China had made these concessions to the British in the hope that at the end of the war large swathes of territory occupied by the Western Powers in China would be returned to the Chinese Government. However, unbeknown to the Chinese, the British and French had secretly agreed with the Japanese Government that in turn for Japan supplying its cargo ships for the war effort and fighting against Germany and its allies, the British and French would make territorial concessions to Japan at the end of the war. This betrayal would have far-reaching consequences at the end of the war.

In the meantime, the Battle of Passchendaele raged on. Eventually Pilkham Ridge was taken by the Allies, but the Gheluvelt Plateau was holding out, and German counter attacks created many allied casualties. The weather over this period was so bad that the Allies called off any further attacks until the 15th of September.

In this period Haig appointed General Plumer as overall commander for the rest of this campaign. This was one of Haig's better decisions. General Plumer was seen by most as a better tactician, encouraging new strategies. He had pioneered the 'creeping barrage' and was now adopting the 'bite and hold tactic' which would prove to be very effective.

In so many previous battles, when large amounts of enemy territory had been gained, the Allies had failed to press home their advantage because of the failure of logistical support. The supporting artillery units fell too far behind the infantry and as a consequence fell out of range. The attacking soldiers very often ran out of supplies and ammunition, and as a consequence, when the Germans counter attacked, they simply had to give up the land they had captured and fall back.

This new method of bite and hold would prove to be more effective. Essentially the advancing infantry would stop at a certain distance, consolidate their positions, replenish their supplies and ammunition, and allow the supporting artillery units and tanks to catch up. In doing so, the infantry would maintain support from the artillery if and when the Germans counter attacked.

The soldiers in these advanced positions would remain in position, becoming the new reserve position, whilst the next wave of infantry advanced past them continuing forward. Each wave of infantry, once reinforced with supplies, would leapfrog each other, consolidating their lines as they progressed.

The Germans had also improved their tactics. They had set up what would become known as their 'Storm Troopers'. These were a small élite of heavily armed fighting units, also referred to as 'shock troops'. Their strength was their speed, fire power and ability to deploy rapidly and attack the weakened areas of the opposing enemy.

In the early days the Storm Troopers were deployed when the allied front had been overstretched. These troopers would attack the flanks, cause maximum damage and then retreat. One of General Plumer's many strengths was that he recognised this German tactic at an early stage and reacted by concentrating some of his artillery on his flanks to repel the Storm Troopers.

On the 15th of September, the Allies renewed their offensive, targeting the German defences at the Menin Road Ridge. The German artillery in this area had caused high casualties to the allied infantry in the area. The Allies continued with their successes and the Australian divisions advanced to the outskirts of Polygon Wood. Again, further progress was hampered by heavy rainfall, but by the end of September Polygon Wood was taken by the Australian divisions.

Disbandment of the Yeomanry Regiment and time off in Rouen

Following their deployment in Mardick, the Yeomans were dismounted on the 3rd of September 1917 and sent to the Third Infantry base depot at the Normandy city of Rouen. There followed a period here before they were redeployed. Whilst writing this book I have managed to salvage an old suitcase that had been retrieved from a skip located at Grandad's old farm in Hartshorne. Contained inside this suitcase is a treasure trove of old family photographs, some of which had clearly been kept by my Grandmother Elizabeth ('Bessy'). Amongst them are three postcards of Rouen dated the 15th and 17th of September 1917. They are addressed to Elizabeth Lees of Greysich Farm.

Ernest has written in pencil, most of the writing has sadly faded and it is difficult to decipher the words, but the gist is that he apologises for not being in touch, and he clearly wants to buy Elizabeth something from the shops in Rouen because he asks her "do you like Pears soap?" Each of these cards has been stamped by the army censor. So, I am under no doubt that Ernest was in contact with Elizabeth at every opportunity. In four weeks', time it would be Elizabeth's birthday.

ROUEN — Pont Boieldieu - 3 arches en acier, 143 mètres de long. 10 mètres de large
Boieldieu Bridge 3 steel arches, 140 mètres long and 10 m. wide

She would be 25 years old on the 16th of September, so perhaps this was Ernest's last chance to buy her a birthday present.

I have seen television tourist programmes about the beautiful city of Rouen. It is steeped in history with a magnificent cathedral. There are a number of other famous buildings, one of which is the 'Joan of Arc Tower'. This is the remainder of the castle's keep, where the famous French hero was incarcerated prior to being burnt at the stake in 1431. My Grandad would have had the opportunity to see the Gothic buildings and other tourist attractions. He must have wished that Elizabeth had been with him.

The month of September was a time of high casualties on both sides. Another Wiltshire infantry Battalion was fighting in the Menin Road sector, south of Passchendaele. This unit, the Wiltshire 6th Royal Wiltshire Yeomanry Battalion, (I will now refer to this Battalion as the 6th Wiltshire for the remainder of this book), would be in the thick of the fighting. They sustained heavy casualties, and as a consequence, some of Ernest's Yeoman cavalry squadron were transferred to the 6th Wiltshires. Private 320252 Burchell and other fellow Yeomans were used as reinforcements to replace their losses. On the 25th of September 1917,

Ernest therefore ceased to be a cavalry soldier. The 6th Wiltshires were an infantry Battalion. This was to be Ernest's first taste of trench warfare.

Bad weather conditions hamper fighting

The Germans were convinced that the Allies would not fight on this front after the month of September, having sustained heavy casualties. The Germans hoped that rain would stop any further attacks. They were proved wrong. To add to their problems elements of their navy had mutinied. This had involved over 400 sailors, many of whom were imprisoned. Two of the ringleaders were subsequently executed.

Following the fighting on the Menin Road Ridge, the 6th Wiltshire were camped at Bois-Carré, a town north-west of Amiens. They had sustained heavy casualties with a total of 113 wounded and 33 dead. The 6th Wiltshires were divided into four companies, A, B, C and D. From the 26th to 28th September all four companies rested and reorganised. On the 27th there was platoon drill, together with a company inspection. The following day, the Battalion was engaged in experiments with the new daylight rocket signals, and the remainder of the month was spent providing working parties for two trench areas, namely the Spoilbank and the Bois Confluent.

At the end of September and the beginning of October 1917 there was further heavy rainfall in the Flanders area. There were further battles around the areas of Zonnebeke, Brookseinde, Saint Jsulien, Langemarke, and Poelcappelle. It was noted that during the period of these battles, the mist and fog favoured the attackers, and the rain gave advantages to the defenders. Part of the Germans' defence plans was to send different coloured flares up in the air in order to alert their artillery as to what was required. However, the mist and fog reduced visibility rendering the flares less effective. Consequently, lines of communication were broken, and the Germans even resorted to the homing pigeons.

Mustard gas was used during this battle. It must therefore have been difficult to differentiate between mist and gas. If the Germans made mistakes, there would be disastrous consequences. Fighting in the trenches was bad enough but wearing gas masks during the fighting must have been a nightmare. The visors misted up quickly and visibility was significantly reduced. Perhaps even more significant was the fact that a soldier wearing a misted gas mask found it difficult to see his rifle sights. This would undoubtedly affect the accuracy of his fire. To confuse the Germans even more, smoke shells were fired to provide extra cover for the infantry.

The German ground observers for the artillery found it difficult to pinpoint targets, and this naturally affected the accuracy of fire.

On the other side the persistent rain slowed the advance to a halt. Supplies were much slower in reaching the troops. Artillery and tanks became bogged down. My experience of walking across ploughed fields in winter, only to have large amounts of mud sticking to my boots, has shown me that this would be tiring in itself. Yet it was so much worse for the soldiers in this battle. They were waiting to go over the top, some had to stand waist deep in cold water before the whistle blew, and then they tried to run across no man's land, sinking as they did so into the mud, carrying a weapon and kit. All of this required tremendous effort to persevere, and soldiers soon became exhausted. Once exhausted, the pitiful men would be desperate to find cover. They were cold and wet, thirsty and hungry for some warm food which seldom came. Fighting soldiers on the front regularly dehydrated, desperate for water, as their canteens did not last long. Some men survived only by finding canteens from their dead comrades or dead Germans.

Ernest begins to serve in the trenches

Wednesday the 4th of October 1917 was 1,069 days since Ernest Burchell had enlisted in the Army. This day was the first he would spend in the trenches with the 6th Wiltshire Battalion. What must have gone through his mind as he marched towards the trenches at the 'Spoilbank'? It was by coincidence his 29th birthday.

It is likely that his unit would have had a guide to take them forward to the fire trench. They marched in single file, with strictly no speaking and no smoking. Each soldier had something to carry to the fire trench. This could have been anything from rolls of barbed wire and iron support fasteners to ready-made duck boards, supplies and provisions, for example food, water, and ammunition.

Ernest had been lucky so far. He had had two horses killed whilst riding to deliver dispatches. Some of his best friends had been blown to pieces whilst brewing tea. Now the odds were beginning to stack against him. He would now be exposed to concentrated shell fire with only the walls of the trench to protect him. There would also be the constant danger of a German gas attack. This would be the first time he would be facing attacking troops of the German Army. Before long there would be another order to go over the top and face deadly German Maxim machine guns, and of course the ever-present snipers.

The trench system at the Spoilbank had by now received several inches of rain water, and Ernest needed to accustom himself to standing in water with permanently cold wet feet. During his days in the Yeomanry, he would have had instruction into the risks of fungal 'Trench Foot' infections. He would have had to apply anti-fungal powder at every opportunity.

Ernest needed to learn to sleep on the earthen ledges which had been dug out of the sides of the trench. He would quickly learn the different sounds of the German shells, starting with the distant blast of the gun going off. The soldiers would then have to judge their trajectory. There would be a distinct difference between the sound of a shell going overhead, as opposed to one descending towards the trench. Someone would shout 'incoming', Ernest would learn instinctively to dive for cover, which at best would be to hug the side of the trench and hope not to be buried alive as so many were. This would be a baptism of fire.

Not all of the trenches were ten feet deep, but some slightly shallower. In these conditions the soldiers had to adopt a permanent stoop in order to keep their heads below the top of the trench. Those who forgot to do this would be targets for the German snipers. A third of all deaths during the war were in the trenches. What must Ernest have thought when he first stood on the fire step and looked through the small aperture into no man's land, the sea of mud and water filled shell holes. He would have to take it in turns with his comrades to take charge of the trench periscope. This was normally two-hour stints. Any significant observations had to be recorded as intelligence or verbally debriefed to an NCO.

As Ernest looked through the periscope, he would see the partially buried rotting corpses of soldiers, some of whom had been there for months on end, having been killed in previous battles. Some of these bodies were covered in flies or crawling with hungry maggots. Other bodies would be draped over the barbed wire, the skin on the skeletal faces black, and the eyes in the sockets long since eaten by vermin and carrion.

Then there were the rats, some of which had grown as big as small cats. By now they had developed a taste for human flesh, and many would bite into the chest cavities of dead soldiers and use the cavity as a nest. Can you imagine the first time Ernest saw rats scurrying out from a dead soldier's body? How would he ever forget those images?

In typical British Army fashion, the sandbags forming the top of the trenches were laid out in neat level rows. This was in contrast to the German trenches. As Ernest looked through the periscope, he would see what at first appeared to be an untidy series of undulating mounds. This in itself made it difficult to make out the edge of the German trench. This was not untidiness on the part of the Germans, but on the contrary, these mounds concealed a series of well-hidden loop holes, which, over 80-100 yards of the German trench, would allow the Germans to deploy their marksmen and snipers. They would have a choice of 20-30 different loop holes, simply because so many were created. Once the sniper had fired his Mauser, he could rapidly change his position to another concealed loop hole further down the trench. This clever tactic would keep the British constantly guessing as to where the sniper was located. The trick on the part of the British would be to try to induce the sniper to fire at least two rounds from the same location, thus allowing one of the British snipers to eliminate his German counterpart.

There can be no doubt that Ernest would have witnessed the devastating effect of sniper fire in his early days in the trenches. These fatalities would have come so sudden and without warning. A moment of lapse in concentration, or a curious new recruit tempted to peer out over the trenches, only to have his brains blown out. These losses would have a bad effect on morale. Ernest and his comrades would have been reassured in the knowledge that their own snipers would improve their own tactics. Their successes grew and eventually the British took the initiative, with many young Germans suffering at the hands of the British marksmen.

In addition, there would be the smells, many of which Ernest had become familiar with by now, but in the front-line trenches, these smells would be even more intense due to so many rotting corpses. Many of the latrines were overflowing and digging parties struggled to find new unused areas in order to dig new facilities. There was huge indignation at having to bend down together in a line of soldiers to go to the toilet. Toilet paper would be available but not in the form we know today. No doubt it was cut up pieces of scrap paper.

During an artillery attack many a shell landed amongst the latrines with horrible consequences. The resulting aftermath would be one hell of a mess. The soldiers would refer to the toilet paper scattered around as "trench butterflies." They used many other nicknames as well.

Having researched the diet and rations the soldiers were given, I found it sad to discover that some of the soldiers complained when their fruit ration was changed from apples to oranges. The question is why? The reason was that with the lack of water, the soldiers could never wash their hands properly, so they could eat an apple with the one hand which they did not use for wiping their bottoms. They needed both hands to peel an orange. With regard to personal hygiene overall, there was never enough water for washing. The soldiers struggled to spare enough water to have a daily shave. They even resorted to using cold tea to mix the shaving soap and to rinse off. There was always the stale smell of humanity to contend with.

Then there was the smell of poisonous gas. Some types would linger in the soil and on objects in the trenches. After a gas attack special apparatus was used to cleanse the area. This was called the Vermoral spray. It had to be maintained and made ready for the next gas attack. A special solution of 3 gallons of water, one and a half pounds of sodium thiosulphate, and three pounds of sodium carbonate was mixed.

The smell of cordite fumes was ever present, burnt flesh and body contents and the smell of blood. In being so explicit I am trying to understand fully and convey the experiences of Grandad and his comrades, and why he was so reluctant to talk about it.

The trench system called Spoilbank was located to the south of the town of Zillebeke. The main battle for Passchendaele raged on, further north of this area. The Spoilbank Trench bordered the banks of the Comines Canal. One stretch of the trench was to the south side and the other part was to the north side of the Canal. There had been an HQ located here for some time. Perhaps the Germans knew this, because their artillery gunners would send daily salvos. The Wiltshires also fought in nearby trench systems at 'Buffs Bluff', 'Gaspers Cliff', and 'Oaf trench'. There were further casualties in the battalion from shell fire during this period.

When deployed in the trenches, the troops operated in a four-part rotation system. They started in the fire trench, then moved back to the support trench, then further back to the reserve trench. At the end of this stage they would go behind the lines and have a rest period. The time spent actually in the trenches would vary between four to seven days, depending on operational demands and if there was a battle situation in progress, when soldiers could go days without food and drink. Exhaustion was common and with the extra stress and fatigue bodies inevitably had reduced resistance to infection and disease.

Simple lice bites could turn into serious infections. There were numerous skin complaints including scabies. The soil became more and more contaminated, and soldiers with cuts and lesions contracted tetanus and other similar infections. Problems associated with men living too closely together would also bring about outbreaks of measles, meningitis, diphtheria, rheumatic fever, influenza and significantly Spanish flu. The outbreaks of this latter serious illness amongst the soldiers and the civilian population became more and more prevalent as the war progressed. The hard-pressed soldiers had enough to contend with apart from the danger of contracting these diseases, which affected them all, and over a period of time weakened their resolve. There were long periods of despair and a yearning to go home.

Routine in the trenches

Ernest's routine now changed. It ran as follows:

Morning – 'Stand to' one hour before dawn. The soldier would have to be battle ready with a fixed bayonet. Prior to this he would be served up with what was referred to in the trenches as 'Gun Fire'. This would be the first cup of tea of the day. It is likely to have been 'green tea'. If the soldiers were lucky, they would be served the tea mixed with a tot of rum. That would have brought them comfort and a warming sensation after a cold night in the water-logged trenches.

There would then follow the 'morning hate'. To relieve the tensions from both sides, and to prove they were battle ready and alert, each opposing side would start firing their machine guns indiscriminately together with artillery bursts.

Breakfast would then follow. This would be tinned bully beef or other similar tinned food. A common tinned food was' Maconochie', which was supposed to contain a mixture of meat and vegetables. The reality was that it contained very little meat and was unpopular with the troops. To supplement this was tea and coffee. Ernest had to learn how to use the 'Tommy Cooker' to boil his water. If he did not have one, he would soak parts of dry hessian sacking in candle wax to light a small fire and place his mess tin positioned above in a moulded ledge in the clay trench wall.

The soldiers in the trenches received hot food delivered to them from soldiers of the ASC who carried warm food contained in what were called 'hay boxes', which as the name suggests, was a wooden box lined with dry hay, which kept the food hot prior to consumption.

Ernest would learn quickly to open his tin of bully beef with his 'Jack Knife' or clasp which most soldiers would have attached to a lanyard around their necks. Once punctured, if the can made a 'hissing' sound, this would mean the contents were 'off' and inedible. The smells in the front-line trenches were often so strong especially on hot days that it tainted the food they ate!

Water was often in short supply, was contaminated and often tasted of petrol as it was carried in old fuel cans to the front. Many a soldier came down with dysentery as a result of drinking poor quality water.

The rule was that the front-line soldiers were fed before the officers.

Grandad said:

> Sometimes we improvised. If it had rained heavily and the shell holes had filled up, we would use the rain water as it tasted better. I remember on one occasion we'd been using this shell hole for some time, when it started to drain, we noticed the bloated carcase of a dead horse in the bottom of the shell hole! When it rained heavy, we used to put empty food cans on the ledge of the trench to catch the rain water.

Following breakfast, the soldiers would clean their guns. This would be done in shifts in case of a sudden attack. The soldiers had to make sure their uniform and kit was presentable ready for the morning inspection. They would also have to present their bare feet to the officer so he could check for 'foot rot'.

The next period would be daily chores, comprising of filling sandbags, repairing trenches and duck boards, pumping out water and digging latrines.

After these jobs were completed, there followed the daily boredom of the afternoon. Soldiers would try to catch up with sleep which was nearly impossible given the artillery explosions. Then the soldiers would play cards, write letters, and read letters received from home. Some soldiers would sit with lighted candles and take off their tunics and hold the flame of the candle under the seams of the tunic.

After a short while there followed a popping sound of the lice eggs bursting. This was an arduous task but one that gave brief relief to the incessant bouts of itching. It also helped to relieve the drudgery of trench life.

Each soldier took 'iron rations' with him to the trenches which was a day's supply of food. This consisted of a pound of preserved meat, 12 ounces(oz) of biscuit, between five and eight oz of tea, two oz of sugar, ½oz of salt, three oz of cheese, and two cubes of meat extract (Oxo or Bovril cubes). In this free time, the soldier would help himself to his ration.

How many times would Ernest take out the picture of Elizabeth from his pocket and wonder if he would ever see her again. Knowing him as I did and knowing how much he loved her, I would say that the chance of seeing her again would be his motivation to keep going against all the odds.

At dusk there would be the 'stand to'. Again, the soldiers had to present themselves as combat ready.

At darkness there would be the 'stand down'. The night duties would then follow, including regular patrols into no man's land to assess the enemy's defences, repairing barbed wire defences, manning listening posts, and trench raids to capture German troops for interrogation.

Each soldier would have to do a maximum of two hours sentry duty during the night and be alert at all times. Falling asleep, as already mentioned, would result in a court-martial.

So, this was the new environment in which Ernest found himself. I knew him to be a strong-willed man of substance, but every person had their limits. How much longer would Ernest be able to keep his sanity and the will to continue? I ask myself; did he have a choice?

In the long periods of boredom many of the soldiers grew resigned to the fact that they would not be going home, for it was only a matter of time before they would be killed. After they accepted the inevitability of it all, their only wish would be for a quick death. They dreaded the possibility of mutilation, or horrific disfigurement and the prospect of losing limbs and being permanently disabled. Then, when they were in the depths of despair, all of a sudden a letter or parcel would arrive from home, and there would be fresh hope that the carnage would end one day. This shred of hope would somehow keep them going.

The importance of those two million letters per week from home can never be underestimated in keeping up the fragile morale that existed in the trenches.

There was always of course the chance you would get the 'Blighty one' or the 'Blighty wound' this would be a wound which was not bad enough to kill a soldier but bad enough to render him incapable of fighting again, and as a consequence he would be sent home to 'Blighty'.

Having spent four days in the front-line fire trench, Ernest and his fellow soldiers were relieved by another unit and moved back to the support line trenches and then the reserve trenches. Conditions here were slightly better in that they had dugouts where soldiers were afforded some protection from the elements. Each dugout normally had two exits in case one was blocked. There was even a blanket covered doorway, the idea being to give some protection against gas attacks.

At night, the soldiers would try and grab some sleep on the straw filled mattresses. The rats were ever present, and as the war progressed, they became ever braver, climbing over the sleeping soldiers and eating any rations that were not stored away. A rat is normally a timid animal, but these had lost their fear. They would nibble at the soldiers' noses and ears to see if they were dead. It has been proved that rats can be responsible for transmitting over 40 different diseases, and it is little wonder that there were so many infections amongst the troops. To add to this, it was the rats that were responsible for spreading lice amongst the soldiers.

The units that had terrier dogs with them would have taken some comfort at night knowing there was a canine presence in their dugouts, to ward off the rats. There were two terriers with B Squadron when they had their photo taken in Aldershot 1916. I wonder how many rats they killed and if they survived the war. Some nature lovers will no doubt argue that rats serve some purpose in life, but I find it difficult to think of one. Perhaps in the situation of the trenches, acting as alarms for the presence of gas. Soldiers had some warning of a gas attack, because the rats used to come squealing out of their holes when they detected gas.

The 15th of September was Elizabeth's birthday, I wonder if Ernest had managed to remember from his world of the trenches. We know he sent at least three postcards whilst he was in Rouen earlier in the month.

Continuing life in the trenches

The Yeomanry Diary states that the Wiltshires were fighting alongside the 9th Welsh Regiment and the North Royal Lancashires, the 8th Gloucestershires, and the 10th Worcestershires during the early autumn of 1917. The period leading up to the 11th of October saw the 6th Wiltshires carrying out working parties in the trenches in the Spoilbank and Embankment trenches. On the 11th of October they moved to the Rossignol Camp where they rested, trained and reorganised. They received further reinforcements to replace the losses during the enemy shelling.

The regiment spent the 19th and 20th of September repairing the tunnels at Spoilbank. Local research shows that there appears to be a long mound of earth running parallel to the canal where the British excavated tunnels. The Wiltshires spend two days repairing damage to these tunnels caused by shell explosions.

From the 20th to 23rd of September the area received heavy shelling in the trench systems of Belgium Wood, Oaf Trench, and Embankment, with inevitable casualties. From the 24th to the 28th of October the Wiltshires were back in the trenches at the Embankment and Oaf trench. They were relieved on the 28th and proceeded to the Brasserie Camp, located near to Mount Kemmel. The soldiers would have been delighted to have the chance of a bath whilst at this camp. The rest of the month was spent training and receiving further reinforcements from the 3rd Wiltshires.

During those last weeks of October and the first week of November fighting intensified in the area around Passchendaele. It is here that the Canadian divisions would for ever be remembered for their sheer fighting ability and courage. They eventually took Passchendaele on the 6th of November 1917. The area was deserted by the Germans. This final piece of high ground was at last in allied hands.

It had however cost the Canadians the loss of 4,000 soldiers and 12,000 wounded. The total cost for the Battle of Passchendaele was 275,000 allied casualties and over 220,000 German casualties. It had taken over 88 allied divisions to fight this battle, which was about half the entire strength of the combined army.

The Allies had fired over four million artillery shells, and in response the Germans had fired the equivalent of over 27 ammunition trains full of shells. General Ludendorff would later write that 'The Germans never recovered fully from the Battle of Passchendaele'.

My own commemoration of Passchendaele

In 2017 my wife and I were privileged to be chosen together with 5,000 other relatives of this battle, to attend the Centenary Commemoration of Passchendaele. This was sponsored by the BBC. I will never forget the response from the Belgian locals as our convoy of cars travelled towards the car parks of the Commemoration Ceremony. They sat outside the front of their houses smiling and waving and giving the 'V' for victory gesture as we drove past them.

We stood in the Tyne Cot cemetery located near to Passchendaele and listened to the Commemoration Ceremony. We heard moving songs and readings, which were read out by politicians, senior army officers and members of the Royal Family, including the King and Queen of Belgium. I can remember walking along the lines of graves with a heavy heart, reading the inscriptions on the graves and trying to appreciate the enormous sacrifices that had been made. You cannot help but be tremendously moved by the sheer numbers of graves. On many of the graves is the inscription 'Known only to God'. This phrase originated from Rudyard Kipling who lost his son Jack during the Battle of Loos. In front of each grave grows a

The Lady of Shalott rose, on the graves at the Tyne Cot cemetery near Passchendaele

beautiful orange rose called the 'Lady of Shalott'. I have three of these beautiful fragrant roses growing in my garden as my own small gesture of remembrance.

The outcome of the Battle of Passchendaele

I do not wish to become involved in the debate as to who won the Battle of Passchendaele. The sadness for me was that it did not shorten the war.

The Allies gained a few miles of territory but had failed to take the German U-Boat ports. This senseless war would go on.

132

For Private 320252 Burchell, the war continued also. Ernest would be resigned to the fact that he would be spending another Christmas in Flanders. He had recently had his 29th birthday, one he would never forget, for it had been his first combat day in the trenches.

The 6th Wiltshires spend the first week in November doing working parties in the Spoilbank trenches. On the same day that the Canadians finally took Passchendaele, the 7th of November 1917, the Bolsheviks seized power in Russia. Unbeknown to Ernest at the time, this was to have serious consequences for the 6th Wiltshires in the following spring.

Above is the authors impression of a sniper hide secreted under the carcase of a dead horse, this is during an artillery barrage in the hours of darkness. This hide would be almost impossible to detect, only the flash of the snipers weapon when fired and the resulting brief cloud of smoke would give the hides location away to ever watchful eyes of soldiers in the apposing trenches.

Chapter 5

The Battle of Cambrai

It is now the second week of November 1917, and the war had now raged on for three years and nearly three months. Private 320252 Burchell had now been operational in the front-line trenches on the Western front for a little over a month. Like so many of his comrades he yearned to go home, but this dreadful war showed no signs of ending.

The Generals on both sides continued to devise plans to give them that final victory. The Allies' next target would be the strategic town of Cambrai. This had been in German hands for a long time and had become an important hub as it had a series of railways and roads forming communication lines vital to support the German army. If the Allies could break through this town and make a push for the coast, then a significant victory would be in sight.

However, Cambrai was nestled behind the Hindenburg line of defences, and to date the Allies had merely been able to penetrate these defences. A decisive breakthrough had eluded them. The Germans had General George von der Marwitz in charge of their army and he would prove to be a worthy adversary.

The Allies used over 470 tanks to support the infantry in the attack on Cambrai. They also deployed over 300 aircraft and over 1,000 artillery pieces. There were six infantry divisions and three cavalry divisions, being part of the Third Army under the command of General Julian Byng.

The Allies were anxious to disguise the presence of over 400 tanks moving up to the front so as not to alert the Germans of another impending major battle. They did this by large scale low flying aircraft missions in this area so as to disguise the sounds of the tanks moving forward. This tactic appears to have been successful because on the morning of the 20th of November the Germans were taken completely by surprise when the attack started.

One of the first obstacles would be the deep anti-tank trenches of the Hindenburg Line. The Mark IV tanks overcame this problem by carrying large bundles of brush wood strapped on the top of the front of their tanks. Having reached the edge of the deep German trench, the brush wood (called Fascines) would be released into the bottom of the trench, partially filling the bottom and allowing the tank to cross the trench and come up the other side.

Another problem for the tank crews was maintaining contact with the infantry. Each tank had two homing pigeons inside cages, which would be released with a message. This strategy proved to be ineffective as the pigeons, like the tank crews themselves, were overcome with the exhaust fumes. The problem was partially resolved with the use of hand signals

These are the Mark IV tanks loaded with brushwood. Note the five soldiers with their terrier on the front of the tank on the left.

and coloured discs, but this relied on good visibility, which was seldom the case in a battle. The system was supplemented by the use of 'runners', individuals who had the unenviable task of running from the tanks back across no man's land to the front-line HQ's. These brave soldiers would be obvious targets for the German snipers.

The success of that first day of the battle surprised Field Marshal Haig. The allied troops had advanced as much as nine kilometres in places. They had almost reached the top of Bourlon Wood ridge which was a strategic priority.

But like so many of the battles, those early gains would be hampered by the difficulties in logistical supplies reaching the front-line troops. The Mark IV 'male' tanks could only carry about 332 x 6lb shells, and the 'female' tanks could only carry about 7,000 rounds of machine gun ammunition. They would also need fuel to maintain the advance in support of the infantry. The infantry would soon use up their ammunition and Mills bombs.

Further logistical problems with the advance.

Another problem was the lack of water to cool the Vickers machine guns. They rapidly overheated from firing 600 rounds per minute. The resulting clouds of steam would have given the gunners' position away to the enemy. Desperate times called for desperate measures, and the soldiers would sometimes resort to urinating in the coolant cylinders to cool the barrels. Finally, and as always, the supporting field artillery gunners had a constant battle keeping up with the advancing infantry and tanks.

The success of the first day would never be sustained, but the Allies captured over 4,000 German prisoners and many of their guns. This came at a huge cost, with over 180 Allied tanks out of action and over 4,000 casualties.

For the days that followed renewed efforts were made to take the Ridge overlooking Bourlon Wood but without success. To compound the problem, key bridges in the area could not support the weight of the Mark IV tanks and as a consequence they collapsed. This in turn prevented the cavalry from being used to rout the retreating German soldiers. This caused delays which were made worse by some of the allied units looting the vacated German trenches.

The Germans were learning quickly how to counter the threat of advancing tanks. They had now developed armour piercing antitank rifles. Their infantry discovered that the tanks had a 'blind spot' which enabled a brave soldier to climb onto the roof of the tank and throw a stick grenade through the roof hatch. A skilled German bomber could strap several stick grenades together and throw them at an advancing tank. A well-placed throw would disable the tank and put it out of action.

In the towns approaching Cambrai the Germans deployed 77mm Howitzers mounted on the back of trucks. These deadly weapons now had armour piercing shells. Some of the streets were narrow making it difficult for the Mark IV tanks to manoeuvre. They made easy targets for the German gun crews. One tactic to avoid being hit by enemy fire was to carry out a 'zig zag' manoeuvre, this only worked when the tanks had space to do this. Therefore, the fortunate tanks crews were those that broke down. Sadly, the others would have a horrible death entombed in their own tanks.

With the delays in the allied advance General Marwitz was quick to take the initiative and on the 30th of November, he ordered a counter attack. His spirits had been lifted by the arrival of battle-hardened experienced soldiers from the Eastern Front. With the carefully coordinated deployment of German Storm Troopers, air support and gas shells, the Germans were able to recapture a lot of the territory they had lost. They captured over 9,000 British prisoners.

During this period Field Marshal Haig ordered a retreat back to the Hindenburg Line. This was carefully carried out so as not to alert the Germans who, had they known, could have caused serious losses to the retreating allied infantry. They were to some extent fooled by the British who fired flares into the skies above the front, giving the false impression that the front was still active. By the 7th of December 1917, the Allies had retreated back to the Hindenburg Line, retaining the strategic important areas of Havrincourt and Flesquires Ridge. In all the Allies had captured about two and a half miles of territory and captured 11,000 German prisoners in total. It was on this day that the weather broke. A snow blizzard put a stop to any further fighting, both sides appearing to be happy with this situation. The losses were similar on both sides with each side suffering over 40,000 casualties.

The Battle of Cambrai was significant for a number of reasons. The Allies had proved that the Hindenburg Line could be broken through. It was about this time that a change in tactics can be seen. The use of the tanks in support of the infantry, with carefully coordinated artillery support and air support would be the template for future battles. The Battle of Cambrai was a great morale boost which the state censured British press was quick to exploit. However, this war would not be over any time soon.

During the time of this battle there had been significant events on the Eastern Front. The Bolsheviks had asked the Germans for an armistice on all fronts. As a consequence, a week later on the 27th of November hostilities on the Eastern Front ceased. The trickle of German soldiers coming to the Western Front from Russia would soon become a tidal wave of over 46 divisions numbering over 500,000 battle hardened German troops.

Faced with the loss of their Russian allies, on the 6th of December 1917 the Romanians suspended hostilities in the Balkans.

The Wiltshires' training exercises

The 6th Wiltshire Battalion did not take an active part in the Battle of Cambrai. For the second and third week of November they were resting in the area of Mount Kemmel and carrying out training exercises. These exercises were a further development of the skills that had already acquired during initial training.

Firing practice on the rifle ranges – if a soldier could place a minimum of ten rounds on the 'target card' within a minute, he would earn the title 'First Class Rifleman'. This exercise was known as 'the mad minute'.

Bayonet practice – the charging of enemy trenches and impaling dummies stuffed with straw, building fitness levels in order to be able to jump the first trench and continue onto the next.

Rifle Grenade practice – the assembly and firing of these clumsy weapons, the high recoil during firing was difficult to get used to.

Forced marching 10-12 miles per day – with a full pack of kit weighing as much as 109lbs. Soldier's feet would swell up, and those that took their boots off, frequently found it difficult to put them back on again. Because of the swelling, blisters and foot sores would often become infected.

The practice of various forms of attack – Frontal attacks, right flank attacks, left flank attacks, both flank attacks, and night attacks. Each of these manoeuvres would require different demands on the infantry man. The Sergeant Major would bark out the different commands. The soldiers would respond to the whistle to go over the top and would climb the ladders. Different squads had different responsibilities. They would become used to carrying an extra bandolier of ammunition around their necks. Each soldier would carry a pick or a shovel. Some would be bombers carrying Mills bomb. There would be a first bayonet man per squad, the list goes on. In the bombing squads there were two grenade throwers, two bomb carriers, two bayonet men, and two soldiers in reserve.

In the last week of November 1917, the 6th Wiltshires were involved in working parties. I have already discussed some of the duties, but in addition to these, the soldiers would have to load and unload shells at the railway depots. This ammunition was then loaded on to smaller trains which travelled down narrow-gauge lines to the communication trenches. The small trains were often petrol powered so as not to give off large clouds of steam to alert enemy artillery of their presence. In this same week the Wiltshires took part in battalion cross-country sport and football. It was during this week that Private 320252 Burchell received training in the use of the Lewis machine gun.

I want to write about the Lewis machine gun because it played an important part in the events that occurred in the spring of the

The Lewis machine gun

following year. Private 320252 Burchell would not have known this, but the training he received in the use of this gun would probably save his life.

The Lewis machine gun

The Lewis gun was invented by an American army colonel, Isaac Newton Lewis, who designed the gun in 1911. To his surprise the American army was not interested in the weapon, so he took his design to Belgium. The Belgian Army was quick to realise the gun's potential as a highly mobile, light weight machine gun, which could be used in an offensive and defensive situation. The Belgians manufactured this gun at their arms factory at Liège. After this the British Army were keen to use this weapon and managed to obtain a licence to manufacture this weapon at the Birmingham Small Arms Factory in England.

Some historians and critics are quick to blame Field Marshal Haig's 'alleged' attitude towards the use of machine guns, which made the British Army fall behind in its deployment. At the beginning of the war only four machine guns were provided per battalion (845 men). The Germans were a lot quicker to see this weapon's potential, and as a consequence they deployed them in far greater numbers. They had six machine guns per company, or 72 guns per regiment by the beginning of 1918.

Having done some deeper research into Haig, I have ascertained that this point of view is contested by some historians. The ratio of machine guns per battalion was no doubt too low at the beginning of the war, but the BEF was lacking in so many areas, perhaps because of the 'blue water' policy in place in the years preceding the outbreak of war. The 'British War Machine' relied too much on naval superiority.

However, this new war of attrition was mainly fought on land. The British by now had found out a costly lesson that the effective use of machine guns could have a devastating effect on massed attacking infantry formations. It was soon realised that the light machine gun was particularly useful in suppressing German machine gun positions. The Lewis gun weighed 12 kg and was a little over a third the weight of the British Vickers heavy machine gun with similar rates of fire per minute. As a consequence, production was rapidly increased to 50,000 guns by 1916. By 1917 there were 47 Lewis guns per battalion, and by the end of the war the British Army could boast of one Lewis machine gun per infantry section, (eight to twelve men).

The gun had a circular magazine located on the top of the firing mechanism. This magazine rotated as the gun was fired. It was designed to fire in short bursts of six to eight rounds per burst. The pan magazine held 47 rounds of .303 bullets which was the standard British round.

Once the magazine was empty it could be refilled manually one bullet at a time. Naturally in a conflict or battle situation there would be a large quantity of full magazines made ready for use. These were often carried in small ammunition cases which carried six to eight magazines. The Lewis gun had an effective range of about 600 metres, and a fire rate of 500-600 rounds per minute. Because of its lightness it could be fired whilst standing. The gun had a low recoil. Some of the Canadian regiments adapted straps to be attached to the gun so that it could be fired from the hip, but the gun was more accurate whilst fired from the ground supported by a tripod. When in use it was a two- man team that operated the gun. Because of the small magazine, the gun would have to be rearmed with fresh magazines at regular intervals.

The Lewis gun had an adjustable clock type recoil spring, the benefit of which was that the rate of fire could be adjusted. In times of short supply of the ammunition, this would be an important feature of the gun.

The barrel of the gun was encased in a larger diameter cylinder which had an aluminium fin encased down the whole length. This helped to absorb the heat during constant fire. This was another important feature, as the larger and heavier belt fed machine guns had to have water coolant to prevent from overheating. The lack of availability of water as a coolant often led to heavy machine guns overheating and seizing up.

As an example of the consumption of ammunition required, one of the sad facts of the Battle of the Somme was that ten belt-fed machine guns fired constantly for 12 hours and used over one million rounds of ammunition! This fact needs to be mentioned because one million rounds of ammunition had to be carried to the gunners to keep them in action. This caused obvious logistical problems because the soldiers supplying these weapons were often under fire and had to struggle across boggy terrain carrying heavy ammunition cases.

The excess steam from over-heated machine gun emplacements often gave away their positions which both sides were quick to react to with snipers and counter fire. The Lewis gun therefore had a number of advantages. By contrast it did not let off as much steam, which made it easier to conceal during use. It was a highly portable weapon, and the operator could rapidly pick up the weapon and redeploy a short distance away. This made it an ideal weapon that could be used in support of advancing troops.

Another useful feature of this gun was that it had a flash deflector fitted to the end of the barrel casement. This made it harder for the enemy to spot and locate, a feature more useful during night operations.

The Germans respected the Lewis machine gun, nicknaming it the 'Belgian Rattle Snake'. They took every opportunity to seize these weapons from the allied soldiers and captured prisoners, or from over-run trenches. They would then use the weapon themselves.

Following the early successful use of this weapon with the infantry, the Allies deployed this gun in planes, ships, special motor bike machine gun units and in female tanks. There were various courses for the operation of the Lewis gun. I guess the time allowed would depend on whether the soldiers were still in training away from the front or operational near the front.

I have been able to refer to an official army course for the Lewis machine gun lasting over 32 hours. The syllabus would have been carried out over two to three days. The regimental diary shows Lewis gun training between the 26th to the 28th of November, suggesting that this was the course the 6th Wiltshires attended. Not all of the Battalion would be trained at once, rather in batches of men.

I do not intend to go into too much detail on these courses, but essentially there would be an emphasis for the whole squad of men to be fully conversant with the component parts. This gun would have to be dismantled and then systematically reassembled ready for firing. The drill would be repeated so as to speed up this discipline.

This would be an important skill on the front. When guns jammed and were out of use, soldiers with knowledge would be able to cannibalise parts from discarded weapons, or use whatever spares were available. This knowledge was vital in a battle situation and made the difference between holding off an enemy advance or being overrun and captured.

The simple task of refilling the magazines would have complications in the muddy environment, and trying to do this in darkness and with freezing cold hands, keeping the component part clear of mud and debris, would have been no easy task. Cartridge cases would split and cause the gun to jam. Again, being able to free the blockage and unjam the gun, under pressure, would be invaluable knowledge in a battle situation. Sometimes this procedure would have to be carried out in the heat of battle, by weary soldiers, their hands trembling with a mixture of fear and adrenalin.

The simple tasks of loading the weapon, setting up the sites, carrying out accurate fire and the effective grouping of shots would become vital skills. The deployment of the gun would be a key aspect of the course, as well as the concealment when used in a defensive situation. Team work would be essential. The squad would have to service the gun with ammunition to maintain its firing rate to ensure maximum effectiveness.

Likewise, in an offensive situation, soldiers needed to learn the rapid deployment of the gun and how to use it to disrupt and suppress key targets like enemy machine gun emplacements and enemy flame throwers and snipers. This aspect of the training could make the difference between success or failure. The effective use of this gun would give a vital support role for troops advancing on enemy trenches.

Artillery fire

The second half of November and through to December 1917 saw both sides on the Western Front curtail any further major operations. This however did not stop the artillery from each side targeting the opposing trenches. These bombardments were designed to wear the enemy down, play on their nerves, and minimise the opportunities for sleep and rest. It should be remembered that a newly bombarded trench system would have to be re-dug at the first opportunity. The battle-weary soldiers would have to re-dig their trenches, adding to their fatigue.

The 6th Wiltshires continued to sustain casualties throughout this period. Because Grandad refused to talk about the impact of artillery bombardments in detail, I have had to research the subject myself.

I was surprised to find out that 60% of all casualties in the Great War were from artillery fire. All of the armies initially saw it as a mobile offensive weapon. Most field guns were towed by a team of six horses. The French had their 75 which arguably were the best of the bunch, capable of firing 20 shells per minute. The Germans had their 7.7cm Feldkarione 96 Nuese Art, which had a shorter range than the French 75. The British had the 13lb and 18lb field guns. These were reliable but at the beginning of the war the BEF had significantly fewer numbers of these guns than the Germans and the French.

It soon became apparent that the field guns had their limitations, because when the infantry from both sides dug trenches, the soldiers would conceal themselves below ground level. In addition to this the soldiers from both sides now had longer range more accurate rifles which could target and kill enemy artillery crews.

As the field guns had a relatively low trajectory (the French 75 had only 18%) it meant that the gun was not capable of doing what was known as 'Plunge fire'. This essentially meant that for concealed ground troops to be successfully targeted, shells would have to be fired in a high elevation so that the shells fell down on top of the troops. This bought about the increased use of the Heavy mortars, Trench mortars, and Howitzer's.

Typically, at the beginning of the war, the Germans were ahead of the field and had a superior number of heavier guns. One of their main stay weapons was the 10.5cm Feldaubitze 98/09 short barrelled Howitzer. The British had the BL60 lb gun capable of firing a shell six miles, often used against German artillery positions. They also had the QF 4.5inch Howitzer which was used against German trench systems and barbed wire.

Private 320252 Burchell would soon learn the difference between the sounds of various shells as they came towards his trench. The best sound would be a shell that went overhead and carried on beyond his trench. The worst sound would be the scream of a shell dropping toward his trench with only seconds to react.

Grandad once said to me:

> 'We used to hate the sound of the 'Whiz Bang' shell as it exploded near to us, not so much   the damage it caused but the unnerving sound it made'.

Then there were the heavy guns. The British had the 9.2inch heavy siege Howitzer capable of firing a 106kg shell a maximum distance of 10km (six and a half miles). The Germans had a 42cm Krupp known as the 'Big Berthas' which could fire an 800kg shell over five and a half miles. The effect of a shell weighing over three quarters of a ton exploding nearby is unimaginable.

The list goes on. These guns were produced in ever increasing quantities, and as a consequence they caused many logistical problems, with their sheer weight. As the front lines changed and moved backwards and forwards it became a nightmare to move them over waterlogged cratered terrain.

For too long the Generals took the view that a battle could be won by the concentrated fire on enemy front-line trenches for days at a time. Then as the whistle blew and the men charged forward, the supporting artillery would extend its range to target the second and third line trenches and enemy artillery positions, and any concentrations of enemy reinforcements. This was the main tactic which failed so many times, but in any event, it caused horrific losses, and so many young men would not return home.

The tactics changed with the concept of the creeping barrage and the prioritising of key targets prior to offensives. The costs of producing this huge number of shells was enormous. It is estimated that over one billion shells were fired by all sides in the Great War. The factories in America, Canada, the Citroën factory in France and the Krupp's factory in Germany made huge amounts of money making these shells.

Essentially there were two types of artillery fire. One was observed fire, which was when an observer would pick out targets and communicate their coordinates to the gun crews, who would adjust the gun sites accordingly and then fire. As the use of spotter planes become more effective, the planes would fly over enemy lines, locate their artillery and drop smoke flares so the artillery observers could adjust their gun sites accordingly.

As a counter measure artillery crews would rely more and more on camouflage, 'dummy' trench systems and fake artillery pieces. Another counter measure would be to place the artillery on reverse slopes out of view from the ground.

'Flash Spotting' was another tactic used. In simple terms the artillery spotter would pinpoint the flash of the gun as it fires, and using a stop watch, a calculation would be made using the known velocity of the shell and how many seconds it took for the shell to drop and explode.

A slightly more sophisticated approach was 'Sound Ranging' this would involve the use of several pairs of microphones to produce a bearing to the source of the sound. Plotted on a map, the intersection of bearings would be the location of the artillery battery. This system would work if maps were accurate and good communications were maintained between observers and gun crews. However, visibility was significantly reduced during artillery attacks. It could be inclement weather with mist and fog, and in addition there was the smoke from numerous exploding shells, and the enemy's use of smoke shells.

The second type would be unobserved fire. Many artillery units would be deployed on reverse slopes out of view from observers on the ground. They would engage in standing fire. Large areas of enemy held territory would be saturated with thousands of shells over prolonged periods.

At the beginning, in 1914 the French were using 900,000 shells per month, but by 1916 it had risen to four and a half million shells. In the final year of the war the German armies were using 8 million shells per month. It is not difficult to appreciate the carnage these exploding shells caused. It can now be seen as a blessing that so many shells were 'duds' and failed to explode. The casualty figures would have been far higher had every shell exploded.

The 6th Wiltshires faced a number of different types of shells in the coming months, for example the shrapnel shell, which on explosion, produced a cloud of smoke 20-30 metres above ground. I mention this because it had a double effect. It helped the enemy gunners 'zero in' on their targets, because the artillery observers could see their shells explode.

On the receiving end, this cloud of smoke also told Ernest to take cover. Upon exploding, each shell contained dozens of steel circular balls, large ball bearings 20-30mm in diameter, which dispersed in a cone shaped arc covering an area 25m wide by 50m long. This had a devastating effect on concentrations of troops who were not in cover. The dispersal of lead ball shot from these exploding shrapnel shells, was similar to the dispersal from a shot gun cartridge, the difference being that these circular lead balls were much larger in diameter, and their velocity and size caused horrendous deaths and injuries.

Another type of shell was the high explosive shell. These tended to be more powerful, the bigger the shell, the deadlier the effect. They contained different types of fuses, some of which were timed to explode before landing, and these were particularly effective against troop and cavalry concentrations. The flying shrapnel would tear into flesh and dismember limbs causing horrendous wounds. It would no doubt be these types of shells that killed Ernest's two horses when he was a dispatch rider.

One nurse in the field hospital came across a soldier who calmly sat on a makeshift bed, with a gaping hole through his torso. She recalled seeing a distant church through this hole. Sadly, he died moments later. What a horrible image to carry in your mind for the rest of your life!

It was not just the shrapnel that was deadly. Following the explosion soldiers would often die from the 'blast effect'. The expanding air around the explosion travelled faster than the speed of sound. When this shock wave hit the poor soldiers, their bodies would be hurled in the air. The hollow organs inside their bodies, for example the heart and the kidneys, would compress rapidly and then rapidly decompress, causing haemorrhaging, and in the case of the brain, severe damage. This effect would often be fatal. It is not therefore surprising that this effect would lead to 'shell shock'.

Almost immediately after the blast effect there followed a reverse effect, as the outward blast of air then caused a vacuum in that space, which then sucked at the surrounding atmosphere, causing a 'pull' on nearby structures and bodies. Deadly shards would fly back into this area with devastating effects. These were so powerful that they could force a 1200kg horse and carriage off the road and half bury them in the mud filled ditches. As a consequence, many of these pitiful beasts had to be put down.

Some fuses detonated on contact with the ground. These were often used to destroy barbed wire defences. It has already been mentioned that the Germans had barbed wire defences in the Hindenburg Line. These were as wide as 30 metres in places.

Observations made at the time found that four field guns had to fire 600 shells between them, in order to clear an area of barbed wire 25m wide by 30m deep. This gives you some idea of the sheer ferocity and rate of fire that the defending troops behind the barbed wire would face. The intensity of these artillery bombardments, often referred to as a 'drum roll', would be so high that it was impossible to detect individual explosions.

Another type of high explosive fuse was the delayed fuse. This resulted in the shell penetrating the surface of the ground or emplacement before it exploded. It was these types of shells that caused the crater effects on the battlefield. I also suggest that it was these types of shells that would cause the sides of the trenches to collapse tragically burying alive many a soldier.

Other types of shells included gas shells and smoke shells. Sadly, soldiers would sometimes become confused between the two, with disastrous consequences. I mention this because in the second half of 1918 the Allies exploited this confusion.

There were also 'star' shells. These were mainly designed for illumination. The Germans fired a 'shell rocket' and following discharge this would ignite high up in the air during darkness. Its descent would be slowed down by an attached parachute. A typical use for this was in the case of an alarm being raised. The Germans would fire their rockets, illuminating the night sky and enabling their soldiers in the trench to shoot at any allied soldiers who were advancing across no man's land engaged in a 'raiding party' or intelligence gathering expedition.

As if there weren't enough types of explosive devices, there would be mortar shells and rifle grenades from the opposing trenches, and of course the underground mines which both sides used to devastating effect.

Ernest had fortunately survived the effects of one of these blasts when his very unfortunate mates had all been killed as they made tea. He had also survived the effects of flying shrapnel when his two horses had been killed. Would his luck hold out? He must have pondered over this on numerous occasions.

My Grandad in the trenches again

During December 1917 the 6th Wiltshires were deployed facing the Hindenburg Line at Ribecourt. Private 320252 Burchell faced these bombardments, and their intensity escalated in the spring of 1918.

He would witness a number of fatalities. The issue of 'shell shock' will not be discussed until the next chapter for reasons that will become apparent.

I have tried to place myself in those trenches in order to appreciate the effect of artillery explosions on my Grandad. To do this I have explored the sights, sounds, smells and the sheer physical impact on his body.

It is hard for me to imagine the physical effects other than those already mentioned. Ducking down behind the trench wall would offer some protection from the shock waves from the blasts in front and to the rear. The 'zigzag' pattern of the trench system to some extent minimised the effects of direct hits on the trenches, if the shells exploded some distance away. But if soldiers were in the immediate vicinity of an exploding shell and not instantly killed, the air would be forced out of their lungs and the chance was that they would be flying through the air until they hit something solid, or buried under the collapsing trench wall.

If the soldiers were near to the blasts, it would be like experiencing a series of earthquakes. The only way I can perceive the effect would be that it would be like sitting on a firm trampoline when others around are jumping up and down. The very ground you were standing on or lying on would reverberate violently. The intense sounds on your eardrums would be almost unbearable, the hot air that eventually filled your lungs would smell of cordite and death and of fresh blood and ruptured intestines. These smells would be so strong that you could taste them. Soldiers must have had terrible headaches and constant ringing in their ears, indeed partial deafness was common.

After the allied bombardment at the Battle of the Somme many captured German soldiers were both deaf and numbed by the shock of this onslaught. Their British captors found it difficult to communicate with them.

Imagine that you are lying under your ground sheet with debris of all kinds landing on you, soil, spent shards of shrapnel, together with bits of previously buried body parts. If this isn't bad enough, a direct hit on a latrine would add further to the pungent, thick and dense smoke-filled air which filled your nostrils. You try to get to your feet and stumble and walk over the body part of a friend with whom, only hours previously, you have sat and joked with together.

The sounds would fill your memory for ever, the squealing horses and mules suffering from dismembered limbs, followed by the quick crack of a Webley and Scott pistol putting the beast out of its misery.

There would be the cries of agony from the wounded soldiers, some begging to be put out of their misery, many crying out for their mothers. The muffled panicking voices of soldiers buried alive, the cries for help in no man's land, the cries for medics.

The orders being barked out by the NCO's, their voices hoarse at the strain of trying to be heard over the drum roll 'Shoot that man who's crying! Anyone caught returning to our trenches without orders to do so will be shot!'

The constant rattle of machine guns from both sides, the sound of spent bullets hitting the sandbags and earth nearby, bullets flying through the air only inches away from your head, the howl of shells some of which would whiz past with a loud roar only feet away. The screaming rats running from their burrows during a gas attack, the screams of the gas attack victims.

The sights would every bit as bad. Body parts flying through the air, mountains of earth rising up like erupting mini volcanos, flying debris of all kinds, the steam rising from a comrade as his body parts lay scattered all around. Then there would be blood everywhere, and the contents of ruptured intestines and stomachs.

The night would take on a whole new experience. The horizon would be like a huge firework display, with noise levels probably ten times louder. Tracer shells lighting up the sky showing their curved trajectory.

I could go on forever.

Then, after the battle when the guns fell silent, there would be the eerie pitiful mutterings and hum of wounded soldiers in no man's land.

I'm now coming to realise why Ernest used to break down in tears when he attempted to tell me of his experiences. This makes me feel guilty for asking but at the time, I was young and naïve .... sorry, Grandad.

The prospect of another winter at war

Returning to the events of December 1917, we know there was a snow blizzard on the 7th which effectively put an end to any further offensives on the Western Front that year. A small consolation but the soldiers would now have to face the cold of another winter away from their loved ones. Christmas was approaching.

The 6th Wiltshires had spent most of November and the 1st week of December training. They returned to the Hindenburg Line on the 11th of December where they relieved Battalions of Leicester Regiment.

It was during the 1st week of December 1917 that the 19th Western Division transferred from General Plumer's 2nd Army, to General Julian Byng's 3rd Army. The Wiltshires were part of the 58th Brigade who were an integral part of the 19th Western Division. They spent the following six days on the front line at Ribecourt where they sustained four casualties (wounded). On the 18th the Regiment retired to brigade reserve. From the 22nd to the 24th the Brigade rested in Havrincourt Wood. The troops had their Christmas festivities on the 24th before returning to the front line on Christmas Day.

The 6th Wiltshires spent the rest of 1917 in the front-line trenches at Ribecourt experiencing intermittent artillery fire from the enemy, resulting in two further soldiers being wounded.

Meanwhile further afield, 1917 ended with the Allies capturing Jerusalem from the Ottoman armies. This was a huge morale boost for the Allies. A large area of previously held Ottoman territory had been captured by General Allenby's XX Corps and XXI Corps. British Prime

Minister Lloyd George said at the time 'This news is a Christmas present to the British people'. The New York Herald headline on the 11th of December read 'Jerusalem is rescued by the British after 673 years of Muslim rule'. This was a huge psychological blow to the Ottoman Empire, which had suffered irreplaceable losses. Now the Allies had secured the oilfields of Basra and Mesopotamia.

The New Year 1918

What New Year's resolutions would Ernest have made? Perhaps none. His only hope, like that of so many others, would be a speedy end to this crazy war. His hopes and wishes would not be answered for some months to come.

The new year in 1918 saw the 6th Wiltshires in the front-line trenches west of Ribecourt. The 1st and 2nd days of January are described as 'quiet days' with routine patrols sent out. The regiment was relieved on the 3rd of January by the 9th Welsh Regiment, and they moved back to a support trench in 'Nine Wood'. On the 6th of January they were back on the Hindenburg Line in the Kabul Trench and Fork Avenue trench. Here they had two relatively quiet days before hostilities returned on the 9th of January, when they had ten soldiers killed and one wounded during the shelling. They remained in the front-line trenches until the 14th, and then moved back to Valley trench, staying there until the 16th when they were relieved by the South Lancashire Regiment.

The Wiltshires spent the next six days recuperating and receiving reinforcements at Hawes Camp.

The role of the Padre

It was during this period that Ernest and his fellow soldiers attended one of many church parades that would be held on Sundays, this particular one being Sunday the 20th of January 1918.

It should be mentioned that these services were well attended. I would like to think that the battle-weary soldiers took some comfort from the words read out by the Battalion Chaplain, with their prayers and thanks giving for victory.

My Grandad was a very religious man, as were a lot of his generation. He was a Methodist. He would have known the words of many of the hymns that were sung. The horrors that he was witnessing would have tested his faith on many occasions, but he remained a Christian to his dying day.

I had not realised just what a valuable role the chaplains and padres performed. I think that it is only right and proper to make the reader aware of the many tasks they performed.

During the early days of major battles, they would often assist the stretcher bearers carrying the wounded from no man's land to the field hospitals. Some even resorted to using trench ladders for this purpose. Following the battles some of them would go out into no man's land and bury the dead saying the words of committal as they patted the soil on the tops of the graves with spades. They would make sure the dead men had their identity tags removed and their personal belongings put safe. The chaplains and the bearers would make sure that the wounded soldiers had 'wounded labels' attached to them. This label gave vital information as to the soldiers' identity and what initial treatment he had received.

In quiet periods the chaplains assisted the platoon officers with censoring the letters which the soldiers wrote to their loved ones back home. They would handle hundreds of letters from worried relatives, and make consoling replies where appropriate. This was traditionally the role of NCOs but at times they just could not cope with the sheer numbers of casualties. Many a poor terrified young soldier would seek comfort from his chaplain or padre. It is difficult to put a value on the kind reassurances they gave. They must have played a key role in maintaining the fragile morale amongst the troops.

When the casualties arrived at the field hospitals the chaplains and padres would become invaluable to the Regimental Medical Officers (RMOs). They gave valuable assistance in the hospitals. In the heat of the battles, when the medical staff were struggling to cope, they would be that extra person who would dress wounds, even administer anaesthetics during operations, assist with X-Ray equipment, and even double up as hospital postmen.

Can you imagine the emotional stress that the nurses and chaplains would have gone through? Imagine the scene... the ward is full of wounded moaning soldiers, a soldier with half of his face blown away and severely dehydrated, tries to communicate, begging for water, the padre gently puts a straw in what's left of his mouth and he tries to suck the fluid, and moments later he dies.

Perhaps the saddest sight of all was the gentle trickle of tears rolling down the face of a dying soldier, his face grey, as life ebbed away, he lies in silence when all around is chaos.

I'm getting emotional writing about this never mind being there, witnessing this scene so many times over and over again.

The chaplains and padres had the unenviable task of attending the dying soldiers in the 'Moribund Wards', leading countless communal services and prayers of absolution and giving last rites and consolation to men at the end of their lives. At the sad end of it all they would conduct burial services for the dead and even help fill in the graves. I hold my hat off to these brave and compassionate men.

I recount a sad memory of a time when I was a uniformed Police Officer in the 1980's when I had to break into an elderly lady's flat. Her neighbour, a retired nurse, accompanied me. As I tried to sit the lady up in bed to make her comfortable, she died in my arms. So, I can empathise with the nurses and chaplains who would have witnessed death so many times.

That's not all, for many of the chaplains would ensure that the numerous cemeteries had the correct battalion's name embossed on the signpost. Where possible they created maps with the location of every man buried. This proved invaluable to the War Graves Commission and the thousands of relatives who would later visit these graves. The suffering soldiers in the winter months resorted often to using the wooden crosses for fire wood. A situation that evokes pity.

Work and rest

The 6th Wiltshires returned to the trenches on the 22nd of January, where they remained until the 25th. They were shelled by enemy artillery which caused ten casualties, six dead and four wounded. The writer of the regimental diary describes this period as 'a quiet period'. Perhaps by now he is becoming immune or numb to the losses and casualties.

At the end of this tour of duty, the regiment were relieved and had a rest period at Hawes Camp where they cleaned their equipment and clothes, and even had the chance of a bath.

Can you imagine having a bath in the open air in the middle of winter? If you were lucky, you would be one of the first in the bath. The water would still be hot and reasonably clean. Bad luck if you were at the end of the queue.

Prior to the return to the front-line trench on the 29th of January 1918, Ernest would no doubt have attended another Church Parade.

The battalion move back to the front and relieve the 10th Worcester Regiment. They received enemy shelling on the 30th. On the 31st, during

Bath time behind the front line

the morning 'stand to', the enemy shelled their positions, some shells being poisonous gas. This would seem to be the first time that Ernest experienced a gas attack whilst in the front-line trench. True he would have seen the effects of gas attacks, whilst in a support role at the front. He and his fellow soldiers must have been well trained and prepared with their masks, as I see no evidence of any casualties in the regimental diary.

The use of gas

It might be a good time to write about the gas attacks and the effects on morale and physical wellbeing of the troops in the front line.

I have already mentioned the use of gas in the earlier battles of this war, but I want to explore how the threat of such an attack would affect Private Burchell and his comrades. I think it is widely regarded that the horror of gas attacks was not the casualties that resulted, but the psychological effects on morale and the sheer terror which they caused amongst the soldiers.

Rather than bombard you all with facts. I wish to state that out of the millions of casualties in World War 1, there was a relatively low number of men killed by gas, about 100,000. The majority of these were Russians on the Eastern Front. Only 3% of the soldiers who were exposed to the gas actually died, however 2% of those exposed were permanently incapacitated. A case in point was that of my wife April's Grandfather, Joseph Brooks. Sadly, she never met him.

Joseph was in the North Staffordshire Regiment, which was also part of the 19th Division, as was Ernest. Having been exposed to a gas attack in the early part of the war, he was returned home. He suffered a slow and agonising death in front of his wife and children. My father-in-law's only memory of his father was when he died at home.

Frank Brooks (my father-in-law), a child of five, climbed into his father's coffin in the front room of their family house. He did not want to leave his Dad. The resulting hardship in the family was typical of the soldiers' families who suffered in a similar way.

I have discussed chlorine gas and its effects, but by far the deadliest was phosgene gas. It was colourless, and thus difficult to detect, but with the smell of mouldy hay. It had the disadvantage for the users in that it could take as much as 24 hours for symptoms to show. As a consequence, soldiers could carry on fighting until the effects took hold the following day. This gas accounted for 85% of all gas deaths.

The most publicised and effective gas was mustard gas, not because of the number of deaths it caused, but rather the sheer agony it inflicted on the victims. It was a real terror weapon. Can you imagine the agonised screams caused by the huge yellow blisters? The sounds of these screams would haunt the survivors for the rest of their lives. The worrying aspect was that gas masks were ineffective against mustard gas.

The incapacitation caused by the use of gas was an advantage to the attackers, as it became easier to overrun trenches. However, this gas did not disperse and it impregnated the soil and lingered in trench systems. The attackers ended up occupying contaminated trenches with all the associated problems that would cause.

How would poisonous gas affect Private 320252 Burchell? Again, he refused to discuss the subject with me, sleeping in the trenches would have been hard enough, due to the discomfort, noise and general stress, but being under the constant threat of a gas attack would sometimes make sleeping impossible. Many of the officers had canaries in cages, similar to the custom in coal mines. If there was a gas attack, an audible alarm would sound to alert the troops.

The lack of sleep would add to the 'wearing down' of the individual, lowering his resolve and ultimately his morale. When I visited the Imperial War Museum, I found some interesting facts. Indeed, the soldiers would raise the alarm when gas was used, but there were also tell-tale signs. Sometimes the attack was so bad that the thick gas used to stop the watch mechanisms on the soldier's wrists. It would also turn the brass buttons on their tunics green. During some of the gas attacks, the rats would run out of their burrows squealing in panic.

It is interesting to note that the gas shells fired by the Germans on the 31st of January did not result in a German infantry attack. Again, a misconception on my part, for I always assumed that the use of gas shells would mean an imminent attack. Not so. Both sides used them as 'terror weapons' designed to wear the enemy down, and destroy their morale.

The use of gas masks added to the discomfort. They were unbearable on a hot day. In addition, the visors would steam up and seriously affect visibility. Even the dogs and horses were given crude masks, but if it saved their lives, then all to the good.

I myself have had to wear visors and masks whilst using power tools. They are very uncomfortable. I often took them off because I sweated too much and my vision was impaired. The soldiers standing in a cloud of poisonous gas would not have had that choice. Those that did rip off their masks would suffer agonising consequences.

The War in January and February, 1918

Although the month of January 1918 was a period of relative calm on the Western Front, both sides carried out artillery attacks, as has been seen. These killed and maimed 100's of soldiers on both sides.

The Allies were now beginning to sense that Germany and its allies would make one more push for a final victory and make that 'knockout punch' to end the war, or at least be in a position of advantage should a truce be called. The big question was where would the Germans attack? Even though the American Army continued to build up its strength, there clearly was a window of opportunity as the German divisions were being released from the Eastern Front in ever increasing numbers. There was a period of two to three months when they had numerical superiority. The German Generals Hindenburg and Ludendorff were by now running the show. They were acutely aware of the American presence and growing threat.

Field Marshal Haig was also aware of the possible German attack and he and his Generals continued to press Prime Minister Lloyd George and his coalition government for more troops. The mass slaughter of recent battles had deterred Lloyd George from letting Haig have these extra troops.

He was beginning to lose faith in Haig. He favoured the Allies going on the defensive on the Western Front, and would have been happy for no further major campaigns in 1918. To Haig's annoyance Lloyd George still favoured a decisive breakthrough in the Italian theatre and in the Balkans.

It was over this period that there emerged a power struggle between Haig and Lloyd George. In Haig's favour was the fact that he enjoyed much support from the Tory side of the coalition British Government. He was also close to King George V. Haig's wife had worked at the Royal Household when George had been the Prince of Wales. Field Marshal Haig regularly corresponded with the King who valued his opinion. Had it not been for this, I suspect that Lloyd George would have dismissed him.

Being the shrewd politician he was, Lloyd George effectively circumnavigated Haig. He appointed General Sir Henry Wilson as Chief of the Allied General Staff. He took charge of the British troop depositions and eventually the deployment of reinforcements.

On the 30th and 31st of January the Allied Supreme General Staff met at Versailles near Paris. The result of this meeting was that Field Marshal Haig and the other Army Generals of the First, Second, Third, and Fifth British armies located on the Western Front from north to south, were ordered to remain on the defensive. To compensate for the lack of reinforcements, Field Marshal Haig reduced the size of his divisions from twelve battalions to nine.

One particular army group suffered the most, this being General Gough's 5th Army, who because of their acute losses had to reduce the strength of their divisions from 12,000 men to 6,000 men. Two months later the Germans exploited this weakness.

How would this shortage of troops affect Private 320252 Burchell and the rest of the 6th Wiltshire Battalion, you might ask? They did not receive the desperately needed reinforcements on the front line. The period between leave was extended, and the trenches they defended were occupied by fewer troops. All of these factors served to drain morale even further. The work in the trenches would now be even harder as there were fewer soldiers to carry it out. In Britain there remained over

600,000 trained soldiers ready for deployment. These soldiers to a large extent were kept in Britain whilst the German menace grew and grew.

The German High Command met towards the end of January 1918 where options were discussed as to where the thrust of their attack would be carried out. The options they had were

To the North, near the coast and the town of Ypres, defended by the British 2nd Army Group whose commander was General Sir Herbert Plumer.

Further South was the 1st Army whose commander was General Henry Horne, occupying Vimey Ridge and Loucette Ridge.

South of this Army group was the 3rd Army commanded by General Julien Byng occupying the Arras area.

South of Arras was the 5th Army commanded by General Hubert Gough who controlled the Somme area.

Following much deliberation General Ludendorff decided that the initial attack would be targeted against the British 5th Army. This Army was deployed both sides of the canal in the Saint Quentin area, extending north to the River Scarpe. Preparations continued, with the offensive planned given the name 'Operation Michael'.

On the 20th of January the German military command completed a memorandum which stated that 'for the up and coming offensive, the Air Squadrons would support ground troops with suppressing aerial fire'. Was this the start of the 'Blitzkrieg' tactics that would later be used in 1939, you might ask?

On 18th of January a full American division was deployed at the front for the first time at the S'aint Mihiel salient. This American division was full of fresh troops, well equipped with the French Renault FT17 tanks with their revolutionary rotating turrets. As I have already mentioned, the French Citroën factory rapidly expanded over the war, making considerable profits out of supplying the American Army and other Allies. The Americans also bought airplanes, shells, ammunition, rifles, machine guns, and artillery from the French over the coming months.

The American General Pershing had refused the French requests to have his soldiers absorbed into their army. To compromise he supplied the French with regiments of black soldiers, who prior to this had only been allowed in a support role. These soldiers soon earned tremendous respect from their French comrades. The American procedure smacks to me as racist. Sadly, racial inequality was still rife in America. The Black Civil Rights Movement was still in the distant future. Martin Luther King would not be born until the 15th of January 1929.

The month of January also saw the Germans step up their bombing raids on Britain. Their bombers attacked London, parts of Paris and the strategic docks of Calais, Boulogne and Dunkirk. The civilian population sustained hundreds of dead and wounded.

The British Naval blockade continued to bring severe hardship on the civilian populations of Germany and Austria, with thousands of hunger related deaths. The Austrians had a mutiny in their navy involving 6,000 sailors, the four main instigators being eventually court martialled and executed.

Cracks were appearing, as the Bolsheviks tried to encourage other nations to join in their revolution. The question was, which side would give in first?

The month of February 1918 saw the 6th Wiltshires in the frontline trenches near Ribecourt. Then, on the 2nd of February, they were relieved by the 9th Royal Welch Fusiliers. From the 2nd to the 5th of February, they rested at the Vallulart camp. On the 6th of February they returned to the trenches at Frescault where they relieved the 8th Gloucestershire Regiment. They spent the next four days in the frontline trench. There was heavy shelling in the Trecault and Ribecourt areas resulting in ten killed and one wounded.

On the 10th of February the 6th Wiltshires moved back to the intermediate trench. I' have not come across this name before, but it would appear that the Intermediate Trench was an old German trench system.

On the 13th the Regiment was relieved by the 4th Bedfordshire Regiment and they retired to the Rocquigny Camp. They spent nine days at this camp during which they received 106 reinforcements. Further training was carried out including musketry on the firing range.

On the 22nd of February the 6th Wiltshires took part in a 'Brigade tactical scheme' which I assume was the practice in manoeuvres of mass formations of troops, a brigade being between 3,000 to 5,500 troops consisting of three to six battalions. The 6th Wiltshire battalion was part of the 58th Infantry Brigade.

On the 23rd of February the 6th Wiltshires moved to another camp at Haplicourt where they spend three days doing further training, and afterwards they attended another Church Parade on the 24th.

On the 27th the Regiment was in a supporting role doing work parties in the forward areas of the front. This would likely to have been assisting in the moving of supplies and ammunition to the front. The last day of the month was spent doing company training.

German planning for the major offensive

In March, the Germans continued to plan for their major offensive. They mustered 191 divisions of infantry on the Western Front, together with over 80 divisions in reserve. This represented over 3.4 million men.

Ludendorff changed the makeup of the Assault Divisions. These soldiers would be predominantly younger soldiers aged between 20 and 35 years. A large proportion of these frontline divisions would be given a three-week intensive training in the modern tactics. The German infantry field manual was rewritten to include these new tactics. Ludendorff also placed his most successful generals in charge of his three army groups facing the British, these being:

General Otto von Below in charge of the 17th Army
General Georg von der Marwitz in charge of the 2nd Army
General Oskar von Hutier in charge of the 18th Army

Surely this vastly superior Army would overwhelm the British.

One important fact which would become significant in the months to come would be the logistical support. The allied armies had over five times as many supply trucks as the Germans. Because of the allied success of the naval blockade, Germany could not import rubber to make tyres, so they had to make do with steel wheels which, over prolonged periods, damaged road surfaces by causing deeper ruts and breaking up the surface much more quickly than air inflated rubber tyres.

The Germans delayed their major offensive until the situation on the Eastern Front was secure. The events over this period are very confusing. There appeared to be wars within a war in the East, and major conflicts in Finland and Ukraine. Whilst the Russian Army attempted to disband, there was civil war between the Red Army who supported the Bolsheviks and the White Army loyal to the old government.

The Bolsheviks were convinced that there would be revolution in Germany, and consequently they tried to play for time until this happened. There were peace demonstrations and rioting in Germany, but these were dealt with an iron fist. Over 50,000 protesters were subsequently conscripted into the German Army. To keep pressure on the Bolsheviks the Germans advanced their armies across the whole Eastern Front taking huge swathes of land. Eventually Lenin and the Bolsheviks come back to the negotiating table.

On the 3rd of March 1918, a Peace Treaty was signed between Russia and Germany. The Brest–Litovsk Treaty, signed on the 3rd of March, allowed the victorious Germans to hold on to vast swathes of Russian Territory which amounted to over 700,000 square kilometres of land containing over 50 million Russians. This area of land included large amount of mineral resources with obvious commercial gains to be had.

This treaty prompted the American President Woodrow Wilson to say 'The German idea is a World Empire of gain and commercial supremacy!'

As already stated there had been peace overtures made over the last 12 months, especially with the Austrian government. However, Germany's reluctance to give up territory gained would mean that the war would continue. America's attitude towards Germany hardened in the months ahead.

By now the Germans had amassed a formidable arsenal of weapons which included over 6,000 heavy guns and 3,000 mortars. They now had more aircraft than the Allies on the Western Front. They had over 360 serviceable aircraft to 261 Allied aircraft.

To maximise the element of surprise, the German Army had moved its divisions up to the front during darkness, marching only at night so as to avoid detection by allied reconnaissance planes. The time was rapidly approaching when the Germans would be ready to attack, but the big question was where? General Haig supported by recent intelligence was of the opinion that the main thrust would be in the Flanders area. As a consequence, he placed the bulk of his reserves behind the 3rd Army commanded by Julian Byng, just south of Arras.

The scene was set! The German idea was a World Empire of gain and commercial supremacy!' The Germans need no longer look over their shoulders at the Eastern Front. Zero hour was rapidly approaching!

Chapter 6

As the month of March 1918 progresses the end of winter is in sight. The land begins to dry up making the movement of troops, supplies and heavy guns slightly easier. The days are growing longer, and with that the daily sense of impending major conflict. Rumours are rife amongst the men in the trenches.

On the home front the civilian population of Britain was going flat out to produce munitions, material and supplies for the war machine. It was imperative that Britain and its allies kept up, or even out-produced Germany and the Central Powers. By 1918 the Ministry of Munitions had over 20,000 factories. In charge of this production was Winston Churchill, and since his appointment in July 1917, production had increased significantly. Factories in Canada and North America, as well as France, made a vital contribution.

The nature of the labour force in these factories had undergone changes. Now women formed the bulk of the workers. They worked 12-hour days on half the pay of men. The munition factory girls were nicknamed 'the canaries', as repeated exposure to chemicals and explosive materials gave them a yellow complexion. The Germans in contrast were using captured prisoners, disabled soldiers, older men, and also their women, in order to maintain their production. Their factories were running flat out. The weapons of slaughter were being produced in ever increasing quantities.

Of the British population of approximately 42 million, at this time over one million men were used in the production of coal. The efforts of these miners, who worked in very difficult conditions without the benefits of today's health and safety regulations, should not be forgotten.

The hatred for the Germans persisted. Hundreds of thousands of British soldiers, husbands, fiancés, fathers, sons, and best friends would never return home. To add to this there were the bombing raids, by both Zeppelins and German bombers. The resulting civilian casualties galvanised the public resolve to sustain the fight. The state-controlled press fanned the flames of this hatred of the Germans through propaganda posters which depicted the Germans as inhuman devil-like creatures.

The factory women were making bullets, bombs, aircraft and weapons for their men in the trenches. Without this effort their men would have been overwhelmed by hordes of evil Bosch soldiers. There was no choice but to work tirelessly, no matter the hardships, and the mental and physical strain this caused. This determination to carry on was often strained to almost breaking point. Running alongside this there remained a determination by women and the working class to improve working conditions, pay and women's rights.

During the period 1915 to 1918 there were 3,227 unofficial strikes in Britain. This figure far exceeded that of France and Germany. There was a price to pay one day for this supreme effort made by our civilian population.

However, General Ludendorff misjudged the morale of the British. He was convinced that this next battle would be decisive and that the British, once defeated would sue for peace but Germany would be able to dictate the terms. He would be proved wrong. He saw the defeat of the British Army as a priority. He believed that when the British gave in, the rest would follow.

During the course of the war the Germans captured over 185,000 British prisoners. The total for all the other allied prisoners captured far exceeded this amount. Many would be put into forced labour.

Preparations for conflict

In the weeks leading up to the end of March, German airplanes dropped thousands of leaflets on the British lines in an attempt to weaken morale further. The gist of these letters was 'What are you fighting for? The Americans will not be with you in strength for another year. Your situation is hopeless!'

It is highly likely that Pt 320252 Burchell read one of these leaflets. Knowing him as I did, he would have treated the leaflet with utter contempt.

On a political front, during March 1918 Lloyd George continued to out manoeuvre Field Marshal Haig, but fortunately the control over the use of the reserves on the Western Front remained temporarily in the hands of Field Marshals Haig and Pétain, who by now had formed a good relationship. Haig trusted Pétain to come to the rescue should the situation become critical, as and when the Germans attacked.

On a tactical note Haig was convinced earlier in this same year, that the Germans would not launch a major offensive in the near future, but would favour smaller scale offensives like the counter attack at Cambrai in 1917. He suggested another offensive in Flanders to take the initiative away from the Germans. He did not have the chance to carry out these plans.

The build-up of German troops on the Western Front still concerned Haig. The appointment of his new Chief of Intelligence, Brigadier Edgar Cox, appeared to have given him a new impetus, but the Germans were quick to mislead the Allies. They constantly changed the radio codes, making the work for the intelligence gatherers increasingly more difficult. The early morning mist and fog, prevailing in Belgium and northern France at this time of the year, frustrated the efforts of the allied air reconnaissance crews. They found it difficult to detect well concealed German artillery which was often hidden in wooded areas and under effective camouflage nets. By now both sides were improving their counter surveillance.

Based on the intelligence he had, Haig had to make a decision as to where he could most afford to give up ground, should any German advance become successful. He chose General Gough's 5th Army as it was based in the weakest and most thinly stretched area. Haig gambled that if it came to the crunch, General Pétain would assist with French reinforcements.

Ernest in March 1918

The first three weeks in March saw the 6th Battalion of the Wiltshire Regiment mainly in training and carrying out work parties. Since December 1917 they had been transferred from the Second Army to the 3rd Army. They were still part of the 58th Brigade, one of three brigades forming the 19th Division, the other two being the 56th and 57th Brigades.

The 6th Wiltshires spent most of their time behind the front line at the Sanders training camp at Haplincourt, doing a mixture of musketry and platoon training. Then, on the 9th of March, they moved to Doignes. It was here that there was a subtle change in the training. The officers carried out training in counter attacks, and the men practised deployment of advanced assembly positions. This was no easy task as the coordinated movement of large amounts of troops was difficult, especially under the cover of darkness. Very often tapes were rolled out to guide the troops in the right direction. This was carried out under strict silence so as not to alert the enemy.

I suspect that by now rumours were rife that something big was brewing. At the beginning of the 3rd week of March, the 6th Wiltshires carried out exercises with the Royal Welch Fusiliers. If I know Grandad, he would be preparing himself mentally for the inevitable.

On the 9th of March, the German artillery started an intensive bombardment on the Western Front. Over several days they fired over half a million shells at the Allies, and these shells contained phosgene and mustard gas.

The 6th Wiltshires attended Church Parades on the first three Sundays of the month. Ernest would no doubt have Elizabeth on his mind during these services. He would picture her playing the piano and organ at Hartshorne Chapel, and hear in his mind that lovely singing voice as it resonated throughout the congregation. He would have used this three-week period to write to Elizabeth.

The importance of sending and receiving letters from loved ones cannot be underestimated. Whilst strictly censured, it gave the soldiers a thin thread of contact with home, and something to look forward to. Whilst writing these letters, Elizabeth would have no idea about the hardships and danger that Ernest was facing.

Can you imagine the joy of received an item, whether it be food or a material object, knowing that only two days previously it had been held and dispatched by someone you so dearly loved? Just to have a scented handkerchief, or a small cloth bag of lavender to hold to your nose, to give you brief respite from the putrefying odours of war. It is impossible to put a value on it.

Elizabeth's two brothers Albert and Daniel were also on the Western Front. Albert Leese was a cook in the Army Service Corps, attached to the Royal Artillery Regiment. His brother, Daniel Leese, was a stretcher bearer in the Royal Army Medical Corps, attached to a Battalion of the North Staffordshire Regiment. Like Ernest's regiment, the North Staffordshire's were part of the 19th Division temporarily attached to the 3rd Army. I wonder if their paths ever crossed, Ernest never mentioned it to me.

When attending the Sunday service at Hartshorne Chapel, Elizabeth, like so many others in the congregation, would pray for the safe return of Ernest and her brothers. Every Sunday service the Vicar would read out a list of any soldiers killed in the parish. Sadly, thirty-three brave men from Hartshorne did not return home. Their names were engraved on a memorial at St Peter's Church, Hartshorne, some 60 metres away from Ernest and Walter's former bakery.

Whilst the battalion was resting at the camp close to the village of Rocquigny, they had better opportunities for more sustaining meals.

Behind the lines there were better cooking facilities. Field canteens were geared up to cook large quantities of food in a short space of time.

This was in contrast to the tinned food that the soldiers had to endure in the front-line trenches. This food was barely adequate. Soldiers were bored with eating the same food day after day. Bully beef, Maconochie's tinned broth, and biscuits, these front-line rations were barely tolerated, but the soldiers had no choice.

Albert and Daniel Leese, brothers of Elizabeth and later brothers-in-law of Ernest

Behind the lines Ernest would see the Aldershot Oven in action. This was essentially a long domed shaped brick oven, which was steel lined. It worked by lighting a substantial fire inside the oven, which was allowed to die down. The oven, having retained most of the heat, would then be used to cook a variety of stews, including plain stew, Irish stew, brown stew, brown curry stew and many other concoctions. Other ovens included the Combined Oven and Trench Kettles, designed to feed 150 soldiers, and there were the Soya Stoves. When circumstances permitted, soldiers in camp would be fed a variety of food, a diet of meat, dried fish, bacon, vegetables and fruit.

Perhaps it is a good time to pay tribute to the merchant ships that ran the gauntlet of patrolling German submarines to safeguard food supplies, in order to provide the soldiers on the Western Front with around 4,000 calories per day.

During this period, Ernest put his baking skills to good use. He became popular with the other men of his company who nicknamed him 'The Rissole King'.

This rissole consisted of a mixture of meat, suet, flour, bread, onions, pepper and salt, with mixed herbs. This minced up mixture, was moulded into sausage shapes then fried and subsequently covered in gravy. This would have made a welcome change from some of the tinned food that the soldiers had to endure. I know these details to be true, as my dear Aunt Margaret, one of the two surviving daughters of Ernest, informed me of the story of the 'rissoles' when giving me information for this book. Even after the war, Ernest would often cook this meal for his family.

I will always remember a time when I was a young boy on Ernest's farm in Hartshorne, Derbyshire. It was harvest time and my Grandad had just bought out a large jug of chilled water containing slices of lemon, for the farm workers, as it was a very hot day. As they drank the cool liquid, Ernest turned to me and smiled as he fetched a whole raw onion out of his pocket, he then started to eat it as if it was an apple. I cringed at this sight, saying to Grandad 'How can you eat that onion? It's raw, won't it make you sick?'

He replied, laughing, 'I got a taste for them in the trenches. They used to keep better than apples.'

Musketry practice

In March 1918, the 6th Wiltshires also spent a lot of time doing musketry practice. There would have been an emphasis on rifle drill and sustained accurate concentrated fire. I can just imagine the Sergeant Major barking out the command '15 rounds rapid fire!'

Having had experience, myself of the constant use of a firearm, I can appreciate the effect this had on the weapon itself. The barrel and firing mechanism would rapidly heat up, making the exposure to skin a real hazard for burns. During rapid and constant fire some of the bolt mechanisms of the Lee Enfield rifles would expand under the intense heat, and then jam. In practice the soldiers would have to learn to improvise and unjam the rifle. If all else failed, he would have to salvage a discarded weapon from a dead comrade. With constant use, the length of the barrels visibly extended with heat expansion. The advantage of the Lee Enfield rifle was that the barrel was almost entirely surrounded by the wooden stock minimising exposure to the hot barrel of the rifle.

By now Ernest had become an accomplished rifleman. Not only would he and his fellow comrades have to be accurate, but they would also have to be able to rearm the rifle with fresh magazines at speed. To add to this, Ernest would have to practise firing the weapon whilst wearing his gas mask. This would have been very difficult when the visor started to steam up. Just focusing on the sights of the rifle and the target would have been difficult. The accuracy of fire to a large part would involve the correct adjustment of the rifle sights. Maybe this could be seen as an easy task, but in the heat of battle, I guess many soldiers, out of sheer panic, or just a rush of adrenalin, forgot to correct their sights as the enemy got closer. I can imagine this is where the NCOs would have to bark out the commands 'remember to adjust your sights lads!'

As if there was not enough stress wearing gas masks, the soldiers' heads would rapidly overheat, the heart and lungs would have to work harder to oxygenate the blood, as the confines of the mask and filter restricted the flow of air into the lungs. Sweat would begin to pour down the wearer's face. Can you imagine trying to focus on an enemy soldier 300 yards away, 'sighting' him with your rifle, and all of this whilst wearing a misted-up gas mask with beads of sweat rolling down your face, stinging your eyes.

The trainers would try to create an artificial battle situation in order to put the soldiers deliberately under stress, so as best to prepare them for what no doubt lay ahead. This time to practise would have been useful for the future. When going to battle, the soldiers already knew what they were about to experience. It was therefore not so much of a shock.

Ernest would not have known this at the time, but in the coming weeks the targets would be German Storm Troopers, dressed in grey uniforms, armed to the teeth. Many of them would be wearing body armour, making them even harder to stop. They would be running towards him, weaving in and out of shell holes. Unlike in training, these troops would be firing back at Ernest, throwing grenades, and some would even have flame throwers. In addition, the Germans used the cover of the creeping barrage. Shells would be exploding around Ernest's trench, causing the defenders to keep their heads down, thus allowing the advancing Germans to approach ever nearer. Would Ernest's nerve hold? Only time would tell.

The German enemy

The 6th Wiltshires would be facing elite divisions of German Storm troopers, who over the winter months had gone through a period of intensive training. General Ludendorff was relying on these elite divisions to make a rapid breakthrough. Their tactics would revolve around speed, mobility and flexibility. It was not their job to destroy the allied defences, rather to penetrate the weak points, make rapid moves forward and eventually encircle the enemy. The regular German Army divisions would take the British trenches and follow the rapidly advancing Storm Troopers to the next objective.

These young soldiers had been carefully selected. The criteria for selection was that they had to be under 25 years old, in peak physical fitness, unmarried, mentally strong, and aggressive. Their reward for being selected was that they would have better food and rations. On the flip side, their casualty rate was expected to be high.

Some of these soldiers were part of the Jäger Corps, which was essentially light infantry, specialised in woodland combat and fighting amongst ruins. They were excellent sharp shooters. They had a decentralised command with junior officers, who had been handpicked for their ability, and they were allowed to make tactical decisions on the spot. The Jägers were supported by the Pioneer Corps. Again, these were small highly skilled units, experts in grenade throwing, with low level command structures. They were also skilled at erecting and breaching obstacles.

The Storm Troopers were heavily armed, equipped with rifle grenades, light trench mortars, and flame throwers. It is easy to see why they were also seen as 'shock troops'.

The Flame Throwers, 'Kleine Flammenwerfer', which would eventually become known as the 111 Garde-Reserve Pioneer Regiment, consisted of two-man teams. One soldier would carry the fuel strapped to his back, the other soldier would hold the flame gun and direct it towards the enemy trenches. This weapon was deployed to flush out the defenders in the trench. Once they were above the trench, the poor soldiers beneath would be 'mown down' by rifle and machine gun fire.

The Storm Troopers could also call on a new type of hand grenade which was much smaller and lighter than their 'stick' grenades. It was known as the 'egg grenade.' The Storm Troopers were supplied with over

A German 'Egg Grenade'

1 million of these smaller 'egg grenades' which had been deliberately chosen for them as they were able to carry them in larger quantities. The Bombers could also throw them much further and therefore the explosive impact would affect the enemy soldiers, and not the advancing Storm Troopers.

To cap it all these elite soldiers carried large quantities of light machine guns. The main weapon was an MG08-15 light machine gun of which six were supplied per company. They would also have shortened Mouser 98K Carbines, and Danish Madson light machine guns.

A young German officer who had used these tactics to great effect on the Italian Front, was transferred to the Western Front. His name was Irwin Rommel, a name that would become legendry in years to come.

The Storm Troopers had also been trained in the use of allied weapons. This enabled advancing soldiers to seize the Lewis machine guns, ammunition and other weapons in the event that they became short of ammunition themselves.

The bulk of these Storm Troopers were deployed to attack General Gough's 5th Army group which was located to the south of General Byng's 3rd Army. This was a bit of good fortune for Ernest, but he would not have known this at the time.

A key to the early German successes was the new artillery tactics pioneered by General Georg Bruchmüller, whose methods had been very effective on the Eastern Front. The tactics of prolonged artillery bombardments over days, followed by a mass attack of infantry over a broad front would now be replaced. The new system would involve a three phased artillery attack taking place over a period of about five hours. The intended targets would have been meticulously identified by reconnaissance and interrogation of captured prisoners, and the results subsequently recorded on detailed maps.

Phase One – This initial barrage would be aimed at troop concentrations and communication hubs. This would be mainly gas shells.

Phase Two – A two-and-a-half-hour barrage aimed at enemy artillery as identified by aerial reconnaissance, involving 50% gas shells and 50% high explosive shells.

Phase Three – A two-hour bombardment aimed at infantry and artillery. Towards the end of this bombardment, the guns would readjust their sights to give creeping barrage support for the attacking German infantry.

The gas shells used would be divided into three categories, namely Blue Cross, Green Cross, and Yellow Cross.

The first type to be used would be the Blue Cross, this being a non-lethal gas, and non-persistent gas, deliberately designed to clog up the defenders' gas masks, forcing them to take off the apparatus.

The next being the Green Cross shells, these being lethal but non-persistent.

The final type being the Yellow Cross, this being persistent, lethal, and causing blistering to exposed skin. It is likely to have been mustard gas. During the creeping barrage the Germans would fire the Blue Cross

A line of British Soldiers having been exposed to a German gas attack

and Green Cross shells in front of the British trenches, and then fire the Yellow Cross shells at the rear trenches. This was designed to cause maximum confusion and reduce the enemy's capability of fighting off the attacking German Storm Troopers.

Can you imagine the chaos caused by gas attacks? These gassed soldiers are on their way to the field dressing station? The pain and agony endured does not bear thinking about. To add to this, there would be the psychological effect which this sight had on Reserves moving up to the front.

New improved German tactics

To make things even worse for the British, the Germans had modified their planes with thicker armour on their underbellies, enabling them to move lower to the ground, and thereby giving much more effective ground support. As the German infantry advanced, their planes would strafe the British trenches with bombs and machine gun fire. A young German pilot would do his bit to cause chaos in the British trenches. His name was Hermann Göring, who years later would become in charge of the German Luftwaffe in 1939.

Ernest and the 6th Wiltshires had no idea what was in store for them. They were about to have the shock of their lives. The new reinforcements supplied to the 6th Wiltshires were young conscripts. Would these new soldiers hold their nerve? They would certainly have to rely on the older experienced members of their platoons and sections.

In situations like this some men emerged as natural leaders. Private 320252 Burchell would not have known this at the time, but when the situation demanded, he would rise to the challenge.

The first day of fighting, March 1918

At 04.40 hours on the morning of Thursday the 21st of March 1918, the silence was broken by an almighty thunderous raw of exploding shells, the 'Kaiserschlacht', the Kaiser's battle. The final battle that General Ludendorff had promised the German people, had begun. 'The British will surrender. Victory will be Germany's!'

The next six days from the 21st of March to the 26th of March 1918 were Private 320252 Burchell's first experience of being confronted by masses of German infantry, who were advancing towards his position in the trenches.

I have referred to accounts from the 6th Wiltshire diary together with the diary of the 58th Brigade and the 19th Western Division. I will leave the detailed accounts to the military historians who naturally have and will do a lot better job than myself. I will try to simplify the course of events.

On the 21st of March 1918, the 58th Brigade were in camps located at the Bertincourt to Haplincourt road. At 05.23 hours the battalion was ordered to stand by. At this news I'm guessing that the adrenalin was beginning to rush through Ernest's veins. This was the battle that they had all been expecting. A total of 21 officers and 478 other ranks joined Ernest in the march towards the front.

During this colossal barrage the brigade marched to Gaika Copse which was located south-west of Velu Wood. As they marched forward, dawn began to break at 06.45 hours, the 19th Division, of which they were a part, were being deployed in reserve behind the 47th, 63rd, and 17th Divisions. This area was part of the 5th Army Corps. The location is at the Flesquires salient.

The Allies were able to field 18 divisions (plus 11 in reserve), this against 78 German divisions. Ernest would not have known this but he and his comrades would be significantly outnumbered in both men and artillery pieces.

As was so often the case in this war, the defenders tended to have the advantage over the attackers. The main reason is that the attackers have to break cover, move out of their trenches, making themselves dangerously exposed to flying shrapnel, and concentrated machine gun and rifle fire. More significantly, it is a hard fact that it was easier to resupply the defenders than the attackers.

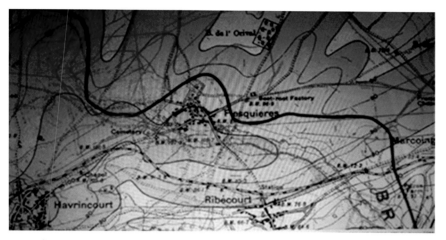

Flesquires salient, March 1918. The black line on the map indicates the front line.

With the onset of daylight, a picture of chaos emerges. The brigades at the front were seriously hampered by the morning mist. This was compounded by the millions of exploded shells, some of which were gas and smoke shells reducing visibility even further. This made the job of allied artillery spotters almost impossible. The mustard gas caused chaos amongst the soldiers, leading to seriously impaired vision, blisters and vomiting. Some of the effects were not felt straightaway and residues of the gas impregnated uniforms, which after a few hours not only affected the wearer, but other soldiers that came into close contact.

At 07.00 hours masses of German troops appeared through the mist and moved rapidly towards the Allied trenches.

During the time spent at Gaika Copse the brigade experienced intermittent shelling during the morning and afternoon.

At 16.00 hours in the afternoon, they were ordered to a ridge west of Hermies where they entrenched. Can you imagine the sheer physical effort of digging these trenches whilst under constant threat of gas attack? The 6th Wiltshires were assisted by the 82nd company of the Royal Engineers and a company of the Pioneers.

It was during this period that Divisional HQ received the news that the Germans had taken Louverval and Doignes. It soon became apparent that the Germans were trying to take the salient on both sides in a pincer movement designed to encircle the 5th Corps.

There then followed a series manoeuvres by the allied brigades to carry out tactical withdrawals. This was done by rear guards, supported by machine gun regiments and mortar crews. These brave men remained behind, facing masses of German infantry. They slowed their advance to allow our soldiers on either flank to retreat. Many of these units were wiped out.

This is where the training in previous months on rear guard and flanking manoeuvres came to fruition. Over the days that followed, this pattern was repeated on numerous occasions. Heavy losses were inflicted on the Germans whose progress was slowed, but eventually, by sheer weight of numbers, they forced the Allies to continue retreating.

At 20.30 hours the brigade was ordered to move on block to an area west of Lebucquire and dig in behind the Hermies Ridge. By now Ernest and his comrades must have been exhausted both physically and mentally.

However, there was no time for rest. At 23.25 hours the brigade was ordered 'to be in a position of readiness', to send out patrols towards Morchies, and to keep in touch with the Morchies – Beaumetz line of trenches.

The evaluation of Days one and two

The speed and progress of the German Army on the first day of 'Operation Michael' shocked the Allies. It prompted the British Prime Minister Lloyd George to make a direct appeal to the American President Woodrow Wilson. He informed him 'The situation is critical; you need to send troops now!'

The President spoke to General Pershing who informed the British and French to deploy his American troops as they see fit.

The British public would not know the true results of the first day of Operation Michael, but the reality was that the German Army on this first day had in places advanced over 7 kilometres (4.35 miles). The British and Allied Army had sustained over 38,000 casualties, of which 8,000 soldiers had been killed. Over 21,000 soldiers had been taken prisoner. A vast majority of these casualties had been sustained by the Germans unleashing around 3.5 million artillery and mortar shells. This would go down as the second worst day in British military history. The Germans had gained over 100 square miles of territory, this being the biggest gain by any army in the war to date.

These gains however came at a price. The supply lines were beginning to become extended. The German transport and logistical mechanised support was nowhere near as strong as that of the Allies, and the cream of the Storm Trooper divisions were beginning to sustain heavy casualties. The German reserves were being used to replace these losses. The long-term effect of this would be significant in later phases of the German campaign.

How long would they be able to sustain this advance? Only time would tell.

It was now Friday the 22nd of March, day two of the German offensive. The 6th Wiltshires received orders from Division to move to the trench system on the north-east side of Beugney, near to the mill crossroads. They stayed at this location for the remainder of the night.

How long have these weary soldiers been awake, how much food and drink remained? I'm guessing very little. Their biscuits and water canteens are likely to have been long since consumed. They may have had chance to open their tinned food whilst on stand-by, who knows? The strain would be beginning to take effect. Their bodies ached with fatigue, but they had to keep going.

At 11.00 hours the 6th Wiltshires received orders to march towards Morchies, about one and a half miles north. They took up a position east of the sunken road near to the location of the ruins of the sugar beet factory on the Bapaume to Cambrai Road. They moved into position alongside the 9th Royal Welch Fusiliers and elements of the 10th Cheshire Regiment. Machine gun units were also present in support. Later in the

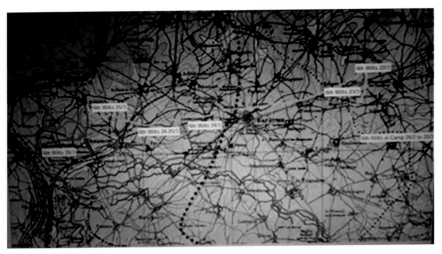

*This map shows the deployments and tactical withdrawals of the 6th
Wiltshires during the first week of Operation Michael. The red line between
the white boxes denotes the approximate line of withdrawal.*

afternoon observers noticed a large concentration of German infantry
on high ground to the area of Vaux, north-west of Morchies. Repeated
requests were made for artillery support to target these masses of grey
uniforms, but to the officers' frustration these requests went unanswered.

As part of the new German tactics, the Allied Artillery Units had been
subjected to a prolonged bombardment. Much of the exploded shells
contained mustard gas causing chaos. This had not only killed gunnery
soldiers, but it had destroyed some of the guns and killed some of the
horses that were used to move them. It is obvious to me why they were
unable to cope with the demands made on them.

About 15.30 hours the Germans make a frontal attack on the 'Crucifix'
trenches occupied by the 9th Welch. As a consequence, Lewis guns, rifles,
and Vickers machine guns opened up at a range of 1,200 yards. They had
a devastating effect on the German infantry, many of whom fell to the
ground. However, the survivors continued to pour over their trenches
towards the Welch lines. At one point the German Cuirassier Cavalry
could be seen in the distance. The Germans were clearly confident of
making a breakthrough.

Ernest's Lee Enfield must have been becoming quite hot by now. He would be thankful for the hours of rifle drill. Now it was for real, would the line hold? The situation was developing into a desperate situation, when all of a sudden, to the rear of his trench came the roaring sound of the six-cylinder Damier Foster engines of the Mark IV tanks.

The cumbersome Iron monsters slowly appeared out of the smoke and mist. The 8th Battalion Tank Corps pushed forward at four miles per hour, supported by infantry. The counter attack could not have been better timed. The 'cranking grating' sounds of those metal monsters must have been music to Ernest's ears. This must have been a welcoming sight for the troops. On seeing the tanks, the German Cavalry had a change of heart and disappeared. By 20.00 hours the enemy advance was halted. They made one last ditch attempt to raid the left flank of the 6th Wiltshires' trenches, but were repulsed. Sadly, of the 25 tanks involved in the counter attack, 16 were destroyed or disabled. Many of the 108 crew would not return home to their loved ones, and their dismembered, charred body parts were entombed inside twisted and mangled steel coffins.

Ernest and his comrades had a brief respite. His pulse slowed down and breathing returned to normal. He wiped the sweat off his forehead and was thankful at being still alive. The remainder of that night was thankfully relatively calm. The 6th Wiltshires sent out reconnaissance patrols during the night, discovering that the Germans now occupied the village of Morchies and had taken up position in the Crucifix Line.

Ernest now had time to replenish his empty ammunition bandoliers with another 150 rounds. He could clean and oil the working mechanism of his rifle. The experience in the trenches had taught the soldiers to wrap a cloth sleeve around the bolt and firing mechanism. This would give some protection against dirt and foreign bodies, if kept in place. Ernest could try to have a drink and eat what was left of his emergency rations.

As he did this, he listened to the distant moaning sounds of the wounded and dying German soldiers in 'no man's land'. He may have caught a glimpse of the shadowy figures of the German stretcher bearers as they struggled with the mass of wounded soldiers. I wonder how he felt, did he feel any pity? I suspect he did.

By now Ernest would know that his battalion was faced by superior numbers of enemy soldiers. How long would they be able to hold out, what would be the Germans next move? Tomorrow would be a new day when the chaos of war would return out of the mist of dawn.

Day three

It is now the morning of Saturday the 23rd of March and the 6th Wiltshires were relieved at having had food supplies brought up during the night. Whatever it was, it would have been gratefully received. Elizabeth's brother Albert and the rest of the ASC would have had to supply the battle-weary troops under extremely difficult conditions, and all this under constant threat of sniper fire and flying shrapnel. The likelihood is that they would have carried some of the food in 'Hay boxes' to keep it warm. God bless them all.

The feel of the warm food inside his stomach would somehow reinvigorate his tired aching body and give Ernest a slight 'kick start' and ready him for the fresh challenges that lay ahead that day.

The 6th Wiltshires remained in their trenches as daybreak improved their view across no man's land. Between 07.00 hours and 08.00 hours they saw small parties of German troops travelling in a north-easterly direction across their front. Reading this account from the diary I am wondering if these were small units of Storm Troopers. This was all happening as the Germans opened up with their artillery.

The 6th Wiltshires received orders to withdraw to the 'Green Line' of trenches. This they did, and by 13.30 hours they were entrenched facing the Bapaume road.

Over the period that follows the 6th Wiltshires discovered that Shropshire's who previously had been on their right flank, had been forced to withdraw leaving the Wiltshires dangerously exposed. They had no choice but to withdraw further to the outskirts of the village of Beugney.

It is here that they were engaged in heavy fighting. Would this be their last stand? If this was to be the case, then the Germans would be made to pay dearly! They would face concentrated rifle fire from the Lee Enfields, the British Tommy that would be supported by the trusted Lewis light machine guns and Vickers heavy machine guns and light trench mortars. The long days of training would now be put to the test.

It is now 16.00 hours and spotters in the allied trenches began to see large numbers of German infantry moving around the flanks of the sugar beet factory to the right, and the village of Morchies to the left. This was a classic German tactic of encircling the enemy. The officers had delayed further withdrawals prior to this period because of the 'lay of the land.' Behind our soldiers, the land sloped upwards and their exposure to enemy fire would be severe. It had been hoped that if they could hold out until nightfall, casualties would be minimised under the cover of darkness. However, it would not be dark until 19.00 hours, could they hold out until then?

By 16.30 hours the Germans had almost completely surrounded the 6th Wiltshires, and the situation was critical. At 17.00 hours the order was received to withdraw further east of Fremicourt along the 'Green Line' trench system. The surviving soldiers would 'slip the noose' in the nick of time.

Having retired behind Fremicourt, what remained of the 6th Wiltshires was reorganised. At 18.00 hours on the evening of the 23rd of March, only six officers remained, two of whom were wounded, and 32 other ranks. When they regrouped, they were eventually reinforced by 64 men from the depot. What were the odds of Private 320252 Burchell being one of these survivors, but he was! So many of his friends were not so lucky. In the coming weeks it would be their names and not his, read out during the Sunday morning services, in the towns and villages of Wiltshire.

The rear-guard actions of brave men hindered the advancing Germans just enough for what remained of the survivors to escape. In this case it was the 9th Welsh who performed the gallant action. Over the coming weeks this story would be repeated so many times.

Overnight from the 23rd to the 24th of March, the survivors received intermittent shelling and machine gun fire. This would have been deliberate tactics designed to wear down the British soldiers, who were trying, almost impossible, to catch up on sleep. Their frayed nerves would be strained to almost breaking point.

The army behind the front

The actions of the Engineers and Pioneer Regiments should not be forgotten. Whilst the front-line soldiers were engaging the enemy, they were busy frantically digging shallow trenches to the rear. This would afford retreating front line troops some protection later on in the battle.

Also, there was the unforgettable bravery of the runners who, under constant threat of machine gun, rifle and sniper fire, ran the gauntlet from the front-line trenches back to Brigade and Divisional HQs. Hundreds were shot trying to deliver vital messages. Their actions allowed senior officers in the field to deploy reinforcements, and concentrate covering artillery fire where it was most needed.

The nurses and medical officers of the 56th, 57th and 58th Field Ambulances deserve a special mention, as their actions saved countless lives.

Prisoners of War

After the initial shock of the first days of Operation Michael, the retreats slowly became more and more planned and organised. However, in those first few days, thousands of British soldiers were taken prisoner. Some of these prisoners were reinforcements heading to the front line. The sheer pace of the German advance had not been anticipated and many were taken prisoner before firing a shot.

The Storm Trooper tactics and the new artillery tactics were having dramatic results, and in those first few days Kaiser Wilhelm was quick to claim victory to the German people. However, the resolve and determination of those brave British, French and Empire soldiers was to prove him wrong.

Retreat

As daylight broke on the morning of Sunday the 24th of March, the German artillery started to gain pace and intensify. The 19th Division straddled the main Bapaume to Cambrai Road. They had the 41st Division to their left and the 2nd Division to their right.

For the next 19 hours the sequence of events was a series of withdrawals by these three Divisions who made a number of brave stands to slow the masses of German infantry. Each division tried to cover their flanks so that an orderly withdrawal could be made. Like other regiments along this front, the 6th Wiltshires, who were by now reinforced, carried out a number of counter attacks to try to relieve the pressure on regiments on their flanks. Their busiest period was after 14.30 hours. Private 320252 Burchell now had to leave the cover of his trench and run with fixed bayonet towards the German lines.

Heavy casualties were inflicted on the advancing Germans, and valuable time was gained to allow further withdrawals to be made. By sheer weight of numbers, the Germans advanced into Bapaume. By 21.00 hours the Wiltshires were down to 270 rifles, and the whole of the 19th Division were down to 2,200 men, representing a loss of over 75%. During the withdrawal through Bapaume, cooks, engineers, pioneers and anyone else capable of firing a rifle was pushed into the front-line trenches in a desperate attempt to make up the losses and slow the German advance.

By about 02.30 hours the 6th Wiltshires had entrenched in the village of Irles about two miles west of Bapaume. Ernest and his battle-weary comrades then had chance to catch their breaths, as the remainder of the night was relatively quiet. The Germans had won the Battle of Bapaume, but at a great cost. Again valuable reserves had been used to make up for their losses which were mounting up rapidly.

The Allies soon had to retreat over the ground gained during the Battle of the Somme in 1916. The huge losses sustained in that battle would be all in vain if the Germans were to win now. Surely this could not be allowed to happen. The British and their Allies would fight on with dogged determination. Uppermost in their minds would be the sacrifice of thousands of men who had died in the Battle of the Somme. For their sakes they would keep fighting.

Ernest survives a second retreat

It is now the morning of Monday the 25th of March, day five of Operation Michael. The 6th Wiltshires were entrenched in three lines to the right of Bapaume Road at Grévillers-Thilloy. They were deployed over a length of trench some 150 yards long, each post having eight men. At 08.00 hours it had been light for about an hour, and the Germans began concentrated machine gun fire on these trenches. They did not yet, however, advance on a frontal attack.

About three hours had elapsed when grey uniforms were seen to the right and left of the Wiltshires. The Germans were trying their flanking manoeuvres again. It was clear that they were capable of overrunning the allied trench, so the brigade carried out an organised retreat. In doing so the 6th Wiltshires deployed rear-guard units who carried out flanking manoeuvres. The effective Lewis gun and rifle fire suppressed the Germans for a short while to allow a steady retreat. The situation deteriorated further when the Germans start to use gas shells, and in addition, the suffering Wiltshires started to encounter misguided friendly artillery fire. These shells began to burst around their trenches, adding to the growing list of casualties.

Picture the scene. Ernest and his surviving comrades were all wearing misted up gas masks. They were filthy, covered in mud and dirt, exhausted, thirsty and hungry, their heads were pounding and their lungs screaming for air. They tried to take cover to avoid flying shrapnel. Soldiers and their body parts were flying through the air, screams came from the wounded and dying. The noise of battle was deafening.

I am wondering how on earth the NCOs communicated with their men under the noise of battle, and whilst wearing gas masks. A quotation from the 6th Wiltshire Regimental Diary at this time states 'Organised retirement was difficult.' What an understatement that was!

But somehow Grandad and his fellow soldiers managed to withdraw at 13.00 hours that day. They managed to scramble to high ground to the west of Grévillers. The enemy who were on high ground to the south of the Bapaume road, saw this withdrawal and opened up with their heavy machine guns. At 14.00 hours those that survived, including Ernest, had to retreat further to an area west and north-west of Loupart Wood. This area proved to be a good defensive position, but an opportunity was missed to consolidate. The Germans managed to sneak nearer the defenders who were partially hidden by a dipped area in the land in front of the British trenches.

The equipment that the battle-weary troops were having to carry has already been described. Prior to the engagement with the enemy, some of them may have wondered why they were ordered to carry empty hessian sacks, but they became invaluable during these frantic and desperate periods of the battle. Having retreated, Ernest and his comrades would quickly fill these sacks with earth, and hide behind them. This would afford them some protection against the deadly bullets of the 'Bosch' Maxim machine guns.

Again, the numbers of grey uniforms were overwhelming, and a further retreat was ordered, but not before making the Germans pay a high price. The 'killing fields' were littered with their bodies. Ernest would have been relieved to see three allied planes strafe the advancing Germans with their machine guns. Some of these planes would be frantically tapping away the Morse code signals to the Allied HQs, listing the coordination's of the enemy troop concentrations.

What was left of the brigade eventually managed to withdraw through Miraumont and to ground east of Puisieux. The Germans had won another battle, but despite all, Ernest had again survived.

The 6th Wiltshires are withdrawn from the front line

On the following day, the 26th of March, the 6th Wiltshires withdrew further to the town of Hébuterne, and then on the 27th they continued through Foncquevillers and then to Bayencourt. What was left of the regiment formed the third line of defence at Beaumont Hamel-Serre. From the diaries at my disposal it appears that they took no further part in Operation Michael.

Captain Alan Garthwaite writes in the Regimental Diary: 'The subsequent retirement from Fremicourt through Bapaume to Grevillers and thence to Bayencourt was only one endless and stubborn fight. Suffice to say that only 1 Officer, one Sergeant and 18 other ranks came out of the struggle.'

Reading his account, I was amazed at the detail he gives, given the chaos of the battles. These figures could be misleading as during the retreat, survivors and stragglers would join other regiments in the melée of the withdrawal.

It is now the 28th of March 1918, and Private 320252 Burchell and the rest of the survivors of the regiment are behind the lines having been relieved by the Canadians. The total casualties for this period was 18 officers and 497 other ranks, killed or wounded. Each and every one of these losses would be tragic for their families.

Included in the casualty list was Major Charles Selwyn Awdry, who had been reported missing on the 25th of March during the Battle of Bapaume. Like so many others, his body was never found. He died aged 41. There is a headstone memorial to the Major at Pozieres Cemetery, France. I mention him because initially he had been Major of B Squadron of the Wiltshire Yeomans, but upon arrival in France 1916, he went on to become Second-in-Command of the battalion and is pictured with Ernest and the rest of the Squadron in Chapter 2.

He was well regarded and popular with his men. It is thought he died during an artillery bombardment whilst trying to organise a withdrawal.

What state would my Grandad have been in, after seven days of combat! He would have been starving hungry, exhausted through lack of sleep, dehydrated, and in a filthy state. His whole body would be caked in mud with his trousers and boots sodden, he would have several days of stubble, his body would reek of battle, gas residues on his clothing, together with the lingering smell of cordite and stale earth.

He would have bruises on top of bruises. I doubt if he would have been recognisable. His hands would be swollen and reddened with constant handling of the Lee Enfield rifle, and his ears would be ringing from the constant exposure to exploding shells. It is likely that he would have been partially deaf. I am guessing that his hands would be trembling. In short, he and his comrades would be in a state of physical degradation and profound shock.

One thing that really annoyed the soldiers was the soil which used to fall down the back of their shirts. This would happen during artillery attacks when mountains of earth would erupt from the surface of the ground, only to land on nearby soldiers. Relatively trivial though this may have been, in a situation where soldiers could not wash, this experience just added to their misery and discomfort. In addition, Ernest would have an unbearable yearning to shed his clothing which was impregnated with poisonous gas residues and have a good bath.

Overnight from the 28th to the 29th of March, the battle-weary survivors including Ernest were required to march with a full kit from Famechon to Candas. This is a distance of over 13.5 miles and takes a little under six hours. The knowledge that they were moving away from the front would certainly have spurred them on. They arrived at 17.45 hours. Upon arrival the soldiers boarded trains and spent the next eight and a half hours on the journey to the Birr Barracks at Locre in Belgium, south of Poperinge. Doubtless Ernest and his comrades would have used this journey to catch up on some much-needed sleep.

The German advance but to their cost

Back home in London, the politicians were stunned at the progress the Germans had made. As is so often the case, they looked for someone to blame other than themselves. The buck stopped at the feet of General Gough of 5th Army, whose seriously depleted divisions had borne the brunt of the German Storm Troopers. On the 28th of March he was relieved of his command. Most historians would say that this was harsh, but given the impossible odds he faced, most agree that any other General would have suffered the same result.

In the period between the 28th of March and the 31st of March, the British and Canadians made a counter attack, taking land around Moreuil Wood. The German advance slowed to a walking pace. However, they had opened up a 50-kilometre gap between the French and British armies.

During this period the French General Ferdinand Foch was made overall commander of the allied armies on the Western Front. This is met with approval by Field Marshal Haig, who was confident that the French would support the British when needed. The dilemma for both of these armies was that the French government had insisted to their Generals that if it came to the crunch, the French armies would protect Paris at all cost. Likewise, with the British, if the situation became critical, their priority would be to protect the Belgian and French ports so that the British Expeditionary Force could escape back to Britain, and live to fight another day.

The Germans were quick to exploit this situation by the constant bombing of Paris with their newly deployed Paris guns. The civilian losses were in comparison insignificant, but the effect on morale was beginning to tell. The result was that thousands of Parisians were starting to evacuate the capital.

Although the situation was becoming critical, there was a ray of hope for the Allies. After several days of advancing, the German supply lines were becoming stretched, and their front-line soldiers were running out of ammunition, food and water. The German soldiers had been told that the British soldiers were seriously short of food and supplies and that their resistance would crumble. To their great surprise, when they overran British supply depots, they discovered ample amounts of bread, food, wine, and rum. These depots were looted by exhausted German soldiers, who rapidly got drunk and refused to advance any further.

Back in Germany the civilian population was starving and severely malnourished. The weary civilians were resorting to digging up lead water pipes in the cities to provide much needed lead for the production of bullets, and even melting down church bells to provided steel for the war effort.

On the 31st of March, General Ludendorff called a halt to the advance, in order to allow supplies to reach the new front and his heavy artillery to move forward for the next phase of the offensive.

At some stage in this period the 19th Division re-joined the 2nd Army under the command of General Sir Herbert Plumer, who had recently returned from operations in the Italian theatre of war.

Chapter 7

The struggle continues

The German advance to date had surprised everyone, but with all this extra territory gained nothing of strategic value had been captured. General Ludendorff had failed to press home his gains in those early days of Operation Michael. He failed to grasp the strategic importance of Amiens to the Allies, and by the time he decided to act, the French armies had been allowed time to move up to Amiens in support of the British, and the opportunity had been lost.

The factories in Britain turned out in force on Easter Monday. There was a determination to supply our troops with vital ammunition and supplies. This was total war that affected the whole population, with everyone doing their bit for the war effort.

Monday the 1st of April 1918 saw the formation of the Royal Air Force. Over the weeks and months that followed there was an increase in use of combined weapon systems and better coordination of armoured and air support during infantry assaults. Both sides were more effective using these combined tactics, but the slaughter continued.

During the next three weeks the Germans restarted their offensives. Their armies continued to push forwards towards the French ports, and they attempted to take land to the south the Ypres salient. They regarded the taking of the Hazebrouck railway junction as a priority, because if they could take this railhead, then they would be able to cut off the supply lines from the French ports to the British army. Attempts were also made to recapture the old Somme battlefields.

Operation Georgette commenced on the 7th of April 1918. The line of advance stretched from the River Lys in the south to the north of Ypres. There was no let-up in the use of deadly poisonous gas, and in April the Germans fired over 2,000 tons of deadly mustard gas during the Battle of Lys.

Between the 10th of April and the 18th of April 1918, Private 320252 Burchell and his comrades took part in three further battles, namely the Battle of Messines on the 10th of April, the Battle of Bailleul on the 13th of April, and the Battle of Kemmel Ridge on the 17th of April.

Considering the battle line from the north coast of Belgium and moving south, the Belgian army was deployed from the coast down to Sir Henry Plumer's 2nd Army, and below this was General Horne's 1st Army Group. Opposing these armies are the German 4th Army to the north, and the German 6th Army to the south. In concentrating on this area, I will be dealing with where Ernest was deployed, with 19th Western Division being part of Plumer's 2nd Army Group.

On Tuesday the 9th of April, the 19th Division was deployed holding a subsector of ground to the east of the Messines and Wytschaete Ridge. The survivors of the 6th Wiltshires who were part of the 58th Brigade were holding a line of trenches between 'Junction Buildings' and the 'Wembeke' trench system. They had the 57th Brigade to their right. At 03.30 hours the night sky was lit up by a deluge of exploding artillery shells. The noise must have been deafening. In amongst the high explosive shells were numerous gas shells. The alarm was raised and the gas masks employed.

Experience warned Ernest and the other soldiers that the 'Bosch' were making ready for an attack. The soldiers strained their battle-weary eyes and tried to focus into no man's land in front of them, anxious to see any signs of figures moving forward towards them in the clouds of mist and gas that was becoming thicker by the hour. At 06.00 hours grey uniforms could be seen in the distance, about 2,000 yards away, the ghostly figures of Germans starting to appear from the swirling mist of no man's land. They were massing together ready to move forward. A call came out to check the rifle sights.

Dawn began to break, and the land in front of the trenches was described as a 'Scotch mist'. The anxious British soldiers stirred restlessly, instinctively wanting to open fire at these ghostly figures in the distance. The NCOs barked out the order to 'hold your fire!' Lessons had been learnt, not to waste valuable ammunition on out of range targets. The soldiers therefore bade their time and waited for the order to open fire. The Lewis gunners adjusted their sights and tried to pick out the forward advancing German machine gun units. The British now had a lot more Lewis guns and they put them to good use as the Germans come into range. The order was given, 'Fire!'

The main German advance concentrated on the 57th Brigade to the left. During this advance the Germans were setting off coloured flares to indicate to their artillery where to concentrate their fire on the allied trenches. Due to the effective Lewis gun and rifle fire the grey uniforms were slow to make ground, but their artillery became more and more effective. By 16.00 hours the brigade was ordered to abandon the front-line trenches and retreat. The Germans seized on this opportunity and by 17.30 hours they had occupied this front-line trench. Any further advances were checked by accurate effective Lewis machine gun fire. This was only a temporary respite. The constant enemy shelling was causing high casualties and at 18.00 hours the 58th Brigade was ordered to withdraw to the reserve line of trenches.

At 19.00 hours the exhausted survivors including Private 320252 Burchell, rallied and took up positions between Damstrasse and Wytschaete. The battalion tried to reorganise and busy themselves trying to help the survivors make it back to the reserve trench. Effective covering fire allowed a further 75 stragglers to make it back.

The wounded

Remember these wretched soldiers had tried their best to help their wounded comrades back with them. Their only medical kit was two wound dressings, each contained in a small waterproof bag. One dressing was for the entry wound and the other dressing was for the exit wound (if applicable).

Private Daniel Leese, the brother of Elizabeth (Bessy) Leese

A soldier who was badly wounded would have to rely on comrades to apply these dressings. At this time the stretcher bearers would have had an almost impossible task of moving the fallen wounded soldiers back to safety. Many soldiers would have assisted in carrying their mates back.

I think this young man deserves a special mention. Private Daniel Leese was the brother of Elizabeth (Bessy) Leese. As already stated, he was in the Royal Army Medical Corps. He was attached to the North Staffordshire Regiment and in 1918 he would have been 26 years old. I wonder if he ever came across Ernest. It would have been Daniel Leese's job to carry wounded soldiers either on stretchers or on his back, and all this while under constant threat of sniper fire.

All Daniel had with him was a small khaki field bag containing the following:

1. A dozen sterile vials each containing a sterile piece of silk. This would be used when stitching up a soldier's wound.
2. A tourniquet – This was a length of webbing similar in appearance to a belt with a tightening device at the joint.
3. Ready-made slings to support broken arms/collar bones.
4. A large gauze shell dressing.
5. Spirit of ammonia.
6. Needles, scissors and thread.
7. A small lantern.
8. A copy of the nursing dictionary.

Indeed, not much for saving lives, but many a life was saved by these brave men.

Having recovered the wounded soldiers, it was Daniel and his partner's job to take the casualty back to the Regimental Aid Post. Each trip into no man's land to recover a wounded soldier, was referred to as 'a carry'.

Field Marshal Haig reacts to a desperate situation

To the south of the 2nd Army, a major battle had taken place involving the German 6th Army who attacked the British 1st Army in strength. The unfortunate soldiers of the Portuguese 2nd Division stood no chance against the masses of German Storm Troopers. Ironically it was this week that the Portuguese were due to be relieved and sent back behind the lines. They had been totally unprepared for the German Storm Troopers. They were acutely short of officers, and the Germans quickly overran their trenches. In a matter of one day the Germans advanced over a 10-mile front advancing as far as five miles in places. They reached the town of Estaires near to the banks of the River Lys.

By the morning of the Thursday 11th April the situation on the Western Front had become desperate, so much so that Field Marshal Haig sent his famous orders out to his front-line troops:

There is no other course open to us but to fight it out, every position must be held to the last man. There must be not retirement. With our backs to the wall and believing in justice of our cause, each one of us must fight on to the end. The safety of our homes and the freedom of mankind alike, depend on the conduct of each one of us at this critical moment.

You wonder just how many of our troops received this message and when. In any case, upon receipt of this message, there would have been mixed reactions, but history and the events that followed tend to suggest that the majority of our troops reacted favourably. Sadly, many soldiers over the next few days and weeks fought to the last man. It is these brave men that compel me to watch the televised Memorial Parade outside the Cenotaph in London every November. It has also inspired me to write this book, for these pitiful men, and Ernest, and the survivors!

The Spanbroekmolen crater

Back to the events of April, and to be precise, the 12th of April. The 58th Brigade had been withdrawn to the Rossignol Camp near the town of Kemmel. The Battle of Messines has been fought and lost. In the aftermath of this first battle, of the 11 officers and 580 other ranks of the 6th Wiltshire battalion, who went into the front line, only five officers and 270 other ranks survived.

The 58th Brigade was desperately short of soldiers, and fortunately they received 270 reinforcements, divided up into the depleted regiments, including the 6th Wiltshires. Most of these new soldiers had only received six weeks basic training. They would look up to Private 320252 Burchell and the survivors as experienced troops who would be their role models.

On the following day the 13th of April, the brigade received orders to stand by at 10.30 hours. Following this order, the 6th Wiltshires marched with full kit about half a mile along 'Suicide Road'. This was a notorious

*The Spanbroekmolen crater taken during the winter of 1917 to 1918,
the trench system would have been around the top of the crater*

stretch of road connecting the towns of Kemmel and La Clytte. They waited for further orders at this location, which came eventually. They were sent to relieve the South African Brigade at the Spanbroekmolen crater.

This was a strategically important ridge of high ground, being part of the Messines Ridge that had been captured by the British and Allies the previous year, when the underground mines had been detonated.

In the previous year, on the 7th of June, the British detonated 41,000 kg of explosives in the Spanbroekmolen tunnel. When ignited the effects were devastating. The circumference of this crater is 250 feet, and the bottom of the crater is 40 feet from the ground surface. The above picture shows the partially filled in mine crater.

In 2017, I walked around this crater with my wife April, and I tried to imagine what it was like 101 years ago when Grandad and the 6th Wiltshires were in the trenches. The area has been restored to farmland. There were a number of post-war fatalities when the plough shears hit unexploded bombs.

This is an aerial view of the crater now called the' Pool of Peace'. South of the crater you can see Peckham Farm. 19 Mines exploded on the 7th of June 1917. An unexploded mine is located under one of the farm buildings.

As indicated on the aerial view, this is what remains of a German bunker on the north-west edge of the crater

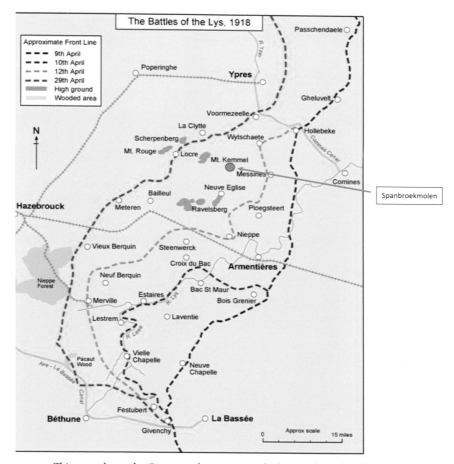

This map shows the German advances towards the Hazebrouck rail junction

Many lives had been lost in 1917 during the 1st Battle of Messines, therefore the British were not about to give this land up cheaply. The 58th Brigade including the 6th Wiltshires marched to Spanbroekmolen during the night of the 13th to 14th of April and deployed themselves in an 800-metre trench system which spanned each side of the of the Spanbroekmolen crater.

The map (by courtesy of the Commonwealth War Graves Commission) shows the German advance during Operation Georgette.

The village of Spanbroekmolen is located between Messines and Kemmel. As you can see Spanbroekmolen crater was located just behind the front lines on the 13th of April. The trench stretched in front of the crater north to south. The crater was strategically important to the Allies. Facing the Germans, from top left, were the 9th Royal Welch Fusiliers, and moving south down the trench was A, B, C and D companies of the 6th Wiltshires. To the right of D Company were the Royal Irish Rifles (RIR). The Wiltshires were in the front-line trenches by 06.00 hours on Sunday morning the 14th of April.

This part of the front line was unusually quiet on this day, the reason being that about five miles to the south of the Spanbroekmolen trenches, there was a major battle taking place for the town of Neuve-Église. Private 320252 Burchell would not have known this. The flashes on the horizon and din of exploding artillery shells to the south would be just the familiar background noise to which they had become so accustomed.

My Grandad and his fellow soldiers would be grateful for this lull, they would use this time to steady nerves and try to reassure the new raw recruits. The older soldiers would no doubt have been bombarded with countless questions from these young soldiers. These new recruits would have been nervous and apprehensive as were the older soldiers, but most of the older soldiers had learnt how to disguise their fears with bravado and trench jokes, and general banter.

They would take time to eat their rations because in the heat of the next new battle, a soldier would never know when his next meal would come. All water bottles would be full, ammunition pouches filled, and if there were any available, the soldier would try to find at least one extra bandolier, giving him an extra 150 rounds of ammunition. They would also clean and oil the rifles, and made sure there was 'one in the spout'. The gun sites would also be checked.

It has occurred to me that the bandoliers which the soldiers carried over their shoulders held 150 rounds. This may seem to be a lot of bullets, but in the heat of a battle, when faced with hordes of attacking German infantry approaching, our soldiers would be engaged in rapid fire. They were trained to fire a minimum of fifteen rounds per minute, which only equates to ten minutes of rapid fire.

The training sessions and musketry practice that these soldiers had undertaken were therefore of crucial importance. They had been taught to reload as speedily as possible, as it could mean a matter of life or death. One has to assume a ready supply of ammunition, but this was not so in many cases. Many battles would be lost or unnecessary withdrawals made just through the lack of adequate ammunition to hand.

As the day progressed tension grew. The question in the minds of the soldiers would be not if the Germans would attack, but when. The NCOs, aware of this rising tension, would 'busy' the men as best they could, filling in damaged sandbags, carrying supplies, inspecting their weapons, making sure adequate supplies of ammunition were at hand, refilling empty Lewis gun magazines, anything to occupy the soldiers' minds.

How many times would Ernest have reached into his tunic pocket to take out the picture of his dear 'Bessy'. He would sit in a quiet corner of the trench and read a selection of mud stained letters, all of which had already been read dozens of times over. He could recite the sentences word perfect. He would pray silently to be spared and for the chance to go home and to be with his family and Bessy again.

Before they knew it, night descended on the trenches, and the horizon glowed with the distant artillery explosions and rolling thunderous noise of war. The soldiers would take it turn to stand on watch, the others would drift in and out of consciousness, with cloudy memories of home and loved ones drifting through their thoughts and dreams.

'Take cover, in coming!' The morning silence is shattered by the howl and roar of overhead shells. It is Monday morning, 05.40 hours and the horrors of war return to the trenches at Spanbroekmolen. Tons of earth and debris are flying through the air as the high explosive shells of the German howitzers explode around the men. The screams of the dying and wounded soldiers are almost drowned out by the sheer volume of the explosions. This is a terrifying experience for the new conscripts, a baptism of fire, you might say. The NCOs and older soldiers try to calm their nerves. 'Steady lads, hold your positions!'

Brigade HQ located 300 yards behind the front-line trenches is taking a pounding. Runners are dispatched to pass the news to Division that masses of grey uniforms are attacking to the right of the 6th Wiltshires. This is the location of the Royal Irish Rifles, who, in the chaos of the barrage are attempting to withdraw, and their line is being penetrated by grey uniformed soldiers. Other parts of the trenches are 'strafed' by enemy machine gun fire and snipers. This suppresses the defenders in the area, but others who are not affected, manage to hinder the German advance with the effective use of Lewis gun and British snipers.

But the hordes of German soldiers keep up the pressure on those thinly manned front-line trenches, so much so that by the evening of the 15th, the Wiltshires receive an order to withdraw. This is carried out during the night, initially B, C and D companies, with A company last to withdraw.

The Battle of Bailleul is not going well for the Allies. The gallant soldiers make a brave stand, inflicting heavy casualties on the Germans but there is little or no protection against accurate concentrated artillery barrages. Many of Ernest's friends and new recruits are blown to pieces. Hundreds will be reported missing over the next three days.

To make matters worse two more German divisions are deployed against the thinly stretched allied trenches. The range of our own guns were inaccurate and 'friendly' shells fall and explode amongst the soldiers in khaki uniforms. Men are hugging the sides of the trench walls for what little protection they offer. Surely no one could survive this onslaught.

It is little wonder that friendly shell fire is misdirected. The reason is that over this period of time, the Allied Artillery Units to the rear are being sought out by the German Howitzers. This results in a total of 259 brave artillery gunners killed or wounded.

However, it is not all bad news. To the south the German offensive in the Somme area is brought to a halt. The brave soldiers of the British and Australian Regiments push the Germans back at Villers-Bretonneux. Further to the north, the Belgian Army manage to hold back and repulse a German attempt to break through. It is over this period that German General Ludendorff calls a halt to the Battle of the Somme. He states 'The enemy resistance is beyond our powers!' Further north, the Allies decide to do a tactical withdrawal and give up all the territory that they had gained at Passchendaele the previous year. The ever-defiant Field Marshal Haig was quoted as saying 'Think how much worse it will be for them when we drive them back!' Was this bravado or not? Only time would tell.

Ernest's supreme act of bravery

Meanwhile in the trenches near to Wytschaete a withdrawal was carried out overnight, but their right flank has been extended by 400 yards, which means that even fewer men will face the German hordes when daylight breaks.

Significantly the area around the Spanbroekmolen crater is seriously exposed when the 120 soldiers of A company leave the trenches. They are replaced by nineteen battle-weary men of the 7th West Yorkshire Regiment who over the next 24 hours cannot possibly hold out against vastly superior numbers of enemy infantry. As a consequence, this area falls to the Germans who retake this important high ground.

It is during the next two days that isolated units become trapped between the advancing Germans. Is this the time when Ernest's luck will eventually run out? According to his military records, he and ten other soldiers become isolated. The order to retreat had been received by some of the forward units and unbeknown to Ernest's group of eleven gallant soldiers, the rest of the battalion had already withdrawn. They were in danger of being surrounded. This is the time that Ernest rises to the challenge.

Moving forward in time 57 years, I'm sitting in my grandfather's kitchen in the old farmhouse at Manor Farm, Hartshorne. The old grandfather clock standing against the wall chimes five times, it's tea time. I sit opposite Ernest. 'Go on Grandad, please tell me what happened?'

Ernest takes a deep breath and sits up in his chair. He looks across the table and briefly smiles at his expectant grandson.

'Well, it was April 1918, we were in the trenches in Flanders, it was a major battle and the Germans were winning. We were outnumbered, all around us were the bodies of our friends and comrades. All the officers had been killed. We were in a sorry state.

I can't remember how many of us were left. We were hungry and tired, but we had one thing to our advantage.

We were in a good defensive position with a clear view of no man's land in front of us. In order to overrun us, the Germans had to get through a narrow gap in the barbed wire about 50 yards away. I had one of the Lewis machine guns and fortunately a good supply of ammunition. Each time the Germans tried to get through the gap in the barbed wire, I fired the gun in short bursts. They fell to the floor in increasing numbers. But they still kept coming.

We held out for two days and as the ammunition started to get low, some of the younger soldiers wanted to surrender, but I refused. On the second day we were reinforced, and then managed to slip away during the night back to what was left of our battalion.

How many Germans did you kill, Grandad?' 'I don't know son, but I hope you never have to go through what we did, there's no glory in war.

Ernest then broke down in tears and that was the end of the conversation.

That brief conversation had little impact on me at the time. True I was proud of my Grandad but I did not have a clue what the poor man and his friends and comrades had been through. I was young and naïve. It is only now that the true horror of what he told me is beginning to sink in.

If you read the battalions diaries over this period, at the end of a conflict the senior officer writes a summary of events and points to where lessons could be learnt for future battles. One such entry refers to the fact that small units of well-placed men can hold out and suppress vastly superior enemy forces. These eleven brave men clearly proved this fact to be true, but it could have only been a matter of time before the German artillery zeroed in on Grandad's trench. One well-placed high explosive shell would have blown them all to pieces. It is easy for the ranking officers to suggest that territory was given away too cheaply when unnecessary withdrawals were made, but survival is a strong instinct!

On the 17th of April elements the 58th Brigade including the 6th Wiltshires were sent to relieve the 9th Welch Battalion in the area south of Store Farm. The beginning of the day was relatively quiet. At 13.30 hours the peace was shattered by 'in-coming' artillery fire. The Wiltshires were manning the parapets and made ready. No attack materialised but the soldiers were pinned down by heavy machine gun fire. Later that night the 58th were relieved by soldiers of the 22nd Division. The Battle of Baileul was another victory for the Germans. They continued to press forward to take what remained of the Messines Ridge. They concentrated their efforts on Mount Kemmel, which is not what the name suggests, rather a village nestling next to a small hill on the western edge of the ridge of high ground.

For the remainder of the month of April the 58th Brigade were moved to the rear and billeted near Abeele, via La Clytte and Reninghelst. They took no further part in the Battle of Kemmel. By the 26th of April Kemmel Hill and the village had been taken by the Germans.

The chaos in the second and third week of April was such that the Regimental diaries had not been completed. It was during this lull that NCOs and surviving officers took the opportunity to catch up with their accounts. Countless acts of bravery and self-sacrifice were acknowledged. Someone had witnessed the brave stand of Private 320252 Burchell and the ten other soldiers.

Naturally I have tried to identify this brave group of men but to date I have been unsuccessful. I intend to keep trying, even when I have completed this book. However, from the investigations to date, there are two possible NCOs who could have witnessed the stand made by the 11, these being Sergeant 204270 E.H Butler and Sergeant 11881 J.E Ackland, both of whom were in the Wiltshire battalion at the time. Like Ernest they were both recognised for their bravery and resilience against overwhelming odds during April 1918.

The Red Baron

On the 21st of April 1918 the infamous 'Red Baron', Manfred Albrecht Freiherr von Richthofen, was forced to land his plane in a field near the front at Vaux-sur-Somme.

Prior to this, he had been pursuing a British reconnaissance plane. The British pilots, sensing imminent death, resorted to flying low over the British lines. This was a desperate tactic hoping to draw friendly fire at the pursuing enemy plane. Naturally the Red Baron gave chase, as he had done so already on numerous occasions, this next kill being his 81st. But on this day, his luck ran out. Upon seeing the distinctive Red Albatross D lll in pursuit of the British plane, Australian soldiers below in the trenches, fired at the Red Biplane. During this burst of gun fire, a bullet penetrated the Red Baron under his armpit and exited near to his left nipple. The wound proved fatal, but the Red Baron just about managed to land his plane. His last word to a soldier who tried to pull him out of his cockpit was 'kaputt'. There is some debate over who shot the Red Baron. Most people have credited Sgt Cedric Popkin of the 24th Australian Machine Gun Company with the kill.

This was a significant blow to morale for the Germans. Because of his class status the Allies buried him with full military honours.

I will let you the reader make up your own mind whether this was right and proper, given that he had shot down 80 allied aircrews, most of which would have suffered horrific deaths. The average life expectancy for a pilot during the early stages of the war was a mere three weeks.

Most pilots carried their own revolver. In the event their plane caught fire and caused them to be trapped, these brave pilots would hold the revolver to their head and kill themselves rather than suffer a slow agonising death by being burnt alive. It was surprising for me to find out that pilots were not given parachutes as it was thought that it would encourage them to give up easily and bail out of their aircraft.

Considering the burial of the Baron and all the publicity that followed, was it a shrewd propaganda move on the part of the Allies, or am I being cynical? Or was it an act of respect and honour? I was surprised to find out that one of our fighter aces, Albert Ball, crashed his aircraft behind enemy lines in May 1917. The Germans buried him with full military honours. His grave is in the War Cemetery at Annœullin.

Counting the cost

As the month of April drew to an end, the opposing armies counted the cost. I do not intend to quote the figures, but again the casualties are in the hundreds of thousands killed, missing or wounded. Tens of thousands of prisoners had been captured, many of whom would have felt relieved that this was the end of their war, whatever the hardships of forced labour lay ahead. This war of attrition was set to continue. The Germans had used up all of their reserve divisions, and many of the cream of the Storm Trooper divisions had suffered significant losses.

On the 30th of April 1918 General's Ludendorff and Hindenburg called off the Battle of Lys. By now the Germans had captured over 1,200 square miles of territory but significantly the allied line had held and the important ports of Calais, Le Havre and Dunkirk were still in allied hands. This meant that they could continue to supply the allied war effort. The cities of Paris and Amiens had not fallen to the Germans, and to summarise, the Germans had not captured any land of strategic value. Even with their temporary superiority in numbers, they had not managed to have their decisive victory.

The Germans were increasingly aware of the ever present growing American Army which in the coming months would swell to over a million soldiers.

One important fact remained. The Germans and Central Powers had to draw replacements and reinforcements from a combined population of 150 million. This was considerably lower than the 1.25 billion population of the Allies and their Dominions which could be called upon.

Logistically the Germans would now be at a significant disadvantage. Some of their supply lines had been extended by as much as 80 kilometres (49.71 miles). A large number of horses remained on the Eastern Front, and as a consequence the Germans were short of draught horses to pull their supplies and artillery.

I mentioned the important invention of rubber pneumatic tyres by John Boyd Dunlop in Chapter 1. I did this because in the latter years of the war, these inflated rubber tyres used by the Allies on their vastly superior number of mechanised trucks were very significant. The Germans under the continual naval blockade had to resort to steel wheels as they could not import rubber.

The consequence was that the roads on the extended German supply lines suffered under constant use of these steel wheels, which made deep ruts and slowed down supply convoys significantly. In contrast the allied mechanised transport moved more quickly and efficiently. Any repairs to these roads were carried out by willing Chinese and Dominion labour gangs. The inflated tyres meant a smoother ride which enabled the trucks to travel at faster ground speeds. It was soon discovered that lowering the tyre pressure led to increased traction, again this was a big advantage.

In contrast the Germans had to resort to forced labour gangs of captured allied prisoners. These severely malnourished individuals could not possibly cope with the demands made upon them, and their work rate was significantly lower. Both sides indeed had steel tracked vehicles, which were similar to tanks. Some of these were steam powered and had good traction, but their gear ratios and design made them slow moving.

Another significant factor was that since the Germans had gained new territory, and the forward troops had left the strong defences of the Hindenburg Line, new trench systems would need to be dug and strongholds constructed. In turn they would require supplies in order to build them.

On a positive note for the Germans, they had been able to seize a significant amount of abandoned supplies that the Allies had left during their retreat.

These battle-weary troops would now have to use their spades and picks and start digging all over again, and this with less and less food and drink to sustain them. However, they would be grateful for the captured food depots they had overrun. Yet with the vast number of mouths to feed, these supplies would soon run out.

It is the end of April 1918, and like so many other divisions the 19th Western Division are counting the cost of the German Spring Offensive to date. I've already mentioned the losses to their artillery crews. The total number for killed, missing, or wounded was 3,774 men.

The 6th Wiltshires had suffered huge losses. The numbers of men going into the front line on the 7–8th of April was 11 officers and 580 other ranks. When they came out of the front line on the 12th of April there remained only five officers and 270 other ranks, representing a loss of over 54%.

On the 13th of April 10 officers and 380 other ranks went into the front line. On the 19th of April only four officers and 250 other ranks survived, representing a loss of just under 35%.

These losses were appalling, but the Allied lines had held. True they had lost territory, but the Germans had been made to pay a high price. Many elite troops would never fight again. Their replacements would get younger and younger, and with less and less training.

Desperate time calls for desperate measure, During April the British Parliament had passed the Military Service Bill which essentially raised the maximum age for conscription up to 50 years, with a provision that should circumstances dictate it necessary, it could be raised further to 55 years. The cream of youth in Europe was being consumed by the beast of war.

The days of the 6th Wiltshires were numbered. They would soon be disbanded, but not before one more period in the front-line trenches between the 1st and the 10th of May, when they would be deployed the Voormezeele sector. Following this deployment what was left of the 6th Wiltshires was absorbed into the 2nd Wiltshire Regiment and others carried out training duties with elements of the American Army.

Private 203241 Ernest Burchell was formally transferred to the 2nd battalion of the Wiltshire Regiment on Monday the 13th of May 1918. On the morning of the 14th of May, the 2nd Wiltshire's Parade for inspection at 09.30 hours which was conducted by their Commanding Officer, Lieutenant Colonel G.F.E. Rapson. The next two days were spent reorganising and at 23.30 hours on the evening of the 16th of May, the 2nd Wiltshires marched to Rexpoede, where they entrained at 04.30 hours the following morning. There then followed a 190-mile train journey to Chalons-sur-Marne arriving at 18.15 hours on the evening of the 18th of May. Ernest would have welcomed this long journey, time to try to relax and catch up on some much-needed rest. It would have been great to be away from the front in the relative safety and comfort of the train. This journey would not have been without risks as many a train was attacked by patrolling German fighters. The Regimental diary suggests that this journey was thankfully uneventful.

It is interesting to note just how busy those train drivers were. Statistics reveal that to move a division of 11,000 soldiers took 40 train journeys, each division carrying over 1,000 tons of supplies. It is little wonder that the Germans tried to capture important railheads and stations. Steam power and coal were still of prime importance. The railway network in northern France continued to be vital for the Allies.

Having left the trains, the battalion then marched just over two miles, crossing the River Marne and arriving at Vésigneul-sur-Marne at 21.30 hours on Saturday evening, the 18th of May.

On Sunday morning, the following day, there was a voluntary Divine Service held at 10.00 hours. I wonder which Chaplain took the service. I have covered their work in previous chapters. Records show that the Reverend W.L. Waugh served with the Wiltshire Yeomans between 1903 and 1928. I ask myself, would he have transferred with Ernest and the other Yeomans to the 6th Wiltshire Regiment in September 1917, and then to the 2nd Wiltshires in 1918? The truth is that I do not know.

I am sure that Ernest would have attended this service. He was a devout Methodist. In his prayers he would have been thankful at being spared, and he would have prayed for his lost friends and their families.

The end of May and back to the trenches

The 2nd Wiltshires spent a large part of May carrying out training exercises and reorganising. The Regiment did not really become active again until the 29th of May when they were ordered to occupy an area of high ground north of Bouluse in northern France. It is in this area, near to Treslon and Germigny, that heavy fighting took place. The 19th Division were supported by elements of the 8th and 25th Division who were to their north. I assume that Private 320252 Burchell was still fighting and not reported sick.

Also, at the end of May, the remainder of the 2nd Wiltshires, being four officers and 163 other ranks, proceeded to Sarcy, where they joined the 19th Division. On the morning of Thursday, the 30th of May 1918, the 2nd Wiltshires were deployed in the trenches. They came under attack early in the morning, and under increasing pressure they had to give ground to the advancing Germans. Having withdrawn, they were involved in heavy fighting in the area of Germigny aerodrome. The German heavy machine guns swept backwards and forwards across their entire front-line trench.

At 14.00 hours the order was given to withdraw to a position east of Sarcy. Here they dug in and organised a position of defence, with the battalions of the Cheshire to their left and the Shropshire and Staffordshires to their right. They put up stiff resistance.

The Germans continued to pile on the pressure, using smoke shells to thwart the Lewis and Vickers machine gun units. This brief advantage enabled the attacking Germans to expose the Wiltshires' flanks, necessitating a further withdrawal to the banks of the River Adre. The Wiltshires suffered heavy losses during this period.

At 21.00 hours, after 15 hours of fighting, the Wiltshires were ordered to return to their previous position south-east of the village of Sarcy. On arrival, they discovered that the French were already occupying these trenches. The Wiltshires were therefore able return to the trenches west of Bligny, arriving at these trenches at about 05.30 hours on Friday morning.

Going through these events in the Regimental Diary it is easy to overlook the length of time these soldiers were in combat. Adrenalin has been rushing through their veins for well over 24 hours by now. Again, these battle-weary soldiers would have been close to exhaustion, but survival meant that they had to keep going. Can you imagine just how many rounds Ernest must have fired during this period? Fortunately for Ernest and his comrades, they were able to stay at this location for 12 hours. There would have been time to take water and eat up any remains of their rations.

At 17.30 hours later that day, these tired soldiers had to muster themselves ready for a counter attack, for a brief period they were held in reserve.

It would soon be Ernest's turn to leave the trench and charge the 'Bosch'! The Battalion received orders to move forward and at 19.20 hours they attacked a farm located north of Chambracy and the high ground north-west of the village. This attack took place in the dark. I am trying to put myself in Ernest's place as he charges forward with fixed bayonet. True you would have taken some comfort knowing your friends are at your side. But the hazards would have been many.

Each shell crater potentially harboured enemy troops concealed inside. There was the ever-present risk of sniper fire, and mile upon mile of rusty barbed wire. Your breathing is heavy, the adrenalin is pumping through your veins, your head is pounding, sweat runs down your face and back.

You have to stop or slow down in order to reload your rifle. You don't want to be left behind, you fumble in haste, you start forward again, you stumble and fall over, friends at your side fall from gunshot, you know you can't stop to help them. You look ahead of you and hope the lead team are going in the right direction, all around you mortar shells explode, the sky above you is illuminated by different coloured flares, you strain to hear the commands of the NCOs.

At any moment it could be your turn to be hit. Bullets hiss past your head, you must keep going, your legs get heavy as fatigue starts to set in, your eyes try to focus ahead of you, images become obscure, you ask what hidden dangers lie amongst the swirling smoke clouds, any moment a figure in grey uniform could jump out at you, you can feel your heart pumping in your chest, pumping the adrenalin rich blood around your body, you call on reserves you never thought you had.

Eventually the farm buildings come into sight, grenades are thrown, you dive to the ground as they explode, then there is the hand-to-hand combat, the screams of soldiers having been bayoneted in the chest and abdomen. The battle crazed soldiers with empty rifles resort to the use of clubs and coshes, and soldiers literally try to 'pummel' each other's brains to bits with these crude weapons.

In desperation the grey figures in front of you hold their hands up in surrender. Sometimes these pleas for mercy go ignored and helpless young soldiers are dispatched with bayonet or bullet. Both sides were guilty of this behaviour. Remember the older soldiers have witnessed their best friends being wounded and or killed, dying in agony. It would have been hard for the soldiers to use restraint, the hatred of the Germans had boiled over in a frenzy of killing.

Not all of our soldiers would have shared these feelings. It should be remembered that some of the young conscripts would have had only six weeks training, thrusting bayonets into dummy soldiers stuffed with straw. Few of these young men actually wanted to kill another human being. Only months previously they had been bank clerks, shop keepers, semi-skilled apprentices. All of a sudden, they landed in a German trench, and for those brief few seconds, they were in a 'kill or be killed' situation. A moment's hesitation could see a bayonet buried into their own chests with agonising consequences. Seeing the life ebb away from a young German soldier you had just stabbed, their pitiful eyes piercing your soul, these images would for ever haunt some of these young conscripts.

There were heavy casualties reported on both sides. After the charge to take the farm only five officers and 120 other ranks remained. However, they had succeeded, having reached the ridge, the 2nd Wiltshires form a line with the French to their left. Shortly afterwards the depleted ranks of Wiltshires were reinforced by the Royal Welch Fusiliers.

There would be no time for rest. The men were ordered to consolidate and strengthen their position. This meant digging, filling and moving sandbags, and repairing barbed wire defences. All of this was to be done by battle-weary, exhausted soldiers.

On the morning of Saturday the 1st of June, the Germans attacked again. This time it was the turn of the French in their front-line trenches. By 14.00 hours the French informed the Wilts that they were being forced to withdraw. In doing this, it exposed the 2nd Wiltshires' left flank, where the Germans maintained the pressure with heavy machine fire.

At 19.30 hours the 58th Brigade was ordered to withdraw to Bois de Courton. They take up position astride the main Chambrecy to Bligny road. Having arrived here, there is even more digging to do, as there is a need for more trenches for protection.

It is now Sunday morning. Fortunately, the previous night had been relatively quiet, but the work continued throughout the day, with further trench digging and the strengthening of this new position. On the following day, because of the heavy casualties, the stragglers were formed into a 'composite' battalion, which included survivors of the 9th Welsh Regiment, the 9th Welch Fusiliers, and the 2nd Wiltshires. The battalion remained in this position for the next three days.

On the evening of Tuesday the 4th of June, the battalion redeployed to cover a perceived attack on the right flank, but this attack did not come as expected. In the early hours of Wednesday, the 5th, the battalion was ordered to 'stand to' but again the attack did not materialise. There were however artillery exchanges between 02.00 hours and 03.00 hours. In the early hours of Thursday the 6th of June, the German artillery opened up. At 02.15 hours the Germans targeted the front line and reserve trenches. Thankfully there were few casualties. This bombardment concluded at 04.15 hours.

The soldiers in the front-line trenches are now alert, expecting an attack. They strain their eyes in the darkness in front of them. At 04.30 hours ghostly figures start to appear, about 200 German infantry start to advance uphill towards the South perimeter of the village of Chambrecy.

Not to be daunted by these numbers, Lieutenants Collier and Marsh muster 40 men and with the support of Lewis guns and rapid rifle fire, they charge towards the German soldiers who sustain heavy casualties. They turn and run back to their trenches. Perhaps it's just me, but I'm beginning to sense a weakening of the Germans' resolve.

During this same day the Welch Regiments on the right of the Wiltshires come under heavy attack. This attack is repulsed. Again, heavy losses are inflicted on the enemy. The Germans try to break through at Montagne de Bligny but are again repelled. The Gloucestershires also hold their ground.

By the evening the line was intact, and further moves were made to consolidate the area. The Wiltshires were ordered to reinforce the Royal Welch Fusiliers. At about 01.30 hours, in the early hours of Friday the 7th of June, the composite 58th Brigade was relieved by the 150th Brigade. Ernest and the survivors then withdrew to Bois de Courton, arriving between 04.00 hours and 05.30 hours.

I will not attempt to hazard a guess as to how long Ernest and the other brave soldiers had been awake during this 10-day period of battle. The survivors would have been dehydrated, hungry and exhausted beyond comprehension. Their bodies would be reeking with stale body odour, battle and the smell of blood.

There then followed a two-month period when the 2nd Wiltshires were reorganised, reinforced, and rested. They also spent time in brigade reserve. My dear Grandad had survived yet another battle, but at what cost. I'm guessing that this is the period when he would have been treated for 'shell shock.'

Shell Shock

Naturally I wanted to find out a bit more about 'Shell Shock' which became prevalent in World War 1. As much as 15% of our soldiers suffered with this condition. In the first six months of the war this was of concern to the War department. This condition was new, and at first it did not have a name. Symptoms of this condition could be suffered in a mild form, but as the shelling intensified, more severe cases were reported. The initial response was that this was 'shirking' and cowardice, a way of being sent back from the front, but as the number of cases increased, the authorities began to take the symptoms seriously.

In March of 1915, the British Doctor Myers was appointed as official neurologist for the Army. This doctor was convinced that the condition was a mental and not physical problem. He described the effects of shells bursts as 'an invisibly fine molecular commotion to the victim's brain'.

By the end of 1915, Britain had over half a million casualties either dead, missing or wounded, and of the wounded soldiers, over 13,000 of them were suffering from shell shock. It was decided that the 'noisy mental cases' would be shipped back to special hospitals in Britain, one such hospital being the Royal Victorian Hospital in Hampshire.

So as not to bring too much attention to this illness, the nurses and doctors tried to segregate the sufferers from the other injured soldiers. This understandably affected their already fragile morale. When the victims were transported back to Britain on trains, the shell-shocked victims were placed in a special railway carriage, which was often painted a different colour from the other carriages. Imagine the stress on the nurses, during these journeys. Mild cases were treated by Doctor Myers and his staff, and they remained in France and Belgium. My Grandad would have been one of these patients.

A long time after the War, Ernest told his youngest daughter, Aunt Margaret, that part of his treatment was half a bottle of Champagne per day. This was probably a convenient treatment as Ernest was resting near the Champagne area in France at the time. In Ernest's case, just rest, and recuperation, would have been enough, and I am also sure he took comfort and reassurance from the ministry of the Padre.

The symptoms of shell shock varied considerably, dependent on the severity of the illness. In less severe cases a soldier could experience shaking, deafness, stammering, irritability, lack of concentration, and insomnia. In more severe cases, it was temporary blindness, loss of speech, uncontrollable shaking and poor mobility.

I am sure that many of you who read this book have seen the pitiful sights of these soldiers on TV in the documentaries. Sometimes on the film footage you see lines of bandaged soldiers coming back from the front. Next time you watch a documentary, look closer and you will see their hands and arms shaking as they walk past the cameras.

This situation deteriorated further in 1916. After the Battle of the Somme, over 35,000 soldiers showed varying symptoms of this condition. The War Office responded by requisitioning more hospitals in Britain so that these poor soldiers 'could be treated and returned to the front as soon as possible!'

In the four years of this war, medical science and surgery developed more rapidly than at any time before or since. The treatment of shell shock was no exception. There were various treatments:

Dream analysis and psycho-analysis – Soldiers would be encouraged to confront their daemons and discuss their traumas with the medical staff. Examples that came to light was when one soldier had accidentally shot one of his wounded comrades who was crawling back towards his trench.

Another disclosure was when a soldier had witnessed a Mark IV tank driving over some of his wounded friends who could not move out of the way in time. Their screams had haunted him to the point of madness.

Hypnosis – Soldiers having been hypnotised were convinced that they could walk properly and stop shaking.

Electric shock treatment – The British in consultation with their French allies discovered a French procedure which involved an electrical shock to the affected area. The French called this 'Faradisation' after the British inventor Faraday, who pioneered electro-magnetic induction. This procedure was found to be very effective when properly administered. A pioneer in this field was a British doctor called Lewis Yealland.

In June 1916 the War Office officially recognised shell shock, but this was not allowed to be used as a defence in a court martial hearing. Many a poor soldier had to stand in front of a firing squad at dawn whilst suffering these symptoms.

The condition of shell shock did not discriminate according to rank. One has to have sympathy with some of the officers, as the establishment would frown on any officer who tried to disclose this illness. It was seen as a weakness. 'Officers should rise above the situation and be stronger willed, to 'buckle' would be a sign of weakness, they had to be an example to their men!'

There were many cases of suicide amongst the ranks. Eventually special hospitals in Britain would be allocated to the officer class. One such hospital was located at Craiglockhart in Scotland.

This horrendous war would eventually send over eight million wounded soldiers back to their homelands. Of these in Britain alone over 200,000 soldiers went back to Britain shell shocked. The sad fact is that even three years after the war ended, over 15,000 men were still receiving treatment for this condition.

I remember a sad story my father-in-law told me. As a young man he remembered walking through the market town of Ashby-de-la-Zouch in Leicestershire, when he saw an old soldier standing on the pavement and shaking uncontrollably. People just ignored him and walked around him, ignoring his presence.

I must confess to the reader that my knowledge of what my Grandfather was doing from the beginning of May 1918 for the next few weeks is very hazy. There is no reference to his shell shock treatment on his medical records. Grandad never discussed his shell shock with me, and as a consequence I do not know how long he was treated for this condition. I am guessing it would have been a few weeks at least.

However, after studying the 2nd Wiltshire's deployments, it is clear that they were engaged in conflict between the 29th of May and the 7th of June. Thereafter, there followed a lengthy period when the 2nd Wilts were training or in brigade reserve. I hope I will be forgiven for assuming that his treatment took place between the 8th of June and the 2nd of August.

Chapter 8

Ernest is treated for the effects of combat

The period of this war has now reached the first week in June 1918. From the 2nd Wiltshire Battalion Diary, it is evident that they spent some time in the Bois de Courton area. This is a small village located in the Champagne area of Reims, between Paris and Verdun.

As stated in the previous chapter, this is the period that Ernest came down with a mild form of shell shock. There is no reference to this in his medical records, a copy of which is in my possession, Army form B 103, together with a copy of his discharge documents, Army form W3997. There is a lack of accurate information covering this period. As already stated, my only source is a brief account from my Aunt Margaret, Ernest's youngest surviving daughter. All we know is that Pt 320252 Burchell had treatment during this period.

I say that it was a mild form of shell shock because of the events that followed. I am guessing that Ernest would have had the 'shakes' and been suffering from a lack of concentration, together with a lack of sleep. Ernest was no shirker and if an NCO recognised these symptoms, he would naturally have been referred to the battalion's Medical Officer. This period in June 1918 would have been an ideal opportunity to have Ernest treated as the battalion was in a rest and training period behind the lines.

It is no surprise that Grandad succumbed to these symptoms given the heavy shelling that he and his comrades had been exposed to in the German attacks from March 21st to mid-April 1918. Literally hundreds of his comrades had either been killed wounded or captured by the Germans. The poor man would have been in a state of exhaustion. No doubt he would also have been suffering 'survivor's guilt', this being a mental condition. Having gone through the horrors of the last few months, he would have asked himself dozens of times, why had he survived and not the others?

The 58th Royal Field Ambulance (part of the 19th Division) would have conveyed Ernest, possibly to a base hospital somewhere in France. He would have spent a brief period of rest and recuperation lying in a hospital bed, with clean bed sheets and a soft pillow. This was luxury. His surviving friends would not be afforded such comfort, as they would be sleeping on lice infested straw mattresses, if they were lucky.

Just to see a pretty faced nurse would have been a tonic in itself. She would give him a reassuring smile and offer him what comfort she could. I have no doubt that Ernest would have been visited by the Army Chaplain who would have given him some spiritual guidance and reassurance.

I make no bones about it, Grandad's faith would have been tested so many times in those early weeks of the German Spring Offensive. As already stated, when the opportunity arose, he had attended the church parades on Sundays. He had bowed and prayed alongside fellow Christians only to see these same young men blown to pieces days later. They had said the same prayers as him, so why had they been killed and not him?

There was an abundance of Champagne in the area. According to Aunt Margaret, he was allowed half a bottle per day as part of his treatment. At least it would have numbed his pain and suppressed the demons in his mind, perhaps long enough for him to catch up on some long-needed sleep. He must have had some nightmares. The horrible images of recent weeks would have featured heavily in these dreams, including the faces of his dying friends with those horrific injuries.

When awake his thoughts would naturally turn to his family back in Wiltshire and that beautiful farmer's daughter, Elizabeth. He would hold her photo to his chest and wonder if he would see her again. In those hospital wards there would be soldiers from all sorts of units and regiments.

The men would be hungry for news from home. I doubt if there would have been any British newspapers to hand, but rumours and speculation would be rife.

Most of us have experienced periods in our lives when we have laid in hospital beds during illness. You tend to have a lot of thinking time, a time to reflect on what future lies ahead. 'Why are we still fighting this war, will it ever end?'. Ernest, like so many others, would have asked himself these questions, so many times over and over again. Most soldiers with Ernest's length of service were resigned to the fact that eventually their luck would run out. As and when the end came, they prayed that it would be quick, and that they would not have to suffer the loss of a limb or a permanent disfigurement. But Ernest would not give up hope.

What kept Ernest going? Perhaps it was his dogged determination to return home and marry 'Bessy'. Somehow these positive thoughts began to prevail in his mind and Ernest began to recover. He was to survive through this ordeal to fight another battle.

The war rages on

Whilst Ernest lay in his bed, the war raged on. The Germans were within 50 miles of Paris. However, the capture of the capital eluded them. General Ludendorff was still convinced that the allied morale was on the brink of collapse. His spies in Paris and the reconnaissance planes had witnessed large amounts of civilians leaving the capital. He reassured the German public that they were on the brink of a famous victory. For the time being he would continue to receive their fragile support, but many were starving to death. The food riots began to intensify.

Over the next few weeks there began to develop an ever bigger salient in the area of Reims and Soissons. The Germans continued to engage the Allies in this area in the hope that the losses incurred by the Allies would lead them to move reinforcements from Flanders to this area. The Germans would then attack in Flanders with superior numbers. Should this be successful, then the Allies would sue for peace, but it would be on Germany's terms!

However, this plan would not work. Instead of moving allied reinforcements south from Flanders, the French managed to persuade the reluctant American General Pershing to provide 170,000 American troops.

Over the second and third weeks in June 1918, a period of heavy fighting took place backwards and forwards across the River Marne, in and around the City of Reims and the town of Soissons. It is likely that Ernest would have heard the distant artillery bombardments whilst he lay in his hospital bed. The more serious cases in his ward would grow very agitated and sometimes lose control, unsettling the other patients. The nurses would sometimes put cotton wool in their ears to dim the noise, and to help settle them.

The Allies had a number of advantages over this period. Firstly, the French intelligence units had successfully deciphered the German communication codes and as a consequence they knew where and when the next German attack would take place. The supremacy in troop numbers enjoyed by the Germans at the start of the Spring offensive no longer existed. This was largely due to the fact that 250,000 American troops were pouring into the Western front every month. Also, a large proportion of the German losses were the elite Storm Troopers and specialist units. These would be replaced by young and elderly troops who were less well trained and inferior in quality. The German supply lines were stretched, with the forward troops having to rely more and more on captured allied supplies. In contrast, the Allies were supplying the Belgian and French coastal ports with 1,000 tons of supplies every day. This was helped by the daily arrival of newly constructed American cargo ships in ever increasing numbers.

As expected, the Germans crossed the River Marne in the second week of June and attacked on a 40-kilometre front. During their initial artillery barrage, they unleashed over 15,000 gas shells. Even though they had anticipated the attack, the French were overwhelmed by the Germans' progress, who captured over 8,000 French prisoners. On June the 11th the Germans were stunned when the French counter attacked with the support of 200 tanks. They managed to catch out the German forward divisions in open ground. Ludendorff had underestimated the French resilience and was forced to call off the offensive in this area after four days of fighting. Over this same period the Scottish regiments had similar gains in the Hinges area.

The American Army engaged the Germans at Belleau Wood. Heavy fighting took place for two weeks ending in an allied victory. The Germans were particularly impressed with the fighting skills of the Americans who proved that they were determined to advance at all costs, even when they sustained heavy casualties. Up until now the Germans had not taken the Americans seriously. This battle had a significant impact on the Germans who were forced to recognise the emergence of a new fighting force with huge resources to hand. Part of their success was the fact that the Americans had amassed large amounts of French Renault tanks with revolutionary rotating turrets. These were faster and more reliable than the British Mk IV tanks.

The reality of this situation with the Americans was beginning to sink in with the German High Command. They responded by making peace overtures, but these failed because of Germany's intransigence over Belgium and territory on her Eastern border.

Ernest is awarded the Distinguished Conduct Medal

All these events were taking place whilst Ernest was in Rest and recuperation, somewhere near the Reims area. Unbeknown to Ernest at the time, moves were afoot to recognise his efforts in the fighting that had taken place earlier in the year at Spanbroekmolen.

I refer to a medal plaque which at some stage would have been presented to Ernest. I mention it now because it was on the 23rd of June 1918, along with 21 other soldiers, that he was awarded the Distinguished Conduct Medal (DCM). The names, including Ernest's with a new number 203241, are listed on this plaque. It is signed by the then General of the 2nd Army, Sir Herbert Plumer.

I ask myself when would Grandad have been told this news? Was it whilst he was in rest and recuperation? I guess we will never know, because he never told us when he received the award and medal.

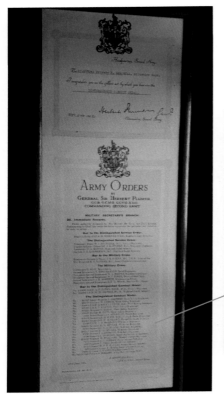

Naturally I have done some research into the history of the DCM, the origins of which date back to the Crimean War in 1854. This medal was first issued to 'the other ranks' for exceptional bravery in the field. This is the next medal down from the Victoria Cross. It was discontinued in 1993 and replaced by the 'Gallantry in the Field Medal'. A total of over 30,000 DCMs were awarded in its 139-year history, and of these over 25,000 were awarded during World War 1.

Do you know for the 16 years that I knew Grandad, I don't think he ever showed me the plaque or the medal! This was probably a measure of the man's modesty. I am glad that the DCM medal is still with the Burchell family. My cousin, Peter Richards (Ernest's 2nd eldest Grandson), is currently the proud owner and guardian of this family heirloom.

I have checked the 2nd Wiltshires' War Diary and there is no mention of any medal ceremonies from June 1918 throughout the remaining period that Ernest remained in France. I can only assume that he was awarded the plaque and medal back in England. To support this theory is the fact that Ernest Burchell is listed in the 3rd of October 1918 issue of the London Gazette.

In the first week of July Ernest was recognised for his leadership skills and ability when he was promoted to Acting Sergeant with pay. I suspect that his period of rest and recuperation was now over, and he had returned to his regiment. I do not want to take any credit away from Grandad, but so many officers were being killed by snipers, machine guns and exploding shells, and it resulted in a chronic shortage of NCOs. The question was, would Ernest be up to the task? I have no doubt that he was!

With this promotion came extra responsibilities. He would be second in command of the platoon (15 to 30 men). He would have three stripes on each arm of his tunic. This was not just a symbol of authority. In the heat of battle, especially when gas and smoke was used by the enemy and in the hours of darkness, the young soldiers had to be able to recognise a supervising officer and be guided by his instructions.

It is highly likely that Ernest would have been one of the oldest men in the platoon. If he were lucky enough to reach his next birthday, he would be 30 years old. Each morning in the trench it would be his job to ensure the men were fit for inspection, with all equipment, weapons clean and ready for the NCO to examine. He would be the first person the young soldier would come to for any welfare issues. He would have administration duties, including intruding into the personal lives of the soldiers, reading their letters before they were sent home, and this would be no easy task. He would be responsible for discipline in the trenches and would now have to coordinate daily tasks. In the heat of battle, he would be expected to show leadership and go over the top with the lads. He would have to support the lieutenant and take up his role if this person were killed or wounded. All this extra responsibility, and Ernest had to try to stay alive as well!

From the day he was promoted to the 6th of August 1918, the 2nd Wiltshires remained behind the lines, in training duties. No doubt over this period Ernest would receive further instruction in his new role as Platoon Sergeant. I have no doubt that the Allies were sensing that the war was going to become more mobile and that in the coming weeks, there would be more troop advances than at any time since the war had started. Because of this, the troops would have to rehearse frontal attacks, and attacks from the right and left flank. Ernest would have the extra responsibility of giving precise instructions during these manoeuvres. The young, confused and sometimes frightened soldiers would be looking to him for guidance and leadership.

Allied success

Over this period of June and July 1918, there had been more significant developments on the Western Front.

A new general emerged from the Australian Army, General Monash, a very skilled soldier who had come through the ranks without a commission. He was not part of the ruling elite class that was typical of the time. Prior to the war he had been an engineer. The War Office was slow and reluctant to recognise his abilities. 'How could we have someone from the Colonies be in charge of 200,000 men?' was the question frequently asked amongst the senior politicians and strategists.

The next battle would have a huge impact on future tactics and battles. General Monash saw the major importance of integrating all resources to work together in one battle plan. He achieved this by the carefully planned coordinated use of artillery, tanks, machine gun units, with air cover to assist an infantry attack.

The Battle of Hamel, when launched on the 4th of July, was a significant success. In less than two hours, all objectives were achieved. Learning from the lessons at Cambrai, General Monash had managed to move over 60 tanks undetected by the Germans to the front. This was achieved under the cover of low flying aircraft, with planned artillery bombardments to disguise the noise of the tanks moving forward. The artillery used some gas shells on the days leading up to the attack, which prompted the Germans to wear gas masks.

On the actual day of the attack, these gas shells were replaced by smoke cannisters, which fooled the Germans, who continued to wear their gas masks. The tanks then advanced behind the creeping barrage. Some of the allied artillery gave them protection by targeting the German artillery units which were threatening to blow the tanks out of action. In order to give additional support to the tanks, the air force strafed any German anti-tank units as they were identified. These same aircraft also machine gunned the German infantry in the opposing trenches. In yet another breakthrough on this day allied aircraft carried out a successful air drop of ammunition for their forward machine gunners.

The Australian infantry did not have to wear gas masks as they knew it was harmless smoke ahead. This gave them a distinct advantage over the defending Germans, who by now had misted up visors in their masks, significantly affecting their vision. They would overheat and sweat. As I have already explained, this would have made it difficult to line up the sights of their rifles and machine guns.

The wearing of gas masks more often than not rendered the forward German army artillery spotters useless, as they were unable to see through their field glasses. Also, German snipers wearing gas masks could not see through their scopes. We will never be able to fully gauge the effect these two facts had on the outcome of this battle. I suspect it was massive!

Because more tanks remained operational during the battle, they were able to provide more cover for the infantry that followed them. General Monash had even held back tanks in reserve, in order to allow for initial losses and breakdowns. More significantly, a lot of these tanks were used to carry much needed supplies to the front-line troops. The success of this battle proved that General Monash and his new tactics had been spot on. His reputation and credibility would be elevated to new heights following this battle. Equally significantly, these new methods and tactics would become the template for future battles to come.

However, just when things were beginning to look better for the Allies, a deadly illness started to take a hold on all the soldiers of the Western Front and other battlefields elsewhere. It was a major pandemic.

The Spanish Flu

Spain had remained neutral throughout the conflict of World War 1, and because the pandemic was widely reported there, the waring countries were quick to name the condition 'Spanish Flu'. It is a fallacy that this epidemic started in Spain.

A soldier would come down with a sore throat, nausea, and severe breathing problems. All of a sudden, dark spots would appear on his body and eventually his skin would turn a blue colour through lack of oxygenated blood. From the initial symptoms, death could follow within 11 days. A sign the end was near was when the victim started to bleed from his nose and ears. The poor soldier would literally suffocate on his own blood and bodily fluids.

The authorities were at a loss as to know how to treat this condition. Remember that this was 1918, and there were no anti-viral drugs or anti- biotics available. Neither of the opposing sides would admit to the losses they were sustaining. Press coverage of the pandemic was strictly controlled by the waring countries. Traditionally the flu virus affected the young and the elderly, but this virus was different, in that it affected a lot more people aged 20 to 40 years, in particular humans who had a low resistance to infection bought about by malnutrition and battle fatigue.

Germany and its central partners had been significantly affected by the Royal Naval blockade, bad harvests, lack of modern fertilisers, and equally significantly, a lack of draught animals (oxen and heavy horses) which were still being used for cultivation and crop production.

The situation was becoming so bad that the Germans had to withdraw their aid to the Bulgarians. There were reports of sand and saw dust being put into loaves of bread. The German soldier was having to manage on less than half his daily calorific requirements, and the consequence of this was that his susceptibility to infection rose significantly. It is estimated that over 500,000 German soldiers came down with the virus.

Over the coming weeks of the war this pandemic was bound to affect future battle plans on both sides. The newly arriving American soldiers were bringing the infections with them, as there was a severe outbreak in the American homeland. The situation become so acute that in September 1918 America suspended the draughting of soldiers abroad.

Did this affect Ernest and the 2nd Wiltshires? The truth is, I don't know. There is no mention in the war diaries, and Grandad never mentioned it to me or his family. I will let the historians argue about whether it prolonged the war or shortened it. The sad fact is that globally this flu pandemic accounted for between 50,000,000 and 100,000,000 deaths. People continued to die long into 1920.

It is quite ironic that as I write this chapter of my book, there is yet another outbreak of a flu, the Coronavirus.

The Second Battle of the Marne

But with all these losses it still did not deter the German High Command. On the 15th of July 1918 they launched the Second Battle of Marne. Using newly constructed extendable bridges, they crossed the Marne in strength. The thrust of the attacks was concentrated east and west of Reims. They faced the French and American divisions, amongst which were the 42nd Infantry Division, known as the 'Rainbow Division'. One of their senior officers was Colonel Douglas MacArthur, who would become much more famous in later conflicts of the 20th century.

Still in possession of the German codes, the Allies were ready. For once the French High Command had listened to General Pétain who was allowed to amass a very strong second line of defensive trenches. The Germans having crossed the Marne, quickly overran the lightly manned first line of trenches, only to be confronted by a very formidable second line.

Again, the exhausted German forces were caught out in the open, and on the 18th of July the French counter attacked, supported with around 400 of their Renault tanks. The French Air Force bombed the newly constructed German bridges over the Marne, and as a consequence the German troops were in danger of being cut off, and were forced to retreat back seven km. This was a massive blow to General Ludendorff, who finally realised that he would never march his troops into Paris. He called off his plans for a major offensive in Flanders, and this was probably the turning point of the war.

This same week saw the execution of Tsar Nicholas II and the whole of his family. The Russian dynasty was destroyed, and the royal blood line terminated for good.

Behind the front-line on the Western Front, Generals Foch, Haig, and Pershing met together to plan the next offensives. They agreed to attack on three fronts. Field Marshal Haig would launch an attack towards the east at Amiens, General Pétain would attack in a northerly direction across the River Marne, and General Pershing would drive south towards Verdun. Their objectives would be vital railway junctions, the lifeline of the German armies on the Western Front.

In those last two weeks of July 1918, the 2nd Wiltshires were busy training their replacements on the rifle ranges, in battle tactics, the use of Lewis guns, and route marching. During this period Ernest would have to become accustomed to barking out orders, which would have been a totally new experience for him. The training continued into the first week of August. The period that followed was later referred to as the '100-day march to victory'.

On the evening of Tuesday the 6th of August, the 2nd Wiltshires were conveyed in a convoy of buses to Chocques, where they waited for nightfall before marching in silence to the front-line trenches at Hinges. That evening they relieved the 1st Gordon Highlanders.

What thoughts must have gone through Ernest's mind as he marched in silence. The familiar night sky would glow in the distance with intermittent shell explosions. The noise of war would grow louder as they approached the front, an occasional flare would illuminate no man's land, and the trenches took on a whole new appearance in the darkness.

The soldiers, including many young newly trained men, would be fighting back their nerves and trying to keep their hands from shaking, taking deep breaths to steady themselves. They would instinctively look into the distance for the unseen enemy. What dangers lay waiting in the shadows?

Their view forwards came to an abrupt end as they entered the trench systems. All they could see was the walls of the trenches as they marched forward in single file along the duck boards. It is likely that they would have been accompanied by a guide since this would have been their first deployment at the Hinges trench system. The guide informs them that they have arrived. The NCOs of the Gordons brief the newly arrived Wiltshires NCOs as to the situation and recent enemy activity, the current risks posed by enemy snipers, any recent gas and artillery attacks, any useful intelligence gleaned, the list goes on.

Part of Ernest's job would have been to sort his platoon into a rota. Some Privates would man the trench periscope for two-hourly stretches. It is likely that these would have been deployed in a forward observation post. This would have been a short length of trench jutting out into no man's land, the end of which would be the nearest point to the German trench. There were numerous forward observation posts spaced along the whole length of the trench systems. The rest of the platoon would be divided into work duties for two-hour stints, followed by rest for four hours. When necessary, trenches still had to be repaired, sandbags filled, damaged barbed wire replaced, and stores collected, as well as many other tasks.

On this particular night, Tuesday 6th of August, word had been received from the neighbouring 4th Division that the Germans were withdrawing from their front. As a response to this news, the 2nd Wiltshires sent out reconnoitring patrols on the right and left flanks. Almost instantly they were met with heavy machine gun and sniper fire and were forced to withdraw. I am not going to speculate if Ernest went on these patrols as there is no way of knowing.

That same night enemy machine guns strafed 'B' company's trench. Observers were able to pinpoint the enemy machine gunners' location which was at Vertbois Farm, and divisional artillery was immediately alerted. They must have had the coordinates of this farm accurately plotted, because the brief bombardment that followed forced the German machine gunners to vacate the area in haste. However, it was not long before they returned.

The 2nd Wiltshires remained in the front-line trenches until the 10th of August, during which period they made a gallant attack on Vertbois Farm, killing twelve defenders and taking two prisoners. A total of 100 yards of territory was gained, but at the cost of fourteen soldiers killed. That same evening the 2nd Wiltshires were relieved by the 9th Welsh Regiment.

The minor battles and skirmishes north of the Somme in which the 19th Division were involved were a deliberate ploy by the Allies to divert the attention of the Germans away from the next main offensive. This was the second Battle of Amiens, located to the south of the 2nd Wiltshires' position. This battle had been launched on the 8th of August.

The role of the sniper

Before going into detail about the Battle of Amiens, my natural curiosity has led me to research the role of the sniper in World War 1. The reasons for this will become apparent in the next chapter. I have mentioned them briefly in previous chapters, but I wanted to know more.

At the outbreak of the war the Germans were typically quicker to deploy snipers, who became very effective once the conflict reached a stalemate, and trench warfare became the norm. In 1914 the German Duke of Ratibor had collected over 20,000 hunting rifles, each with telescoping sights. The British had only a few Mannlichers and Mauser hunting rifles, and a short supply of ammunition for these weapons.

The Germans deployed many soldiers, trained in using their weapons, in each of their front-line regiments. They were allocated a certain stretch of trench, approximately half a mile. Each company had rifles with telescopic sights. Out of every 100 soldiers, six had rifles with telescopic sights. They had special instructions to identify and kill as many officers as possible. The British made this task a lot easier for them by fitting their officers with a tighter fitting trouser, like riding breaches. As a consequence, hundreds of NCOs died needlessly, purely because of their different style trousers.

German snipers were specially selected solders, many recruited because of their experience in field skills, in particular hunting in the forests of Germany. They had excellent eyesight, a steady grip, and accuracy with rifles. They were often deployed alone and had the ability to work on their own initiative. Many of these soldiers were from elite Jäger battalions. The German sniper was feared amongst the front-line allied troops. Signs were erected in the allied trenches warning of snipers in the area. At the peak of their success, the German snipers were accounting for between twelve and fourteen kills per day, and they were beginning to have an adverse effect on morale.

At the beginning of the war, the Germans enjoyed a tactical advantage over the Allies with their deployment of snipers. Their early success prompted them to manufacture purpose-made weapons in much larger quantities than the Allies, who did not really begin to catch up until early 1916. The mass-produced weapon of choice was the Mauser Gewehr 98 service rifle, fitted with a telescopic sight.

They were personal issue, the advantage being that the user could adjust the sight to his own eyes. It became his best friend, and therefore these weapons were well looked after. With typical German efficiency, the manufacturers even put simple instructions on how to set the sights up prior to use. These paper instructions were folded and placed in a small compartment in the telescopic sights.

The Germans sometimes deployed snipers in purpose-built concrete 'pill boxes'. Sometimes they would be deployed alone in no man's land, concealed in the ruins of buildings, in the wrecks of burnt-out tanks, or secreted under the carcase of a dead horse. The list is endless. The sniper would sometimes have the added protection of a steel plate with a peep hole in the centre. This plate would be embedded in the earth.

This is the German Mauser Gewehr 98, a precision-made weapon, deadly accurate

A crude but effective counter measure to this would be to fire at the plate with an Elephant gun. These lead balls fired from a Jeffries high velocity .333 gun would penetrate the steel plate and could kill the sniper behind it.

The German sniper bullet could penetrate a 10-inch thick wall of brick at 100 yards. It could also penetrate a 20-inch sandbag at the same distance. The average effective distance was about 300 yards. The real skill was being able to rapidly identify a target and let off a round within two to three seconds. The muzzle velocity of these weapons was 3,000 feet per second.

With regard to counter measures, the Allies were rather slow to respond. They naively thought that these early fatalities were the result of 'lucky shots' on the part of the Germans. When the penny did drop, all sorts of methods were used to pinpoint the location of German snipers.

A special factory was set up in Amiens, where papier-mâché imitations of human heads were produced. A steel helmet was placed on the head which was carefully raised above the parapet of the trench. Whilst this was being done, there would be a separate team of two, one being the observer with field glasses, the second being a British or allied sniper. Their job would be to spot and identify the location of the German sniper's rifle flash when it fired at the dummy. The British or allied sniper would then fire at the German sniper.

This method had mixed success. The Germans became wise to this method, and a good sniper, having fired his round, would rapidly redeploy to another pre-chosen place of concealment. As you can therefore see, each side was constantly trying to outwit each other with measures and counter measures.

Not to be outdone by the Germans, the British quickly enlisted the services of a certain Major Hesketh Pritchard, a man with money and resources. Prior to the war he had spent some time in Africa shooting game with high power hunting rifles fitted with telescopic sights. He soon developed the skills of stealth, concealment, and accuracy with his rifles. At the outbreak of war, he took his rifles and his knowledge with him to France. He became the natural choice to set up a sniping school behind the front, where he could train and recruit soldiers. He received the support of Major General Lynden Bell and Sir Charles Munroe commanding the 3rd Army.

Major Hesketh Pritchard advocated teams of two, one being the 'spotter' and the other would fire the rifle as directed by the 'spotter'. This role could be rotated, the advantage being that eyesight would be put under a lot of strain during prolonged periods. Having done some deer stalking myself in the Highlands of Scotland, I am aware of the practical difficulties, especially as follows:

Posture – When in a fixed position, especially lying forward on one's stomach, it can sometimes be very difficult to readjust your body when the target moves out of your 'arc of fire', and time is of the essence.

Adverse weather – Cold damp weather can often cause condensation on the telescopic lens leading to poor visibility. The necessity of wearing gas masks compounded this problem.

Wind direction, temperature, and distance – With the increase in distance to the target, one has to allow for the effect of gravity on the bullet which over long distances will fall slightly below the intended target. Experience allows the shooter to aim slightly high of the intended target to allow for this drop.

Likewise, with wind direction, allowances can be made to compensate for the wind direction by aiming either right or left of the intended target.

Air temperature will affect air density. Cold air makes the bullet strike lower and hot air make the bullet strike higher. Training teaches the sniper to make allowances when aiming the weapon.

As a result of this training and the increased production of purpose-built weapons (Lee Enfield MK III) and scopes, the Allies caught up with the Germans by mid-1916. A lot of credit should be given to Asketh Pritchard who together with his training staff managed to train 15 Infantry Divisions, each of which had three brigades belonging to the 3rd Army. This teaching was speeded up by initially training the NCOs who in turn taught their specially selected Privates. Now it would be the Germans' turn to cope with this threat.

Most historians would agree that over the period that followed, not only did the Allies catch up with the Germans, but we overtook them in this method of warfare. The allied snipers' key objectives were to identify and eliminate forward artillery spotters, German snipers, machine gun teams, and officers. A crack sniper unit was called the 'Lovat Scouts'. This unit consisted of Scottish soldiers who, prior to the outbreak of war, had been employed as deer stalkers and guides in the Scottish Highlands. They had natural ability and would soon prove their worth.

As the second half of the war progressed, ammunition was modified and in some cases armour piercing shells were used. These were particularly useful when the German machine gun was in view, but not the operator. A well-aimed shot at the breech mechanism could render the weapon useless. Not to be outdone, the German sniper would sometimes cut off the pointed area of the lead bullet making it blunt, or take the lead out of the case, and reverse it back into the case, blunt end outermost (referred to as a 'dumb-dumb' bullet). When these bullets hit the victim, they caused horrific injuries. Any German snipers captured with this ammunition were shown very little mercy.

The threat of snipers would be uppermost in Sergeant Ernest Burchell's mind when he briefed the young soldiers of his platoon. There is no doubt that Grandad would have witnessed the deadly effects of German snipers during his time in the trenches, and he would advise his subordinates of the deadly risks and consequences.

The Battle of Amiens

Returning to the Battle of Amiens, this was yet another offensive involving the Australian and Canadian Army Corps who by now had gained a reputation as a brilliant fighting force. They were deployed in the centre of the main thrust, the British being on the left and the French on the right. General Monash, and General Currie of the Canadian Army Corps had formed a good working relationship. Both of these Generals were known for their meticulous preparations prior to battle. Both insisted on the best supplies and equipment for their troops. Perhaps significantly, for each ten Australian soldiers, one would have a Lewis gun. The Allies could call on over 800 aircraft to support them during the battle.

Following the Canadian success at the Battle of Passchendaele, the Germans quickly regarded the Canadian Corps as an elite fighting unit. They were convinced that this unit would form the spearhead of any future major conflicts. As a consequence, every effort was made by the Germans to identify where the Canadians were deployed. The Allies used this fact to their advantage.

A few days before the Battle of Amiens commenced, General Currie deliberately marched 120,000 soldiers of his army, in broad daylight, north towards Passchendaele, in full view of the German spotter planes. They were quick to pass their observations on to the German High Command. However, the following day, under the cover of darkness and in complete silence, the Canadians did a reciprocal march back to Amiens, completely fooling the Germans.

During the days that preceded the attack at the start of the battle, allied twin- engine Hadley Page bombers deliberately flew low over the front, in order to drown out the noise of 580 allied tanks moving forwards. A large number of these new tanks were the latest Mark V tank. These new weapons had a number of improvements, being three tons lighter, and fitted with a more powerful new Ricardo six-cylinder petrol engine which gave them an extra ten miles range with a full tank of fuel. In addition, the armour plating was thicker and the male tanks had an extra six-pounder gun, giving the tank a much wider arc of fire. The female tanks had four Hotchkiss MK1 machine guns fitted, replacing the Lewis guns of the Mark IV tanks.

In order to give the tank's the best possible protection during battle, a number of changes had been made to the Allied Artillery whose covering fire would help to minimise tank losses.

Each of the supporting artillery guns had been carefully calibrated prior to deployment. The weapon had been fired through two paper screens located at set distances apart. The precise time the shell passed through the paper screens was recorded, enabling the gunners to calculate the muzzle velocity of each gun.

A dedicated meteorological unit had also been set up by the army. Their knowledge and equipment enabled them to give the battle planners more accurate information on wind direction, air temperatures and weather forecasts. This would be vital when planning gas attacks and determining the accuracy of weapons. Fine adjustments could be made. Equally important, the Allies were perfecting the technique of sound ranging of enemy artillery units.

The Allies had learnt the lessons from past battles and did not open up with their artillery until shortly before the men went over the top taking the Germans completely by surprise. The attack had been deliberately brought forward by two days because the Germans were still withdrawing across the Marne, and did not have time to stop and regroup. They were taken completely off balance.

It has been estimated that during the first few hours of this battle, as much as 95% of the German artillery units were destroyed. The success of the first day even surprised the Allies with over 8,000 Germans taken prisoner. General Ludendorff was quoted as having said 'This was the black day of the German Army'. In making this judgement, he was not referring to the lost territory, but instead to the front-line German soldiers' morale which had sunk to new depths. Their fighting spirit was beginning to wane. In the coming weeks German surrenders would become more and more widespread and in ever increasing numbers.

Just like at the Battle of Hamel, the Allies substituted their gas shells with 'flavoured' smoke shells on the day of the battle. Again, the Germans were fooled and were wearing their gas masks as their trenches were overrun. The allied soldiers would see those dirty faced prisoners as they were marched behind the lines. Gone were the looks of defiance and arrogance, and instead were pitiful looks of despair, hunger and anguish. Many were relieved to have been captured.

The allied soldier's morale in contrast took a turn for the good. An entry is made in the 2nd Wiltshire's diary dated the 21st of August, stating 'The troops were in great spirit!' This was even commented upon by a war correspondent of the time, Phillip Gibbs, who noted 'a distinct change in troop morale'.

In the remaining weeks of August 1918, there followed a series of smaller battles towards the Hindenburg Line, namely the second Battle of the Somme, the Battle of Noyon, the second Battle of Arras, the second Battle of Bapaume, the Battle of Saint Quentin, and the Battle of Scarpe. Each battle was a success for the Allies. The 19th Western Division were not involved in these battles. They continued to fight in the Hinges area, making advances. On the 19th of August they pushed forward 800 yards in one day.

The 2nd Wiltshires started to come across a lot of abandoned German equipment, referred to in the diary as 'salvage'. It was inevitable that soldiers started to take souvenirs, including as a result of searching captured prisoners. These included watches, field glasses, and small arms.

I can distinctly remember Grandad telling me this story during tea in the old farmhouse.

> 'When the Germans started to retreat, I can remember coming across one of their dead officers. He had a holster containing his Luger pistol. I decided to take this with me. A lot of the others were doing the same. I'm not saying it was right, but we did it anyway'.

The 2nd Wiltshires continued to rotate in the trench system, moving from front-line, to support trenches and then rest periods, and periods in reserve. As if they did not have enough to cope with, on the 26th of August, there was an epidemic of diarrhoea. This could well have been a mild form of dysentery as the complaint was common in the trenches because of the poor sanitation, eating with dirty hands, and drinking contaminated water.

It should be remembered that it is now the middle of summer in the trenches and there is no mention of rainfall in the diaries. As a consequence, many of the front-line troops in the trenches would have resorted to collecting water from shell holes. As the water level dropped in these shell holes so would the drinking quality. In many cases the soldiers would boil up the water prior to drinking it. They often referred to a green scum on top of the boiling water, which they would spoon off before drinking.

Soldiers being soldiers, some would be more thorough boiling water than others. You have to feel sorry for these poor soldiers. To add to their misery in the trenches, they would now have to endure stomach cramps,

Night barrage

dehydration, blood in their stools, with numerous visits to the latrines. I pity the soldiers who had latrine duties over this period! Grandad would be alright, because he was now Acting Sergeant and he could delegate these duties! However, these symptoms persisted only for about one week and with the intake of plenty of fluids, most of them recovered.

This chapter ends as the 2nd Wiltshires relieve the 9th Royal Welch Fusiliers in the front-line trenches at Locon.

These are some of the emergency rations Ernest would have had with him during the retreat in March/April 1918, note the biscuits on the left and the tinned rations on the right, in desperation and hunger, he is likely to have ate the contents of the tins cold as there would have been little opportunity to light a fire.

Chapter 9

This chapter covers a detailed account of events that took place on Tuesday the 3rd of September 1918. I have referred to the war diaries of the 19th Western Division, the 58th Brigade Diary, and the 2nd Wiltshire Regimental Diary.

I have taken the liberty of creating a fictional German soldier whom I will name 'Kurt Schlüter' for the purpose of making this account more interesting. I hope you as the reader will excuse me for writer's privilege.

The Wiltshires' position on 3rd of September 1918

On the previous evening the 2nd Wiltshires were in the trenches at Locon just east of Hinges. This map shows the location of the 2nd Wiltshires on the 3rd of September 1918.

Over the previous twenty-six days, the German salient to the north of Béthune has been progressively pushed back towards Lille. As you can see the 2nd Wiltshires are deployed on the southern tip of this salient.

Back in the British trenches Sergeant 203241 Burchell was in the front-line with his soldiers, and the time was 04.00 hours. He advised the men under him to grab a bite to eat and drink as they were all to be ready to 'jump off' at 04.30 hours. The men's spirits were high, as 'Fritz' was retreating, and in their minds, there was hope that there may yet be an end to this crazy war.

The rum was passed around, and eager hands held out their canteens so that Ernest could pour in the belly-warming liquid, which was swallowed up eagerly. More was available for those that wanted it, the maximum ration being a third of a pint per soldier per day.

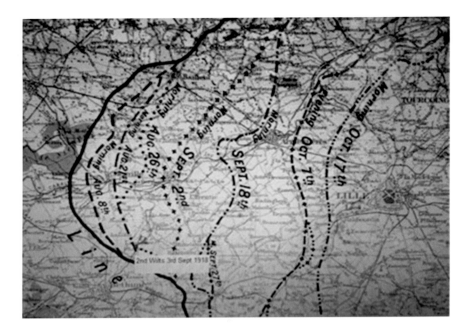

'Make sure your magazines are full, with one in the spout lads. Remember to put your guns on safety until we go over the top'.

Those soldiers who had not already done so, sat and wrote a final letter to their loved ones, in the event that they were about to be killed. They carefully folded this letter and placed it in the breast pocket of their tunics or handed it to one of the NCO's who would remain in the Trench when the men went 'over the top'.

Ernest made a final check of their equipment and just before 04.30 hours Ernest ordered the men to fix bayonets. The men were then ready. There then followed a period which seemed like eternity when the Tommies waited for the order to go over the top.

The German opponents and Kurt Schlüter

The Wiltshires were facing the German 6th Army whose commander was General Otto von Below. This army group consisted of the 55th Corps, IV Corps, 11th Corps, and the 40th Reserve Corps.

There were five divisions in the 55th Corps, one of these was the 38th Division and part of their battle order comprised of the Jäger-Regiment Number two. One of the many marksmen in this regiment is rifleman Kurt Schlüter. The word 'Jäger' is the German word for 'hunter'. A lot of men from these regiments came from similar backgrounds to Kurt.

Kurt had been especially chosen to join this light infantry regiment, as he had proven skills honed in the forests of Bavaria, hunting red deer and wild boar with his father. He had received special training in Prussia at the outbreak of war.

About 700 yards away from the Wiltshires, a lone figure moved stealthily out of the German front-line trenches. He moved from shell hole to shell hole. Mindful of the British observers, Kurt was dressed in a makeshift suit of hessian, the same material used for filling sandbags.

Previously he had daubed the material with clay, and light green and brown paint, designed to blend in with the surroundings. He wore a hood with eye holes cut out, and a slit for breathing. Where possible he had wrapped thin cloth around his Gewehr 98 Rifle, and painted the material in a similar way to his outer clothing.

It was Kurt's intention to deploy for two to three days if circumstances permitted. He had food and water for this period and an ample amount of .323 Spitzer cartridges (8mm). Amongst his ammunition were special bullets that he had adapted, with a pair of plyers. He had removed the pointed lead ball from the case, and then pushed the pointed end first into the brass casing of the cartridge. He had carefully crimped the case around the lead projectile so it would stay in place.

Kurt had done this for a specific reason, because over the last 12 months, his regiment had been confronted with British Mark IV and Mark V tanks. He had learnt that at close range, he could fire these blunt nosed ('dumb, dumbs') at areas of the tank that had thinner armour, and at the spy holes in the tank.

On previous occasions the German Intelligence Unit had examined abandoned British tanks, and as a consequence they knew all the weak areas where the armour plating was thinnest. This valuable information was passed on to all the front-line units. In the next few days of battle, if confronted with tanks, he would use these bullets as a last resort, prior to retreating. Kurt also had half a dozen iron core bullets which would also be used for the same purpose.

His brief was to cover the retreat of his regiment. He and those that remained behind, were to become the rear guard. Part of his tasks would be to protect the machine gun teams, and cover their flanks. At least one other sniper was deployed to protect the flanks. Kurt would naturally take any opportunity to shoot at British officers, runners, artillery observers, and British machine gun units. This would have to be done in a measured way so as not to expose himself to hostile fire.

Kurt carefully moved forward towards the hide which he had finished the previous day. He had selected a partially buried carcase of a horse. The unfortunate beast had been killed by shrapnel several months previously. The rats and blue bottle fly larva had long since feasted on the flesh and stomach contents. However enough of the back bone and rib cage remained intact, and the outer carcase was still covered with brown hair. It was under this carcase that Kurt had carefully excavated a cavity for himself, this had been done under the cover of darkness the previous night. He was then able to place two steel plates, each about 7mm thick, measuring about 900mm square, about three feet apart. The first plate directly faced the British front-line trenches, the second was placed at an angle of 30 degrees clockwise to the first plate.

On the previous day, with Kurt's guidance, the farrier behind the German lines had carefully cut out a groove to accommodate Kurt's rifle and scope in each of the loop holes, the second plate having a much bigger aperture.

Having fitted the steel plates, Kurt secured them by piling mounds of earth either side of them, and as high as the horse's carcase. The weather was still dry, and the freshly moved soil would have time to dry out and blend in with the other soil, so as not to alert the watchful eyes of a British sniper or observer.

The two apertures gave Kurt a view down no man's land towards the British trenches. The scope of the view would give him a 60-degree arc

*Having read this Chapter, this is my neighbours' interpretation
of what the hide would have looked like*

of fire. The second loop hole would enable him to cover the German machine gun team to his right. His position was such that the land in front of him sloped down towards the British front-line. His gun had been 'zeroed' to a range of 300 yards. On the top of his telescopic sights was a circular adjustment for elevation. Kurt had become so familiar with his gun, that if he had to adjust the range, he knew precisely which way to turn the adjuster and how far.

As Kurt neared the hide, British flares lit the skies above him, but he remained still, some 20 yards away from the hide. The flares did not concern him, but experience had taught him to be patient and not to compromise his position. As the light dimmed, he was able to crawl the remaining distance to the hide.

On arrival he instinctively checked the outer facing surface of the loop holes to see if they had been fired upon by armour piercing bullets from a sharp-eyed British sniper. The loop holes remained intact. This fact gave Kurt confidence in the knowledge that his hide had not yet been discovered. Kurt knew that when the sun came up later that morning, any dew would soon evaporate. The soil around the aperture of his loop holes would be left dry, and this dry soil would be prone to turn into a small dust cloud following a shot fired from his rifle. His field craft had taught him to urinate on the soil to dampen the dust around this aperture.

This same field craft had taught him to be aware of bright sun shine, and the effect this had on the front facing lens of his telescopic sights. Some of his comrades had been compromised by the dazzling reflection of their sights on bright sunny days. Kurt had learnt not to present his sights until the midday sun was behind his hide.

Kurt slowly moved around to the back of his hide and entered. He pulled the flaps of the hessian curtain which was hanging in the entrance. The curtain was necessary as experience had taught Kurt that any light coming from the rear of the hide could reveal his silhouette to any advancing Tommie's or sharp-eyed British snipers. So, having straightened the hessian curtain behind him, he then moved inside the hide, removed the leather lens caps of his 'Otto Bocke' telescopic sights, and he again checked the views down the apertures. The 4x magnification did not work especially well in the hours of darkness, and sadly for him there was no full moon tonight.

An occasional flare would illuminate no man's land. When this happened, he would maximise the opportunity to survey his field of fire. He would be on the lookout for anything unusual or suspicious, and any slight movement would alert him to the possible presence of an enemy sniper, one of the the biggest threats to his survival, the other being exploding shells.

Kurt would avoid shooting in the hours of darkness, unless it was absolutely necessary. Firing his rifle would cause a flash of light which could easily reveal his position. The British observers were using powerful telescopes. Their operators would naturally be on the lookout for rifle flashes. Some of these telescopes had been captured. Kurt had resisted the temptation of using one. He found them too long and cumbersome in a confined space, and preferred to use his German Fernglas 08 binoculars.

He took some small comfort knowing he was not alone. There was a machine gun team to his right, and another sniper to his left. The five-man team with their heavy water-cooled Maxim machine gun had reassembled the weapon the previous day, and every effort had been made to camouflage its location. They had been made aware of Kurt's presence in the area. They too, were reassured by the knowledge that 'he had their backs' but nothing would be able to protect any of them against accurate shell fire.

Kurt had positioned himself slightly back of the machine gun unit, so as not to interfere with their line of fire. It would only be a matter of time before the khaki uniforms came out of their trenches to pursue the retreating German Army.

The German rear guard waited for daylight. The time was 04.30 hours, and at this time of year it would not be daylight until about 07.20 hours. Belgium and North-Eastern France were about one hour ahead of British Summer Time.

Kurt Schülter would have a little under three hours to wait for sunrise. He put the time to good use by filling some hessian sacks with dry soil, which he placed in front of himself. He then placed two of these sacks

This is a captured German Maxim machine gun. As can be seen, it was a heavy weapon. Note the body armour which was often worn by the German troops. This photo is courtesy of the Staffordshire regimental Museum Whittington.

just below the apertures of the loop holes. He would use these sacks to rest the front end of his rifle on during firing. He had to balance the need for a steady stance when firing, otherwise movement and the arc of fire would be hindered. Operational circumstances quickly changed and different targets presented themselves at very short notice. This would be a common problem for snipers. Reaction speed and being able to fire at an identified target within two seconds was vital for success.

The position Kurt preferred was lying on his stomach, with the muzzle of the gun as near as possible to the aperture opening. He then attached the leather rifle carrying strap to the clip located at the fore-end of the barrel. He would grip the first four inches of the strap where it was attached to the clip with his left hand, and the uppermost part of his clenched left fist would support the fore-end of the gun. He would then place a small hessian bag partially filled with soil, under his left fist. This bag, the size of half a bag of sugar, would itself rest on top of the sandbag nearest the loop hole aperture. By holding the gun this way, he gained flexibility to alter the elevation of the gun. Movements of his hips and sliding his elbows on the smooth surface of the supporting hessian sacks, together with the subtle movement of his left fist, would all allow Kurt to move the rifle slightly to the left or right. These movements would be only slight, but over a long range, they would be significant, and allow Kurt to pick out targets with speed.

Over the last four years the muscle groups of his body had become accustomed to this firing position and Kurt managed to adopt this position for long periods of time. He would deliberately give himself brief rest periods by resting his eyes, turning sideways, and relaxing for short intervals. Prolonged periods of intense concentration proved to be very tiring for Kurt, so he learnt to manage his periods of observations, so as not to become too fatigued.

Kurt lay in his hide and pulled out his flask and took a small sip of his Schnapps. He pondered over the future. His morale had sunk to new depths, and there was not even an ounce of fat on his body. He had seen a decline in the food rations over the last eighteen months, and hunger pains were now part of everyday life in the trenches. His mind raced back to the months of March and April that year, when for a brief moment he let himself believe that this war could still be won. He remembered when the British supply depots had been captured, and coming across those sides of bacon and beef. His stomach began to rumble at the thought. It was three months since he had consumed a good meal. The German Generals had lied to their soldiers, telling them that the British were starving and on the brink of surrender.

The news from home was no better. Some of his friends returning from leave had told stories of families suffering from disease and malnutrition. There had been food riots in Berlin and other major cities.

Such were the shortages. Wounded soldiers in the field had little in the way of bandages for treating wounds. Captured British troops were by far better equipped with proper field dressings.

In the next few days, Kurt would try his best to slow any British advance, as and when it took place. Once his position in the hide had been compromised, he would move from shell hole to shell hole trying to cover the machine gun units' retreat, should this be necessary. Retreat was inevitable. Kurt had heard rumours that the army was retreating back to the Hindenburg Line.

If the situation became impossible, Kurt's plan was to discard his sniper's rifle and camouflage clothing and hide under a dead German body. Once the advancing British troops passed him, he would surrender himself to the stretcher bearers. He had simply had enough.

This plan was necessary as he had witnessed more than one of his comrades being shot. The khaki soldiers had ignored the snipers' pleas for mercy. The snipers had been shot at point blank range by British soldiers, who were hell bent on revenge. The Germans both feared and hated the Scottish soldiers who showed little mercy to captured prisoners.

Action begins

It was now 05.25 hours and Sergeant Burchell had synchronised his watch with those of the other NCOs. It was imperative that everyone's timepiece told the same time. This procedure naturally went as far back as headquarters and the artillery gun crews behind the lines. In the events that followed, timing was of the essence.

At 5.30am the field guns of the 19th Western Division erupted into action. The Division had about 75 Guns in total, and of these 54 would be 18lb field guns, a tried and trusted weapon of the British Army. On this morning there were piles of shrapnel shells stacked next to each gun ready for use.

These shells were designed to explode in the air. Having been fitted with type 80 fuses, each shell contained dozens of steel balls, which, following explosion, spread in a cone-shaped area below, very much like the dispersal from a shotgun cartridge.

The early models of the 18lb field gun had a range of between 6,000 to 8,000 yards. The guns would have been deployed in rows behind the British front-line under camouflage. Their arc of fire had been carefully

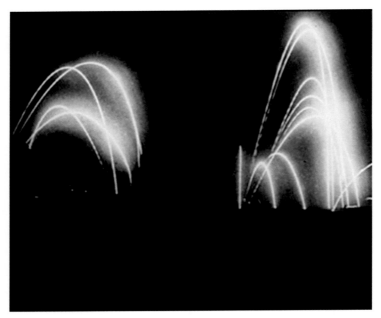

This picture shows an artillery barrage during darkness. Note the different trajectories of the shells. The highest are likely to be Howitzers or heavy trench mortars, the lower trajectories are likely to be the field guns.

calculated, designed to cover as much width as possible of the front-line area across which the allied troops would eventually advance.

Imagine the five-man teams for each field gun. They would work frantically to load, fire, and unload, a routine which they had perfected over the last four years. A good team could fire up to twenty rounds per minute. However, during prolonged fire, this would need to be slowed down to four to five rounds per minute, as the gun would rapidly overheat, expand and firing mechanisms would jam. If the advance was successful, the gun teams would have to hitch the horses up to the guns to move them forward in pace with the advance. Speed was of the essence.

As a consequence, during this first minute of the bombardment, upwards of over 1,000 shells were exploding in the air above the German rear guard, literally thousands upon thousands of steel balls travelling at the speed of bullets towards the Germans below. In the mayhem that followed, observers reported the accuracy of fire, and noted the gun teams' ability to make fine adjustments as necessary. Each minute counted, and minor changes were made to the sights and elevation settings as necessary, so that the range was extended 100 yards further on, at minute intervals. This procedure was necessary to maintain the creeping barrage.

The effect of this barrage was to suppress the Germans' returning fire. Their natural reaction was to take cover from the flying shrapnel balls, which would cause horrific injuries and death if they hit the body. This vital protection enabled the 58th Brigade to move forward to its objectives, and casualties were minimised.

Ernest and the 2nd Wiltshires could see the night sky light up with tracer shells exploding in front of them. To distract himself, Ernest hammered two small stakes in the wall of the trench, each side of the trench ladder, to prevent it from falling over under the mad rush that was bound to follow the sound of the whistle.

The initial barrage lasted for three minutes. The range finders had calculated the shells to explode 200 yards in front of the British front-line trench. On this day, their maths had been correct. On the fourth minute of the barrage, the artillery crews adjusted the elevation setting on their guns to fire the shells another 100 yards further. This marked the commencement of the creeping barrage. The range would be extended 100 yards every minute thereafter.

Ernest shouted to his men over the sound of the bursts of the shells 'Remember lads, to keep pace with me, don't go too fast, and whatever you do, don't get too near to the barrage, keep a constant distance behind it!'

Ernest's trench was now crowded with soldiers of the 2nd Wiltshires. Adrenalin was rushing through their veins, their hearts were pumping in their chests, and they all fought to control and steady their breathing, as the time was rapidly approaching when they would go over the top.

A shout came out 'Make space for the stretcher bearers!' The soldiers knew this was the last order given before the whistle blew.

Many would ignore these medics, some would even be strangely hostile towards them. Perhaps it was the dreaded reality that within minutes of going over the top, they would be their first patients.

The time was 05.40 hours, the Second Lieutenant blew his whistle, and the men climbed the ladders. Ernest was the first up. He was closely followed by the others who having reached the top of the ladder began to fan out in formation. With fixed bayonets at the ready, the men moved forward.

An initial lack of response from the Germans

Kurt lay in his hide, totally unaware of the impending bombardment. He checked his watch, it was 05.25 hours, and all was quiet in no man's land. He rested his eyes briefly and took his eyes away from his rifle sights. He wondered how far his regiment had retreated.

All of a sudden, the skies lit up, followed by the all too familiar crescendo of exploding shells. These appeared to be shrapnel shells as they were bursting about 30 feet up in the air. It was difficult in this light to tell the colour of the smoke. Kurt would be forever on guard for the first signs of a gas attack. He instinctively reached to his side and touched his gas mask pouch for reassurance. He then sniffed at the air through the loop hole, to check for the presence of gas. All he could smell was cordite fumes.

It was not long before the smoke from hundreds of exploding shells started to impair his view of the British trenches, which were about 650 yards away. Any signs of weariness had instantly evaporated, and Kurt was in a state of high alert. He readjusted the focus on his sights in an attempt to penetrate the thickening smoke. If only it would get light, he muttered to himself.

A couple of minutes elapsed, and Kurt sensed something was wrong, but what was it? Then it suddenly struck him. His own artillery was not responding. Were they still on the move? Had they not yet had time to deploy? Kurt began to grow concerned as he shifted slightly to his right in order to look through the second loop hole at the machine gun team.

He saw a feint sign of movement, indicating that they were still in position. They were clearly conserving their ammunition. This time there would be no restocking from their support trenches. At 500-600 rounds per minute, their supply would not last for long. Kurt turned again and looked through the forward-facing loop hole. He sensed that the artillery barrage was coming nearer, this was it! The British had commenced a creeping barrage. This could only mean one thing; an infantry attack was imminent!

The British advance

With adrenalin pumping through their veins the 2nd Wiltshires make steady progress. A few minutes into the advance, an old trench system comes into view ahead of them. Surprisingly the 'Bosch' have not yet opened up. More significantly there is no response from their artillery, other than sporadic misdirected fire to the right of their brigade line.

A young soldier nervously calls out 'What's happened to the Bosch?' He is instantly rebuked by Ernest, who shouts 'Keep your concentration. You'll see him soon enough!'

At that moment the familiar sound of the German Maxims begin their deadly rattle. The air instantly fills with the hiss of lead bullets as they whiz past the soldiers' heads. Instinctively the Tommie's stoop slightly as they continue moving forward. There is a brief respite as the German machine gunners correct their aim. The lead team of advancing soldiers make it to the old shallow trench system, they instinctively dive forwards and bury their heads against the walls of the trench for cover. Sergeant Burchell is in this first group.

Sergeant 208242 Burchell took brief shelter in the old shallow trench. He allowed himself to catch his breath and steady his breathing. His men in their desperation to dive into the trenches had nearly caught up with the creeping barrage. Some of the young soldier's stare at Ernest, waiting for his next move. He winks at a couple of them to try to reassure them. Lead balls from exploding shells hiss overhead. Ernest fights to control his own nerves.

The night skies light up with German flares. The element of surprise had only been brief, and the German machine gunners were fully alert and firing at will. Ernest's nerves remained steady, much to his surprise. He had to keep his men focussed. Less than half a minute elapsed when the shout came out, 'Advance! Move on!'

The men stood up immediately. Ernest glanced around him. He could feel his heart pounding under his tunic. He was so proud to be in their company. If ever there was a moment when he felt genuine love for these brave men, it was now. They all moved forward as one, ready and determined to meet whatever fate or glory had in store for them.

The darkness had now been replaced by the artificial lights of the German flares. They cast shadows on the soldiers as they moved forward. Occasionally a flare would fall, with its small parachute attached, lasting 10-15 seconds before hitting the ground. Ernest guessed that the machine gun teams ahead would have several boxes of flares to hand. By firing two or three flares every minute, the corridor through which the British were advancing was illuminated. This was their killing field.

The forward German machine gun teams had a brief window of opportunity to litter the 'killing field' with British soldiers, before the creeping barrage was on top of them. They then had the choice of hoping they were not hit, and that the barrage passed behind them. Alternatively, they could withdraw, exposing themselves to Lee Enfield and Lewis Gun fire. This would not be an easy choice to make, but they also had another choice.

The machine gun bullets started to take their deadly toll. Far to Ernest's left men started to fall. Some shouted out in agony for help. Their comrades were made to carry on. They were not allowed to stop and assist their friends.

Ernest had taken the precaution of carrying his Lee Enfield rifle. He had seen too many NCOs killed by snipers, because they were carrying their Webley and Scott revolvers. They must have stood out to the ever-watchful German snipers. The only thing that gave Ernest's rank away were the three strips on each arm of his tunic, which in this light would have been difficult to see.

The Wiltshires carried on up the gentle slope towards the German lines. Today was different. Their progress was not hampered by exploding German shells. Some men stumbled and fell over. It was difficult to hear them cursing in the din of the battle.

The Germans continue to hold their ground

The German Maxim machine gun team was now on their second box of cartridges. At this rate they would run out of ammunition within two to three hours. The barrels of the gun were becoming ever hotter. There was always the risk that the gun would jam and be rendered useless. Shortages were such that they had no spare gun to call upon. In the cool damp air before daylight, the hot barrels started to reveal a small cloud of steam. The water-cooling system was at its limits with the constant firing of the old gun. To have poured water over these barrels would increase the risk of revealing their position, but the muzzle flash of the gun would soon be spotted by British snipers anyway. There would come a time when the water option would have to be considered and if there was no water, they would try to urinate over the barrels, as a last resort.

These desperate measures were necessary if only to delay the advancing British soldiers. Behind the German lines other traps were being set. There would be other machine gunners deployed further back, and some troopers would be armed with light machine guns for greater manoeuvrability. There would also be other snipers deployed. Booby traps would be set, and trip wires would detonate carefully concealed explosives.

As each minute went by the risk of being targeted by British snipers grew and grew. These had for some time been using armour piercing bullets to penetrate loop holes. As the British advance drew nearer to them, there would be the added danger of hand grenades, to be precise, Mills bombs.

About 200 yards to their left, Kurt Schlüter lay still in his hide. The time for killing was now upon him. With the illumination of no man's land in front, together with the noise of the barrage and the constant flashes from explosions, he had an ideal window of opportunity to carry out his deadly skills, before he was eventually compromised.

The British would be distracted by concentrating their efforts on pinpointing the German machine gun emplacement. Kurt worked his scopes to focus on a suitable target, as he understood the need to maximise this opportunity. At 400 yards the ghostly figures of the British infantry started to appear in view. His first shot failed, and he was about to squeeze his trigger again, when the khaki soldier fell to the ground, hit by a machine gun bullet.

More and more targets presented themselves. Several soldiers started to cluster in order to pass between two shell holes. Kurt took aim at the lead soldier. In that split second the reticule of his sights zeroed on the centre of his chest, he squeezed the trigger, and the effect was instant. The front soldier fell to the ground, but immediately behind him, another soldier also slumped to the ground holding his chest. Kurt had experienced this shot several times before. He wondered if both soldiers were dead but could not allow himself to ponder on this thought as he worked the bolt action of his rifle and rapidly placed another round in the breach.

Within those few seconds the advancing soldiers were another fifty paces nearer to the Maxim machine gun, a couple of the British soldiers knelt briefly to fire their Lee Enfields. They had spotted the machine gun hide. As they reloaded, other soldiers continued to move forward. Soon they would be in range for the bombers to hurl their Mills bombs.

Ernest is wounded

The Wiltshires were making good progress as they moved further up the slope. The land had dried out under the hot summer days, and instead of mud sticking to their boots, the soldiers kicked up dust as they advanced. The shell holes were nearly empty of water. What remained had a disgusting green film of algae floating on the top. Months of shell fire from both sides had littered the land with numerous craters, some of which were so close together that it slowed the advancing soldiers. Naturally they had no desire to stand the risk of being sucked into the mud and green scum at the bottom of these shell holes. Much to Ernest's concern, the forward units began to cluster as they negotiated their way through these hazards. They presented themselves as an irresistible target.

Yet there was no alternative, because they had to maintain the momentum. A rifleman slowed in front of Ernest as he approached a gap between the two nearest shell holes. Ernest was slow to alter his stride and he nearly collided with this rifleman. At this moment, in a split second, Ernest felt a stinging sensation in the right upper part of his chest, instantly followed by a heavy shock wave reverberating around his upper body, which caused him to slump forward. He briefly saw the rifleman in front of him fall. Ernest's eyes sensed the ground rushing up to meet him as he hit the earth and rolled sideways, facing upwards.

Ernest lay on his back facing the bright lights of battle above him. Delirium was beginning to set in. He was fighting to stay conscious.

He briefly recognised the voice of young Henry Stubbs from his platoon 'The Sergeant's down! What are we going to do?' Another voice shouted 'Sorry lad, we can't stop, the medics will find him!'.

One of the last memories Ernest had prior to losing consciousness, was seeing his rifle, bayonet end first, stuck into the earth at the side of him, a hand reached over him and placed his steel helmet to hang by the strap to the stock of the rifle. Private Henry Stubbs (fictitious name) had done this in the hope that the medics behind them would see his sergeant's body and come quickly to his aid. Some of the soldiers did this to stop the tank drivers from driving over wounded soldiers.

Ernest lay on his back, the noise of the battle continued further up the slope, the sky was flashing with so many colours that for a brief moment it seemed surreal. He fought to remain conscious but his inner strength that he had called upon so many times in recent months, was now beginning to ebb away.

Then came the pain, at first it was a burning numbness, then it intensified because two off his ribs had been splintered by the Mauser bullet. It was no small miracle that he was still alive. The poor Private in front of him had taken the full force of the bullet which would have hit his body at 2,880 feet per second. The kinetic energy on impact would have been around 2,935 joules. The Private had died almost instantly but there was enough velocity remaining in this bullet, to pass straight through him and penetrate Ernest standing immediately behind him. The bullet had indeed slowed by the time it reached Ernest, but it had still broken two ribs in his chest. These ribs had also absorbed some of the energy, and the bullet had buried itself in his right lung. Consequently, there was no exit wound.

As Ernest lay in no man's land his thoughts turned to home, and that beautiful image of the farmer's daughter in Hartshorne. He wanted to reach for her photo inside his tunic, but he did not have the strength. The slow reality that he could be dying began to set in. He did not want to die. He had survived so many battles, surely this wasn't the end?

Ernest began to feel a tingling sensation in his extremities. He tried to move the fingers in his hands. He would not have known this but Mother

Nature was trying to help him. His body was adjusting, his vascular system was shunting his blood to the core of his body in order to protect his vital organs, and as a consequence his extremities were now having to cope with less blood.

Ernest thought he was dying. As he lay there, tears formed and started to trickle down his dirty face, and he blinked constantly, struggling to focus his eyes. Convincing him even further of his impending doom, he started to find difficulty in breathing. As much as he tried, he struggled to fill his lungs with air, and the stabbing pains increased with each breath.

Ernest's right lung was beginning to collapse. The bullet had ruptured the pleural membrane that encased his lungs, and air was being sucked into his body cavity through the bullet hole in his chest. If he didn't have urgent help soon, he would surely die! In the last seconds of his consciousness, he muttered 'God bless my family and Elizabeth'.

Ernest closed his eyes for the last time that day. His senses vaguely perceived a person walking to his side and then there was silence and darkness.

Kurt surrenders

Further up the slope, the situation was becoming critical for the German rear guard. The barrage was about 200 yards away and advancing closer. The intensity of exploding shells was still relentless. Nerves were beginning to fray.

Kurt Schlüter looked out of the side loop hole at the machine gun hide to his right. The soil ramparts were now taking hits from the .303 Enfield's. Kurt could hear the familiar short bursts of a Lewis Machine gun. He frantically searched his field of view for this lethal weapon. The two-man Lewis gun team were well concealed, probably under the rim of a shell hole. As much as he tried, he failed to locate them. Kurt made a sudden decision to leave his hide and move backwards slightly to see if the Lewis gun team were further over to the left of his forward-facing loop hole.

He threw caution to the wind and ran as fast has he could about 50 yards back to a large shell hole and jumped inside. He peered over the rim of the crater between two large clods of earth. The shrapnel shells were now hitting the makeshift soil roof of the machine gun hide. The occupants inside would have but a short time to consider their next move. Then, all of a sudden, the gun felt silent. The soldiers in khaki uniform sensed some advantage and increased their pace. Two Mills bombs landed just short of the machine gun hide and exploded. Then Kurt behaved totally out of character. Instead of giving covering fire and targeting these advancing soldiers, he just lay there, watching the events unfold.

The British artillery gunners, having yet again adjusted their sights, were now sending shells behind Kurt's position. In the minutes that followed he saw a rifle with a white handkerchief attached. This appeared out of the machine gun dug out. It waved backwards and forwards frantically.

The British soldiers approached with caution, after all this could be a trap. Before they reached the soil mound, four Germans appeared, one holding the rifle in the air. A tall well-built khaki soldier trembling with rage in his eyes shouted 'Hände hoch!' The team of gunners complied instantly, one of them dropping the rifle to the ground. They all held their hands up in the air in act of compliance.

Then Kurt held his breath, half expecting a volley of shots that would be the end of his comrades, but to his amazement, the German soldiers were spared. All four were frisked for small arms, weapons and knives. It was now common practice to seize mementos like cigarette lighters, fags and watches before their NCOs could put a stop to it. Kurt had a few minutes while the British soldiers were preoccupied going through the pockets of his comrades' uniforms.

Whilst the attentions of the British soldiers were elsewhere, Kurt threw his rifle to the bottom of the shell hole. Beneath the surface of the water, he took off his outer camouflage clothing, and then crudely wrapped the hessian clothes around some large clods of earth. They too were thrown into the stagnant green water where they sank beneath the surface. Bubbles emerged letting off a pungent smell that briefly made Kurt convulse as he readjusted his grey tunic. He placed his army cloth cap on his head, took out his soiled dirty white handkerchief and held it in the air, as he exited the shell hole and shouted across to the British 'Ich will mich auch ergeben!' (I too surrender).

Ernest's stretcher is carried by the German Prisoners of War

Daylight was approaching, and the group of soldiers stood together, five in grey uniforms and eight soldiers of the Wiltshire Battalion. The Second Lieutenant, seeing this group, strode across to organise them all. 'I want two volunteers to escort these prisoners back, and one to carry the barrel of this Maxim.' Hands were flung in the air, but before anyone had time to speak, Henry Stubbs shouted, 'Sir, can I volunteer?' Henry had an ulterior motive and was quick to make himself ready. The Lieutenant accepted the offer and quickly nominated two others for the tasks. The three British soldiers were instructed to hand over the four German prisoners to the intelligence liaison officer and to hand the Maxim gun to the regimental quartermaster at their first opportunity.

The group of eight soldiers then made their way back to the British lines. Henry Stubbs deliberately chose a reciprocal route hoping that he would come across Ernest's body. After five minutes of marching back, Henry's spirits were lifted. Not only was Ernest's rifle still stuck in the ground where he had left it, but a stretcher bearer was kneeling at the side of his Sergeant's body, frantically trying to cut through Ernest's outer clothing with his scissors.

As the group of eight approached, the stretcher bearer shouted out 'Come over here, quick lads. I think we can save this one, if we can get him back in time!'

They all stood next to Ernest who was unconscious. The stretcher had been laid next to him. With a gentle movement they slid him on to the stretcher. Without prompting, two of the Germans stooped down and picked up each end of the stretcher. The British soldiers were stunned by this act of benevolence. The stretcher bearer walked alongside Ernest as he was carried by the Germans back towards the British trenches. He had heard air being sucked in through the bullet hole and had been instructed in these circumstances to hold a field dressing with pressure over the wound in order to seal it and stop air entering. This was quite common with chest injuries, and by following this instruction from the Medical Officers at the Battalion Aid Post he was giving Ernest a fighting chance of survival.

Ernest's injuries

Whilst this party of soldiers was conveying Ernest back to the 58th Brigadel Aid Post, Ernest's fate was still in the balance. Would he die from shock, as so many others had done before him? Would his breathing deteriorate further, to such an extent that he literally suffocated? Would his lungs fill with blood, and would he drown in his own fluids?

When the bullet went through Ernest's muddy and dusty tunic, a small amount of germ-ridden fibres would have been forced in the wound. Within hours this would develop into a serious infection causing a rapid rise in his temperature. The condition of septicaemia (blood poisoning) would be a constant risk to Ernest. The earth in no man's land was full of pathogenic organisms. Many soldiers died of tetanus, tuberculosis and typhoid and many other soil-borne infections.

Having scrutinised Ernest's medical records, I have discovered that he had been vaccinated on the 7th of February 1916. This is likely to have been against tetanus and typhus. This would to some extent have improved his chances of survival. However, there was a real risk of Ernest haemorrhaging, and literally bleeding to death.

The list goes on. The odds were stacked against him, but survive he did!

The outcome of the battle

Meanwhile the battle raged on, and the 2nd Wiltshires and the 19th Western Division made massive territorial gains on that day. From just outside

Locon to where they eventually called a halt, was, in my estimation, at least four miles. They can be proud of their successes this day, as they captured five enemy machine guns and a total of fifty prisoners. It's quite conceivable that one of the German prisoners captured could have been responsible for shooting Ernest, the truth is we will never know.

The new headquarters had been set up at Harrow Post, in an old British trench, north-west of Neuve-Chapelle. Finally, these battle-weary soldiers could rest and take in food and water.

This success, however, had come at a price. The 2nd Wiltshires had sustained eighteen wounded and six killed. I name these six fatalities because some may well have fought with Ernest, and may have been his friends, some may well have been killed at the same time that Ernest was shot:

36207 William Allen
29249 Alfred Bailey
35071 William Bedford
28201 Charles Best
28216 Walter Fender
28234 Herbert Richardson
19364 Arthur William

You will note that I have listed seven soldiers, there appears to be a discrepancy with the 2nd Wiltshire Diary which states six soldiers killed, but the Roll of honour lists seven soldiers died on the 3rd of September 1918, I can only conclude that one of the soldiers may have died who was not involved in this advance on the Germans but died in different circumstances.

As already stated, the names of Kurt Schlüter and Henry Stubbs are fictional and any resemblance to anyone real is purely coincidental.

There are a number of different possibilities as to how Ernest was shot and under what circumstances. I only ask you as the reader to consider that this account may be one of those options.

I could have invented a story without acknowledging that it was not necessarily true. You, the reader, would be none the wiser. I believe in honesty, and the truth is that Grandad may have talked about the subject briefly during an afternoon tea in the farmhouse, but I can no longer remember any exact details. I do know that he was definitely convinced that he had been shot by a German sniper. In the next chapter I will examine the different options, given the facts that are available.

Chapter 10

Ernest's treatment

The team of stretcher bearers and prisoners made their way back towards the British lines. Their aim was to reach the Regimental Aid Post (RAP) as soon as possible, the likely place of its location being the area of Locon or Hinges. This was no walk in the park as they would have to negotiate shell craters, barbed wire defences, broken tree stumps, and climb in and out of narrow trench systems. All of this was under the constant threat of sniper fire and exploding shells.

These RAPs could be ruins of an old church, or other buildings, or parts of buildings that offered some form of shelter against the elements and of course flying shrapnel. The RAP could be even a tent over a dugout.

Upon their arrival, the German prisoners would be taken to the rear, and Ernest would be laid out at the end of a row of other wounded soldiers. By now the stretcher bearer would have filled in a Field Medical Card. This would contain vital information as to the identity of the patient and his battalion, as well as the extent of his injuries and their location, and any treatment administered, including medication. This last bit of information was vital, because the stretcher bearer would have placed a quarter grain morphine tablet under Ernest's tongue (*sub lineal*). It was vital that this information was accurately recorded, because mistakes could easily lead to subsequent overdoses and fatalities. It was also vital that this medical card was securely attached to Ernest because its loss could also have serious consequences.

This procedure would assist the Medical Officer (MO) to carry out a prompt triage of his patients, a process which basically entailed assessing and prioritising patients' needs for treatment.

They would be divided into groups from; those whose death was unavoidable, those requiring urgent lifesaving attention, all the way through to the walking wounded, and soldiers not needing urgent treatment. Sadly, during some of the major battles of the war, the MOs were put under so much pressure through sheer weight of numbers and time constraints that they often made very brief assessments. Their on the spot decisions could literally mean life or death for the poor man on the stretcher.

On this day the numbers were manageable, and Ernest would have a fighting chance of survival. It would be the MO's job to keep Ernest alive until the ambulance could take him to the Casualty Clearing Station (CCS). The stretcher bearer would then return to the battlefield to recover more wounded soldiers and repeat the process. The return walk back to the RAP was referred to as 'a carry'.

As in all battles there would be other stretcher teams, known as the Sanitary Squads. It was their task to recover the dead bodies for subsequent burial.

The ambulance crews had the task to convey Ernest and the other wounded soldiers to the Casualty Clearing Station (CCS). I have tried

I took this picture of a typical ambulance during the Passchendaele commemoration in 2017

to identify which CCS this could have been. On Grandad's records, the place name La Bassée is mentioned, but I cannot find any record of there being a CCS in this town. One possibility was Number 9 CCS located at Hazebrouck, situated about 10 miles north of Hinges. It makes sense because there was a railway station in this town.

The ambulance used for this task is likely to have been part of the 58th Brigade Field Ambulance of the Royal Army Medical Corps attached to the 19th Western Division. Earlier on in the war horse drawn ambulances were also used. It is possible that some were still in use when Grandad was wounded.

I cannot say for certainty when Ernest Burchell arrived at the CCS, but due to the severity of his condition, I would like to think that it was on the same day that he was wounded, the 3rd of September 1918.

I am trying to picture the scene upon his arrival at No 9 CCS at Hazebrouck. There would be several tents with row upon row of beds. In general, there would be at least six doctors and support staff, including 25-30 nurse's, nursing auxiliaries, anaesthetists, and of course the Padre. To the rear of these tents would be the Moribund Ward. Soldiers were placed in this tent when all hope of a recovery had faded. They still had care but were allowed to pass away in as much dignity as circumstances permitted. To the rear of this tent would be the nurses' quarters and wash tents, where the bed linen and soldiers' clothes were cleaned.

A further triage would be carried out on arrival here. During this process the nurses would try to clean Ernest's body and strip him of his filthy lice-ridden clothes. It would also be important to collect all his personal possessions for safe keeping.

The most important considerations were:

1) To carry out cannular decompression, and by doing so, allow Ernest's right lung to reinflation back to its normal size. This would be a temporary fix.
2) To determine the need for a blood transfusion, dependent on blood loss. This could be done during an operation or post operation.

3) To rehydrate Ernest's body by administering a saline intravenous drip. This would bring his blood pressure back to normal, assuming there was no major pulmonary bleed in the body cavity.
4) To remove the bullet at the first opportunity.
5) To minimize the risk of infection whilst conducting all of the above procedures.

In case you are wondering, no, I am not a doctor, but I have the privilege of having a family friend who is an eminent surgeon in Leicestershire. There are full details in the acknowledgements. He has advised me of the likely treatment which Ernest would have received, given the facts that are available to us.

The large bore cannula decompression would have involved inserting a special needle with a sheath surrounding it. The doctor would measure a distance halfway along Ernest's right collar bone. Having done this, he would then feel for the top rib and then move down two further ribs to the top side of the third rib. It would be important to locate the top side, because on the bottom edge of each rib is a series of blood vessels which supply the rib cage. The needle would be inserted as near as possible to the top edge of the third rib, avoiding the bottom edge of the second rib for the reasons stated.

Having established this position, the doctor would insert the cannular needle three to four inches into Ernest's chest. The point of the needle would pierce the pleural membrane which surrounded the collapsed lung. Inside this cavity would be trapped air, or both air and blood, which over a period of time would put excessive pressure on the major blood vessels and heart, decreasing venous return and thus reducing the heart's capacity to function. If not treated in time this condition, a tension pneumothorax, was often fatal.

Having punctured the membrane, the doctor would remove the needle, leaving the sheath inserted. This would allow trapped blood and air to escape and result in the right lung being able to re inflate, thus allowing normal breathing to resume. The amount of air or blood escaping the sheath following cannula decompression would give an indication to the doctor if Grandad had either pneumothorax or haemothorax, or a combination of both.

I hope I am not going into too much detail for you as the reader, but I was curious to know what these marvellous people did to save Grandad. Remember that in previous battles, in the winter months, these procedures would have been carried out wearing mud covered wellies. Sometimes the staff would be ankle deep in mud, and under constant threat of exploding shells and flying shrapnel! A number of nurses and doctors were killed whilst trying to carry out lifesaving operations. Lest we forget.

Mother Nature designed our lungs to be contained within a membrane which surrounds each lung. This feature creates what doctors refer to as negative pressure. In layman's terms, the atmospheric pressure outside the body is higher than the pressure inside the lung cavity, consequently inflating the lungs is made a lot easier. When that pressure is disrupted, as in Grandad's case, then the affected lung can collapse making breathing very difficult and stressful. This condition is called a pneumothorax.

The other condition is haemothorax. This occurs when blood vessels are punctured in the pleural cavity, which leads to haemorrhaging. This causes a build-up of pressure in the pleural cavity. In Ernest's case the bullet had embedded itself in his lungs. The lungs are vascular, in other words they have many blood vessels and a rich blood supply.

It is the considered opinion of my friend that, given the size of Grandad's scar on his chest, and its location, together with the time he would have spent wounded in no man's land, plus the time it took for him to be conveyed to the CCS, the likelihood is that Ernest suffered from a pneumothorax. Had it been a significant haemothorax, it is highly likely that Grandad would have haemorrhaged and bled to death within five to ten minutes of sustaining the wound.

I have to say that Ernest was very lucky to have been shot on the right side of his chest, and towards the top of his chest. Had it been the left-hand side, the chances are that the bullet would have penetrated his heart or major blood vessels in that area, in particular the aorta. The rib cage protects vital organs and, in this case, the ribs would have absorbed a lot of the velocity from the bullet. Perhaps this was another reason why the bullet did not pass straight through Grandad.

Marie Curie

Before I consider the next phase of his life saving treatment, I want to devote part of this chapter to a very special lady of her time. Her work during World War 1 no doubt helped to save countless lives, including that of Ernest Burchell.

Like so many of you reading this book, I have strongly supported any cancer charities over the years. I have received charity leaflets with the Daffodil Appeal associated with a woman named Marie Curie. I just assumed this woman was some way involved with the fund raising. How wrong can a person be! In every generation there are 20-30 people who make a massive difference to people's lives for generations that follow. This lady and her husband certainly rank in the top 10 of their generation.

Born in 1857 in Warsaw, which is now in Poland, Marie became fascinated with all the sciences. Because of the discrimination against women at the time, she was not allowed to study in her native country. She chose to move to Paris to study at La Sorbonne, and it was here that she met a fellow scientist Pierre Curie whom she later married in 1895.

The two devoted their studies on the radiation properties of plutonium. Their pioneering work enabled them to isolate radioactive elements from uranium ore known as pitchblende. Their dedicated work eventually led to the discovery of two new elements, namely radium and polonium. Marie named this second element after her native country.

In recognition of their tireless devotion to science, Marie and Pierre were awarded the Noble Prize for Physics. Marie had become the first women to receive this accolade. The subsequent funding which they received allowed them to do further research into the effects of radioactivity on living cells, and the field of radiation treatment for cancer.

Sadly in 1906, Marie's husband was run over and killed by a horse and carriage. This tragic loss did not deter Marie, who continued her work. In 1911 she was again recognised for her skills and devotion in being awarded a second Nobel Prize for Chemistry. In this same year she used another invention of Wilhelm Conrad Röntgen, the X-ray machine, and sought to evaluate its use in surgery.

Marie Curie was aware that the British had used X-ray machines in the Second Boer War. She theorised that portable X-ray machines, if deployed to the front- line, could save lives in future wars. At the outbreak of World War 1, her efforts had made it possible to install mobile X-ray machines in motorised field ambulances, powered by portable generators.

Marie Curie went to the Western Front, and personally trained over 150 nurses in the use of these valuable machines. She was hands-on, and she was capable of installing these machines and connecting them to the generators herself. Furthermore, she even funded a lot of the ambulances and the equipment out of her own pocket. So now in 1918 there were X-ray machines at the CCS, as well as staff who were trained to use them.

Part of Ernest's treatment would have been X-ray images of his chest cavity in two positions, the first lying on his back, and the second when he was moved on his side. I am hoping that Grandad was still unconscious during this procedure, because had he been conscious, the pain in moving him would have been excruciating.

The two images obtained from the X-ray machines would tell the doctor if there was any severe haemorrhaging in the chest. They would also pinpoint the precise location of the bullet, and tell the doctor if Ernest's right lung had fully inflated again.

One option open to the doctor would be to use a 'rampley' or similar instrument. This is essentially an elongated pair of forceps, but instead of having a sharpened end, it had a grooved grip designed to locate the bullet. The surgeon would grip the bullet and carefully pull it out via the entry wound. In knowing the precise location of the bullet, the surgeon could extract it causing the minimum disruption to body tissue, and more importantly avoid open chest surgery. The speed of this procedure would allow the surgeon to use local anaesthetic by injecting the area around the bullet entry, thus avoiding the need to use general anaesthetic, which was not without its own risks to the patient.

I have no doubt that the X-ray machine made a significant impact on Grandad's chances of survival. The skills of the surgeon in extracting the bullet would also have been vital. It is estimated that over a million soldiers had X-rays during this war. It would be difficult to quantify how many lives were saved, but the figure is without any doubt highly significant. It is sad that Marie Curie was slowly contaminating her body with radiation. Her hands showed clear signs of over-exposure to radiation as she aged. The end result was that sadly she contracted a form of leukaemia. She did however survive the Great War, dying in 1934 aged 77 years. What a woman!

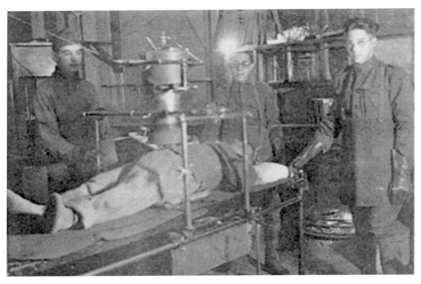

This photo is courtesy of the National Medical Museum. It shows a patient being X-rayed in Boulogne General Hospital. It is interesting to note that the operators are wearing rubber gloves. Clearly there were risks associated with using X-Ray machine, but precisely what the long-term risks and side effects would be, were still not known. It was not appreciated at the time that the operators needed to move out of the room when the image was being taken, in order to protect themselves, standing behind lead screens would afford some protection.

Blood transfusions

The Americans started to have blood banks at the end of 1917, this blood was kept in cold storage. Donors were always being sought after. Some of the healthy soldiers were approached, but because it was a new concept in medicine, understandably some were reluctant to part with a pint of their own blood. Some of the crafty nurses would bribe them with a bottle of stout. Also, it was by no means uncommon for doctors, nurses, and support staff to donate blood, but even for them there were limits before had an adverse effect on their own health.

I have no way of knowing if Ernest was given a blood transfusion during his treatment, or even post operation. At some time after his arrival at the CCS (casualty clearing station) he would have been given another morphine tablet, again under his tongue if he was not conscious. If it had been decided that Ernest needed blood at the CCS, then it is likely that the donor would have lain in a bed at the side of him. It is likely that Ernest's blood group would not have been known.

There was still an element of risk that if the blood groups did not match, clotting could result. There were some fatalities in these circumstances due to severe transfusion reactions in receiving ABO incompatible blood products. Nowadays universal O negative blood can be used in extenuating circumstances, or if there are no means to test for the correct blood group.

All blood groups react favourably to this blood group, but I doubt that this information would have been known at the time of Ernest's treatment.

In the early 1900s two doctors had been pioneers of blood transfusion techniques, namely Alex Carol in 1902, and George Crile in 1905.

The procedure was essentially that the donor had a needle inserted into his vein, which was attached to a pipe which then fed into a 500ml glass bottle. From this bottle would be another pipe with a needle inserted into Grandad's arm. Dependent on the blood loss, the process normally took two to three hours. The process was by no means fool proof. The difficulty was to measure how much blood was being donated and

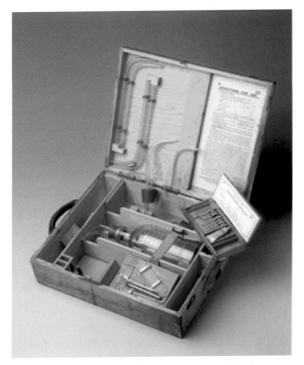

This is a typical transfusion apparatus of the time

at what point Ernest's blood loss was replenished. In order to assist staff, a syphgmometer (blood pressure gauge) was used to measure continually Ernest's blood pressure.

The nurses would also check Ernest's radial pulse and carotid pulse. When the blood pressure and pulse were found to be normal, the process was complete.

A bullet is removed

It is highly likely that during the above processes, Ernest would have regained consciousness. I have tried to imagine how it would have felt for him. A lot of research has been done with people who have come out of comas and been bought back to life from the brink of death. For me personally I can liken it to your brain becoming active again at the end of a deep sleep. I have had many dreams just prior to waking up. Ernest would be enveloped in darkness but as he roused, images would begin to form in his mind, the nightmares of war would return, with all his recent experiences in the battlefield, the sights and sounds of war, the screams of wounded soldiers, shells exploding, soldiers being hurled through the air, dismembered horses screaming in agony, orders being shouted out.

In the darkness a light would appear at the end of a tunnel which would come nearer and nearer. There would be the face of Elizabeth. He would want to reach out and touch her. Her lips would move and form words. 'Ernest, you're with us again, you're so lucky!'

Elizabeth's face in an instant was replaced by the friendly smiling face of a nurse leaning towards him. She had adjusted his pillow and was swabbing the beads of sweat that had formed on his forehead. Ernest slowly realised that he was still alive. An enormous sense of relief came upon him. Tears rolled down his cheeks.

'Take a look at the small bottle on the top of your bedside table', said the soft voice of the nurse as she pointed to his left. Ernest gingerly glanced sideways and saw a bullet in the receptacle. 'You can keep that as a souvenir', she laughed.

I have taken this bullet to a local registered dealer of Antique Firearms. Under close examination, the rifling marks on the body of the bullet can be detected. The bullet fits perfectly into a spent cartridge case of the standard 8mm German bullet. It is fair to say that it would have been fired from a rifle, so that I am going to suggest that Grandad was correct in his belief that he had been shot by a sniper.

I think it is also true to say that if he and his immediate comrades had been subjected to the constant fire of a machine gun, he would have remembered this fact and told us. I remember Ernest telling me one teatime:

'I remember coming round in the hospital ward and seeing the bullet in a small bottle at the side of my bed. Shortly after this, I checked my personal belongings and discovered that someone had stolen my German Luger pistol. I don't know why this

This is the Mauser .323 bullet removed from Ernest's chest

annoyed me, but I was so relieved to be alive. If it weren't for being wounded, I don't think I would have made it!'

...silence, followed by tears.

Recovery

So, Sergeant 203241 Burchell is back in the land of the living. Those first few conscious breaths of air cause intense pain, but as the minutes and hours go by the effects of the morphine start to give relief. Ernest looks around him. He is lying on top of clean bed sheets, and can smell the faint odour of carbolic soap on his body. He blushes at the slow realisation that one of the nurses has stripped and washed him prior to putting on a bed gown. He no longer wears his filthy uniform and underpants. Ernest nervously touches the wound on his chest. It has been sealed with a bandage, but is still tender. He sees the saline drip hanging at the side of his bed.

The bottle of saline now contained a 0.9% salt water solution designed to return Ernest's blood pressure back to normal. This has been explained to me as follows:

As an analogy, consider a central heating system. Because of a leaking pipe or radiator, the pressure in the system has dropped. As a consequence, the efficiency of the central heating pump is reduced. By repairing the leak, the system has to be repressurised by allowing more water into the system to return the water pressure to the optimum pressure. The saline replaces circulating volume in the human body.

But this was not the only surgical appliance that was attached to him. He felt a slight pricking sensation at the right-hand side of his body about five inches down from his arm pit. He gingerly reached over with his left arm and felt a pipe leading down from his side down under his bed, attached to which was a bottle. He could not see the contents, which was probably as well, because the contents would have been a yellowy red colour. This was the chest drain, set up to collect any other fluids from the ruptured lung cavity. It would have been used as definitive management following emergency decompression with the cannula, and chest surgery to remove the bullet.

Return to England is necessary for Ernest

Unbelievably Ernest Burchell had survived yet another ordeal, but he was not yet out of the woods. It was almost inevitable that he would develop an infection or even a number of infections over the next few weeks of his recovery. The chances were that he would develop an empyema in his chest, which would take the form of an abscess containing poisonous puss. The bacterial infection could be tuberculosis, typhoid, tetanus, or typhus, to name a few.

His recovery would depend on the devoted care of the nurses, as well as the constant monitoring of temperature fluctuations, the cleaning of wound dressings and the replacing of lost bodily fluids with the saline drip. The quantity and colour of the fluid drained from his wound would also be under close scrutiny. The broken ribs would heal themselves with prolonged rest and no exertions. The damaged cells in the pleural cavity, together with the membrane, would eventually regenerate themselves. The positive news was that with good care and an uninterrupted period of recovery, Ernest would get better.

The extent of Ernest's injuries clearly meant that he had a 'blighty one'. This would mean the end of the war for him, but at the time he would not have known this. He had witnessed a lot of soldiers returning to the front, having recovered from their wounds. He clung on to the hope, that the war would soon end and that eventually he would be allowed to return home.

Ernest would probably not have been moved from the CCS for at least five days, because the risks to him would have be deemed too great. The train journey, when it came, would be long and sometimes uncomfortable. Most of the trains carried around 440 patients, and when loaded they struggled to travel faster than 10mph. These hospital trains had to make way for the trains carrying troops and supplies, as they were deemed a higher priority. There would often be derailments and repairs to the lines after German bomber attacks. As a consequence, the 30 to 50-mile trip to the French coast would take a relatively long time, I'm guessing several hours at least, or even a day.

The wounded soldiers did not travel alone, as each carriage had one nurse, whose sole responsibility was to look after the patients within that carriage, and to keep it clean and as sterile as possible. The carriage had blinds and blacked out windows. In the hours of darkness there was always a lookout for German planes, and to avoid detection the train would sometimes stop, with all the lights switched off, until the danger passed.

I have looked at the possible train routes from the Béthune and Hazebrouck area to the coast. The most direct route to Boulogne was across country, mainly on a single-track line via Arques, Lumbres, and Hesdigneul. The alternative was a double-tracked route via Calais and then southwards to Boulogne.

The final destination would be the coastal town of Wimereux, about three miles north of Boulogne. It clearly shows on Grandad's Casualty Form B103 that he was hospitalised at this location prior to being transferred on the hospital ship at Boulogne bound for England. There were eight Base Hospitals in and around the area of Wimereux, and also Château Mauricien. I am going to be bold and say that he was taken to number Five General Hospital prior to going to England.

During this period, I would like to think that he would have written to his family and Elizabeth, especially when he received the news that he would be coming back to England. If he was incapable, and knowing the charmer that he was, I am sure that his nurse would have written a few lines on his behalf.

Ernest Burchell, together with hundreds of other wounded soldiers was loaded on to the hospital ship on Thursday the 19th of September 1918. This ship would have steamed to the docks at Southampton. Ernest would soon be back on British soil for the first time in two years and four months. I have no doubt that Ernest would have still been in a lot of pain and discomfort whilst he was on his way back to England. Part of him would feel guilty that he had left his mates behind, and he would be asking himself how many of these would he see again. Being a religious man, I am sure that he would have prayed for them all.

Arrival at Southampton and recuperation in West Yorkshire

Eventually the hospital ship arrived at Southampton docks, and the Captain of the ship waited eagerly for his turn to enter the port. There then followed a lengthy period unloading the wounded soldiers. I can only imagine the scene. There would have been literally hundreds of stretchers waiting to be loaded on to ambulances, ready for the journey to the train station. The administration of all of this would have been a

This is East Leeds Military Hospital, now known as the Thackeray Medical Museum

nightmare. There were hundreds of hospitals scattered all over England, Wales, Scotland and Ireland. Whoever had the responsibility on this day had decided that Ernest's batch of wounded soldiers would go to the East Leeds Military Hospital, located in West Yorkshire. The distance by road is about 235 miles. I am guessing that the train journey would have been a little further, with numerous stops and transfers along the way.

Ernest Burchell arrived at East Leeds Military Hospital sometime in the 3rd week of September 1918. It is good to see that this building still retains its Victorian grandeur. The building is now the Thackeray Medical Museum of West Yorkshire. During World War 1, the hospital treated over 57,000 wounded soldiers. My Grandad would have spent three to four months here. The novelty of sleeping in a clean bed and being able to wash and shave each day would soon be replaced by the daily boredom of life on the wards. However, in those days people were more capable of entertaining themselves. It would not be long before patients had their own magazine of sorts, where they were encouraged to write jokes and stories of interest. Anything to help pass the time of day, of course.

For Ernest there were also the letters and postcards to his family and to dear Elizabeth. The soldiers would be keen to read the local newspapers for news from the front, and to catch up on events in Britain.

There would always be the fear that the war could still drag on, and some soldiers would dread the thought of having to be sent back to France and Belgium. Any new patient coming on to the ward from the Western Front would be interrogated at the first opportunity by the other patients. It soon became apparent that the Allies were making good progress, but also that soldiers were still being killed in their thousands.

I have tried to research if pay phones would have been available for Ernest during his stay in hospital. It appears that pay phones were not available to the public until 1920–1921. They would have been installed in hospitals, but I doubt if the patients would have been allowed to use them, and Ernest would certainly have had to rely on postcards and letters.

Changes in English society

So much had changed since Ernest had last been in England. The streets and roads were filled with cars, trams and buses. There was still horse drawn carriages, but they had noticeably dwindled in number. Ernest read local newspapers which were still under Government censorship.

The socialist party continued to grow with ever increasing support from the poor and working-class communities. There was still a threat of social unrest. Communism and people who preached its philosophy were suppressed and kept under close scrutiny. Meetings were still held but always under the watchful eyes of the authorities. The Establishment still feared revolution.

The Trade Union Movement continued to grow in strength. In August 1918 20,000 police officers in London went on strike, demanding better pay and trade union representation. This act alone must have been a litmus paper test of public feelings.

On the civil liberties and equal opportunities front, there were developments with regard to the rights of women. Earlier in 1918, women of 30 years and over were given the right to vote. At the end of this same year, the Countess Constance Markiewicz was the first women to be elected as an MP. She was unable to attend Parliament because she had been arrested earlier in the year, having been involved in anti-conscription riots. She had been sent to Holloway Prison as a punishment.

On the domestic front, ration books had been introduced for butter, margarine, lard, meat, and sugar. Coal was also rationed. The Education Act raised the school leaving age to 14 years.

All this news would no doubt have stimulated lively debate amongst the soldiers on the hospital wards. The ruling class were still trying to cling on to power. They still had special hospitals for officers. These unfair benefits would feed and fan the flames of envy and social injustice.

I have read a copy of the 'Yorkshire Post', dated the 30th of September 1918. I have no doubt that copies of this newspaper would have been read out to eager listeners, including Ernest, on the wards at the hospital, including those too ill to sit up and listen. Newspapers seem to have changed in the 102 years since this very publication. I would have expected headlines on the front page, but no, the front page looks more like a page in the Farmers Weekly, with lots of livestock sales advertised, and adverts for various products and medicines. There were many jobs advertised, no doubt due to the lack of men to fill these posts. It is little wonder that so many women were taken on to fill the roles.

It is only on pages five and six that the reader comes across articles covering the war. There are various articles that would have been of interest to the patients:

'German troops withdraw from Romania' was one article, another article read 'Late News Special – Attack South of Quinten'. A summary of the article read – 'Our Troops attack on the front Orvillers-Cerisy, the Enemy made 'energetic resistance' was driven out of both villages, which are now in our hands. We have crossed the road from St Quenten to La Fère, 500 prisoners have been counted. Between the Ailette and Aisne we have today made an advance of about two kilometres on both sides of the Chemin de Dames and have occupied Pargney, Silain and Oste'.

Reading these articles, I am amazed at the detail. I am sure that the wounded soldiers would have also been impressed as they read them. It should be remembered that the soldiers on the front were starved of information. They relied on rumour and speculation. Occasionally someone returning from leave would enlighten them of the situation elsewhere in the other theatres of war.

Other articles read:

'The Bulgarian Armistice Proposal – envoys in Salonica – Reuters Agency learns of Bulgarian Armistice proposal – The British envoys insist the Allies be consulted first'.

Another article reads;

'Allies Five – Fold attack in the West – Gains on the whole Battle front, Anglo Belgian thrust in Flanders – Fierce Battle from St Quentin to Scarpe'.

In summary, this last article states that the British were now attacking on a 30-mile front, from Bellenglise to the Sensée River. Lancashire troops had captured Fontaine-Notre-Dame. Allied troops in the Cambrai sector had captured 16,000 prisoners and 200 guns. The whole Western Front from the North Sea to Verdun was in a state of great activity, with very few exceptions, and everywhere, the Germans were suffering. The main Hindenburg Line had been lost. In the first three days of these operations, 22,000 prisoners and 300 guns were captured. The Belgians had captured 5,500 prisoners and 100 guns. General Plumer's army group had captured almost all of the Passchendaele Ridge.

On a domestic front there was even talk of a General Election!

Reading these articles would have been heart-warming to the patients, but in the back of their minds, they would have been picturing the horrible scenes and the heavy price which our troops were paying for this success.

The general public would have had no idea of the true cost, except of course for those relatives who received letters from the Padres and nurses from the Casualty Clearing Stations, and from the hospitals behind the front, informing them of their husband's or relative's death. Many widows had not long been married. The soldiers who came home on leave had rushed to marry, one reason being that there would be a state pension for the widow, should the worst happen. I am sure that these same thoughts would have gone through Ernest's mind, because during his convalescence he decided to propose to Elizabeth.

The newspaper articles would have given Ernest and many other patients a very real hope that the end of the war was near. However, Ernest would have had no way of knowing if he would recover before the cessation of hostilities, so that there was always the risk that he could be sent back to France, even if only for a short period. This uncertainty would have played on his mind.

I am sure that Ernest would have made a number of friends on the ward. Patients would have exchanged numerous stories and discussed family backgrounds and those fit enough would have enjoyed games of cards and drafts. There would be other board games too. But more especially there was plenty of time for Ernest to consider his future.

Would Elizabeth accept his proposal? What would become of the greengrocer's shop in Marlborough? How long would it take Ernest to save up for a cottage of his own? He would like to have his own farm one day. How would he raise the money? These thoughts and many others would have gone through his mind as he lay in his hospital bed during those late summer and early autumn days of 1918 in East Leeds Hospital.

Recovery and the Citation in the London Gazette

It is now the beginning of October 1918 and Ernest Burchell continues to make steady progress. His strength is slowly returning. His optimism remains high, buoyed by encouraging reports in the press, highlighting the Allies' progress.

At some stage Ernest would have been made aware of the citation in the edition of The London Gazette on Thursday the 3rd of October.

```
203241  Pte. E. BURCHELL (Marlborough)
  For conspicuous gallantry and devotion to
duty.  He held an isolated post with ten men
for two days, being continually in danger of
being cut off.  He also maintained continuous
communication with his company headquarters
through heavy shell fire.  Throughout he showed
great ability, and performed most valuable work.
(3.10.18)
```

The above caption shows brief details of his efforts that earned him the Distinguished Conduct Medal (DCM). It is interesting to note that there is no mention of the Lewis gun, but I can assure you, it played a big part in saving the day.

I guess there would have been some leg pulling on the ward at this news, but Ernest was a modest man. He would have witnessed countless acts of bravery during his time in the trenches, and many of these courageous soldiers never got the recognition which they deserved. During the dark hours of the German spring offensive that year, some regiments had been wiped out to the last man. The decision to stand and fight, was, in my view, the ultimate sacrifice. No medal, not even the Victoria Cross, would have been enough recognition for these brave men who died so that others could pull back, evade capture, and live to fight another battle.

There was, however, a group of soldiers who were quick to use letters after their names and display their medals at every opportunity, for their own prestige and kudos. The 'shiny boot brigade' of the officer class revelled in the titles bestowed upon them. I am not anti-authority, but I do resent some of these individuals, as I know Ernest would have.

That is not to say that many officers were not deserving of recognition, they were! I have recently read that over 80 British Generals were killed in World War 1, Major Charles Awdry and Colonel Tyne of the Wiltshires to name a few.

Many others were not deserving of recognition in my view. I'm referring to the 'shiny boots' who lived in relative luxury in the Châteaux behind the lines. The soldiers that 'went over the top' and fought this war were referred to simply as 'other ranks'.

I have checked the Yorkshire Post for the 3rd of October, and there is no mention of Ernest's citation. This is understandable as the paper concentrated on Rolls of Honour for their own Yorkshire regiments. On the other hand, it is interesting to note that the newspaper gave updates about patients' progress in some of the Yorkshire hospitals. Each bed was given a number, and the patients are categorised as very poorly, comfortable, or making good progress. I can imagine this took some pressure from hospital staff, who would have been bombarded by enquiries from anxious relatives.

On this particular date I read an amusing article where a lady train passenger in England had been instrumental in the arrest and capture of two escaped German prisoners of war. They were dressed as Catholic nuns. Apparently, her suspicions were aroused by their muscular appearance. This article would have no doubt caused a laugh amongst the soldiers on the ward.

There is also an article stating that the town of La Bassée had been taken by the Allies. This makes me think that when wounded, Grandad was definitely taken off the battlefield to Hazebrouck CCS, and not La Bassée as stated on his medical records. This must have been a clerical error by whoever filled in this form. The town would still have been in the hands of the Germans on the day Grandad was wounded. Given the sheer enormity of this conflict, it is little wonder that there were so many clerical errors.

Meanwhile in the trenches

Meanwhile back on the Western Front, the 2nd Wiltshires had spent two more days at the front before returning to Hinges for a rest period and further training. They returned to the trenches on the 11th of September where they were deployed in trenches in the Richbourg St Vaast area.

On a wider front the Allies were continuing to make progress. During the end of August and the first week in September, the Australian 2nd

Division had achieved a significant victory at Mont St-Quentin. This was an important area of high ground that would be essential for the next phase of the advance, namely the storming of the Hindenburg Line. Intelligence reports had been received via captured German prisoners, that the Germans would continue to retreat to the Hindenburg Line, and having arrived there, they would not yield another inch of territory. The Germans were confident that this line of defences was impregnable to allied attack. They were to be proved wrong!

The next major obstacle was the Drocourt Queant Line, west of Cambrai. This was a stretch of heavily fortified trenches protecting the southern flank of the Hindenburg Line.

During the period from the end of September to the first week in October, the Allies made massive gains on the Western Front. The little-known British 46th North Midland Division successfully crossed in rafts the canal which formed part of the Hindenburg Line defences. They were supported by a heavy Australian artillery barrage, together with aircraft and tanks, and proceeded to break through the Hindenburg Line.

At the peak of this battle over a quarter of a million shells exploded over the German lines. This was not wasted artillery fire. The shells exploded with pinpoint accuracy as they were being directed by artillery spotters in allied planes flying over the lines. Improved communications meant that artillery units could be redirected, if necessary, within minutes. This effective suppressing artillery fire was a major factor contributing to the success of the Allies.

The unthinkable had been achieved, the Hindenburg line was broken! This was an undisputed major blow to the Germans. Other allied divisions had similar success at the Canal du Nord area, another area of the Hindenburg Line.

As Ernest and his wounded comrades continued to read in the papers about the success of the Allies, rumours begin to spread that the end of the war was imminent. The press, however, did not report to the British public that there was in excess of three million German soldiers remaining in the field on the Western Front. There remained one more major obstacle to the Allies, namely the strategic German military hub of Cambrai. The Germans had deployed three lines of defence containing 200,000 battle hardened troops. If they lost this town, they would lose their strategic mobility to continue with the war on the Western Front.

The British and Canadian divisions attacked. They had significant air support and 324 tanks. The Allies continued to use 'flavoured' smoke shells to fool the German defenders. The Germans destroyed the town as they retreated, and eventually the Allies took the town of Cambrai. The German leader, General Ludendorff, issued a proclamation to his troops on the 25th of October. It read:

'For us as soldiers' capitulation is unacceptable, we must resist with all our might!'

Reflecting on this situation, the Germans now found themselves in a similar situation to the Allies, when in April of the same year, Field Marshal Haig issued his famous telegram to his troops. The question was, would the Germans troops respond in a similar manner to the Allies back in April?

Since August 1918 to the end of the 1st week in November, the Allies captured 375,000 German prisoners. The Germans were giving up in droves.

News of impending victory reaches West Yorkshire

Back in the hospital wards of the East Leeds Hospital, rumours and speculation continued to develop rapidly. No doubt lively debates took place, and I wonder if a few bets were placed as to when the end of the war would be announced.

During those darkening nights in October 1918, other debates would take place. There would soon be a General Election. There was a mood for change. The ruling class were losing their grip on power. The significant changes in voters' rights would soon have an impact on future politics and Government policy.

There were also concerns about the flu epidemic, which was still killing thousands of people worldwide. The soldiers in Ernest's hospital and hundreds of other hospitals would be particularly vulnerable, given the weakened state of health and lower resistance to infection of their patients. It is not clear to me if enough was known at the time about this virus which would prompt the authorities to impose visiting restrictions. The capital London was suffering the most casualties. It is quite strange for me, as I write the penultimate chapter of this book, in the context of history repeating itself with the country currently preparing to lockdown, given concerns about the growing death rate due to Covid-19.

As the month of October 1918 came to an end, the clocks were put forward one hour following the Summer time Act of 1916. There were more encouraging signs that the end of World War 1 was near, as the German Navy mutinied on the 29th of October. On the 30th of October Turkey signed an armistice with the Allies, and the walls of a once mighty Ottoman Empire came crumbling down. Furthermore, the first week in November brought the news that Austria and Hungary had also signed an armistice with the Allies. Yet another once mighty empire had fallen.

The reticent Germans were still reluctant to give in. They were determined to hold on to some of the territory which they had gained at the beginning of the war. On the other side, the overall Commander of the Allied Armies, General Foch, was determined to drive the Germans back to the Rhine, and to drive what remained of their army out of Belgium.

The last battle and victory

There was one last major battle, that being the Second Battle of Mons. There was fierce house to house and hand to hand combat in order for the Allies to drive the Germans out of the town of Mons. General Horne, who was involved in the first Battle of Mons, took great pleasure in liberating this Belgian town, and the local population was ecstatic.

On the 9th of November the Kaiser was forced to abdicate. However, instead of being detained to be held to account for war atrocities, as might be expected based on today's norms, he was allowed to flee to Holland instead.

On the 10th of November 1918 General Hindenburg advised his Government to seek an armistice. The following day, the 11th of November, soldiers on both sides were informed that at 11.00 hours all fighting would cease.

The 2nd Battalion of the Wiltshires were in billets in Eth. On the morning of the 11th of November, having received news of the ceasefire, the battalion band played outside the soldiers' billets.

The locals from the town of Eth unearthed the church bell that had been hidden from the Germans. They reinstalled it in the church and proceeded to ring out that the war was over!

Press reactions in Leeds

I have read the 11th of November's issue of the 'Leeds Mercury'. The newspapers appear to lag behind the events of the day, to allow for overnight printing like in all newspapers. The news of the end of the war can be read in the edition of November 12th.

The headlines on the 11th of November refer to

'The Flight of the Kaiser to Holland'

'The Dramatic change in Berlin – Socialists overthrow the Government of Prince Max, Revolution all over the country'

'Enemy in full retreat – British on the outskirts of Mons'

It is only when you read the following day's edition of the' Leeds Mercury' that you see a real reaction.

'How Yorkshire Celebrates the Surrender of Germany – A crowd of 20,000 gather in Victoria Square, they wave flags and throw their hats in the air, Patriotic songs are sung including 'Rule Britannia'

and 'Hearts of Oak' to the accompaniment of the Police Band. Church Bells ring. Some of the wounded soldiers from the local hospitals commandeered three drays (horse and cart) and proceeded down the street playing trumpets'.

I wonder if Ernest was well enough to join in these celebrations. True the mood would have been of huge relief that it was all over. It is clear from the newspaper articles that some of the wounded soldiers did take part in the celebrations outside. In reality, I doubt that Ernest did, as he had too many tubes attached to him. In any event I am sure that he would have allowed himself to smile. The nurses would have tried to brighten up the wards and I am sure that songs were sung and that there was a lot of hugging and kissing. Hey....... who could blame them?

Now Ernest could concentrate on a full recovery and hope that he would be demobbed from the Army, so that he could return home.

Earnest post war

Chapter 11

The meaning of victory

World War 1 is finally over! The celebrations continued for days, but the soldiers on the front were in a state of exhaustion. The guns had fallen silent, which in itself was a strange experience. There was a sense of numbness amongst the men. They sat in groups trying to take stock of the situation. 'What was it all about? So many dead and for what? What do we do now?' These and many other questions raced through their minds, as the soldiers pondered their own futures.

There were reasons to be kept busy. For a lot of men, namely those who supported the divisions on the front, the work did not stop at the ceasefire. There followed a period of burying what remained of the dead. This must have been one of the most heart-rending tasks. Those who had survived the war, over four million British and Colonial troops, still had to be fed and watered. The administration process continued.

Work had to start cleaning up the awful mess created by warfare. Over seven and a half million acres of land had been put to ruin. Mile upon mile of barbed wire defences had to be taken down, unexploded shells recovered, trenches filled in and drainage systems repaired. This process would take years to complete.

Rebellion from the Chinese Labour Corps

For the Chinese Labour Corps going home was naturally uppermost in their minds, but they had signed three-year contracts, and they were given the unenviable task of recovering body parts for mass burials.

They started to become unruly and restless, some started to riot and a number of them were shot.

This rebellion was fuelled by news from China. Part of the original deal with Britain and China was that in the event of the Allies being successful in the war, then consideration would be given to return land to China which had been occupied by the Germans. However, with typical colonial arrogance and a lack of foresight, the British reneged on this deal. A secret deal had been made with the Japanese at the beginning of the war, by which the Japanese would be given territory occupied by the Germans in China in return for Japan entering the war on the Allies side. Japan would support the Allies by sending troops and war materials, and also allow Japan's cargo ships to be used for the allied war effort.

As the details of this deal were revealed in China, there were many riots. The Chinese ruling dynasty eventually fell, paving the way for an up and coming revolutionary, Mao Zedong, to destabilise the establishment. Years later this led to China becoming a Communist state.

The surviving soldiers return home

Back in Europe, the civilian population of the war-torn countries tried to return to what was left of their villages. This horrendous conflict had killed over 10 million civilians. There were many orphans and widows, and the deprivations continued for many years.

Slowly but surely some of the regiments were allowed home. They took with them all of their equipment, including rifles, but were ordered to leave their ammunition behind. The recently appointed Minister of War, Winston Churchill, set about disbanding the regiments.

The strength of the British Army fell rapidly from over four million men to just over one million. This was a deliberate decision on the part of the Government, as the establishment was still concerned about the ever-present threat of revolution and Bolshevism which was rapidly becoming a growing cancer, spreading across Europe.

Those soldiers who were lucky enough to return home early, arrived at the docks in southern Britain. They found a general public who had no idea about the horrors of the past four years. Many were indifferent and did not want to speak about the subject. There was mass unemployment, and some companies were discriminatory when advertising for job vacancies, with many adverts stating 'Ex Servicemen need not apply'. Can you imagine the effect this had on the returning soldiers? Anger and resentment festered. It took a long time before men were allowed to replace the women who had been doing their jobs. There was no respite in the suffering of poor families.

In the immediate post-war years, social change was evident. Many of the estates of the ruling class had to be sold off in order to pay death duties, as the owners and their heirs had been killed.

Soldiers continued to arrive home and the hospitals continued to receive wounded men. As some of the soldiers began to recover, they were moved from the hospitals to convalescent homes for rehabilitation.

The unlucky regiments had to stay in Europe, some of whom formed part of the army of occupation of Germany. Those soldiers would not be going home any time soon. As for the 2nd Wiltshire Regiment, they remained in France until the 2nd of April 1919, when they marched to the docks at Le Havre and embarked on the USS 'Yale sailing to Southampton, arriving at 18.00 hours. They were home, back in Blighty!

Ernest moves to a convalescent home,
is discharged and demobbed

Sometime in December 1918, Ernest Burchell was moved to the Pitchforth Convalescent Home in Saltburn on the East Coast of Yorkshire.

What a happy bunch of men they look, and can you blame them? They would soon be going home to their loved ones. I wonder how many, if any, kept in touch after they returned home. This photograph is in the form of a postcard which was no doubt sent with an accompanying letter to dear Elizabeth. On the back it reads 'Wishing you a bright and happy Xmas – signed Ernest'.

Photographed in front of the Pitchforth Convalescent Home in Saltburn, I count 38 patients in civilian clothing, with seven nurses. A very relaxed looking Ernest is sitting on the front row, second from the left. He has now shaved off his moustache.

During their stay at Pitchforth, the patients would no doubt have taken part in the General Election. This was held on the 14th of December 1918. It would become known as the 'Coupon Election' because prior to this election, David Lloyd George had sent letters of endorsement to candidates who supported the Coalition Government.

The result of the election was delayed to allow for votes cast from overseas soldiers to be counted. The result was announced on the 28th of December 1918. It was a landslide victory for the Coalition. David Lloyd George became Prime Minister again for another term.

I am sure that there was much celebration, singing and dancing on New Year's Eve in the Convalescent Home in Saltburn. I would like to think that Elizabeth at some time would have caught the train and visited Ernest. The 'romantic' in me wonders if, over this period, the two met up. I can picture the young couple walking along the sea front at Saltburn. Was this the time Ernest proposed to Elizabeth? I can only speculate if this happened. I hope it did.

Towards the end of January 1919, Ernest was assessed by a doctor, partly to ascertain if he was eligible for a War Pension. Captain H. Lee assessed Ernest as fit and well and stated that he did not qualify for the pension. Ernest was described as being of good character and fit and well enough to travel home without an attendant during the journey. His medical report confirmed he had had a foreign body (the bullet) removed from the right-hand side of his chest. His chest expansion was normal, and there were no adverse symptoms, other than aching in the area of his wound. Ernest was discharged from hospital on the

Sergeant 203241 Burchell. I note that he is not wearing his medals. Surely by now he had received them. On this photo you can see three chevrons on his right sleeve, the significance of these is proof that Ernest spent three years on active service overseas, the single chevron on his left sleeve is an indication that he was wounded once during his service.

31st of January 1919. Ernest was demobilised from the Army on the 1st of March 1919.

Ernest returns to civilian life

January to March 1919 would be remembered in Britain for large amounts of snow fall throughout the country. There was heavy snow in the first and last weeks of January. There were further heavy snow falls in March, with over a foot of snow recorded in London. This cold weather no doubt reminded Ernest and the other patients of that bitter cold winter of 1916 in the trenches of Belgium.

Before my Grandad left the convalescent home at Saltburn, he posed for one last photograph. This was produced in the form of a postcard on the rear of which is written in pencil 'Ernest Burchell'. A man of few words.

Well, Grandad Burchell, if you are too modest to show your medals off, then I am not! These are the three medals that Grandad was awarded.

(Photo courtesy of cousin Peter Richards, Ernest's second eldest Grandchild).

From left to right; The gold medal is the Victory Medal, the silver medal in the centre is the War Medal and the medal on the right is the DCM

At demobilisation soldiers were given civilian clothes to wear. I am guessing that Ernest wore the clothes as seen in the photograph of the Pitchforth Convalescent Home in Saltburn.

After all this time, Ernest is standing on the platform of a station in West Yorkshire, waiting to catch the train that will take him back home to his beloved Wiltshire. There would be many other ex-soldiers standing with him. I bet he never stopped smiling all the way home. His sense of elation must have been almost overpowering. It would have been like being released from prison. The shackles of war had been broken away. Ernest was a free man, and he was now in charge of his own destiny.

Between March and October 1919 my story is a little vague. Ernest would no doubt have had a hero's welcome from his mother Ann and the rest of the Burchell family back at the cottage in Calne.

By now his older brother Walter would have returned back from the Machine Gun Corps. The greengrocer's shop in Marlborough was still open for business, having been run by Walter's wife during the war. At some stage in the next few months, Ernest considered cashing in his share of the business in order to raise funds for his up-and-coming wedding to Elizabeth, and their own future plans.

I know it is 101 years ago, but I feel strangely excited for him.

The state of the nations at the turn of the year 1918–1919

It was now New Year's Eve 1918, and the country and its war weary population was looking forward to the New Year and a fresh start. Britain's national debt now stood at £7.4 billion, the bulk of which was owed to the Americans. However, the situation was more complicated, as the other allied powers had been partially financed by the British. This had been done to keep them in the war and finance their arms production. That first week in January 1919 saw substantial falls of snow in Britain. The hardships were bad enough but were now compounded by the rationing of coal.

During the course of the war and as an aftermath, Empires had fallen. Only Britain's Empire remained intact, but its days were numbered.

One country emerged as a new superpower, the United States of America, who were owed over 30 billion Dollars. America was now set to have a massive influence on world affairs, and how the 'New World Order' would form. America provided substantial aid to the Europeans in order to feed and rebuild their economies and infrastructures.

In the New Year President Woodrow Wilson toured the ruins of Europe. On the whole he was well received. Part of his mission was to promote his concept of a League of Nations, designed to reduce the risk of further wars. He also insisted that individual nations should be allowed self-determination and have their own government. This went against the grain with the old Imperial Powers, but this was the price of continued foreign aid from America. American bankers continued to support the Europeans, but the President's conditions were that as part repayment they would buy American goods with the result that America would grow even richer.

Embarking on research into world events of 1919, I was expecting a period of relative calm and stability. Not so! There were literally dozens of conflicts all over the world. Instead of a World War, the conflicts developed into smaller areas of conflict as each country tried to break away from old imperial rule. The spread of Bolshevism was one source of major conflict. Thousands more people in other areas of the world perished fighting under the banner of independence, freedom and self-government.

I would have to write another book to cover all these events, but it is fair to say that the world was still far from being a safe place. There was civil unrest in many countries and across whole continents. The returning soldiers were angry, frustrated, and, above all, many are unable to return to their employment.

On the 28th of June 1919, the Treaty of Versailles was ratified. Germany had to relinquish all of its territories gained prior to the commencement of the war, including provinces in China, Alsace-Lorraine, Poland, and East Africa. They were ordered to pay in excess of 30 billion dollars in war reparations to the Allies.

Controversially the north coast of Germany was annexed to allow Poland to have a coast and port facilities. This caused resentment amongst the German population. This ill feeling grew and festered in the coming years.

In October of this year American President Woodrow Wilson suffered a serious stroke, from which he never recovered. He was rendered an invalid for the rest of his life.

This same month a little-known political activist named Adolf Hitler made his first speech on behalf of the 'Workers Party' in Germany. This menace grew, festering on the ill feeling in Germany about the sanctions imposed by the Allies. Adolf Hitler exploited this ill feeling to elevate himself into power in the next decade.

In November this year, health officials declared that the global flu pandemic had ceased. I hope that by the time this book is published, the current crisis which we are experiencing is over. The so-called 'Spanish Flu', as it was then called, is thought to have originated in America at the beginning of January 1918. At the time the medical name for the pandemic was H1N1. It was thought to have affected over 500 million people world-wide. Over 50 million people died as a result of this virus.

So, you can see that Ernest and his family would have had plenty of news to read, though Ernest remained focused on his future plans.

A happy ending

My story does have a happy ending with an event on a particular day. To help me gain a feel for this, I have read a copy of the Derby Daily Telegraph for Thursday the 2nd of October 1919. I also referred to an article in the Friday's edition of the Derby Advertiser, dated the 10th of October 1919.

This was a very special day for Ernest and Elizabeth, as it was the day of their wedding at Hartshorne Wesleyan Church in South Derbyshire, a day that marked the start of their new lives together as husband and wife. The weather forecast for the Midlands area was moderate west to north-westerly breeze, variable cloud, showers, moderate temperature.

The Leese family did not have far to travel, as their Greysich Farm was about two miles away from the church. However, as in all farms

OCTOBER 4, 1919.   TELEPHONE Nos. 485, 486 & 487.   ONE PENNY.

MISS E. LEESE MARRIED AT HARTSHORNE

"Burton Daily Mail" Studio

The marriage at Hartshorne, last week, of Miss E. Leese and Mr. E. Burchell.

The newly weds exit Hartshorne Methodist Chapel, Ernest is looking a very happy man can you blame him!.

Elizabeth's brothers would have had to get up and milk their cows that morning. I would like to think Elizabeth would have been excused this chore. There would have been a frenzy of activity in the farmhouse, with Elizabeth's sisters Selina, Mary and Lydia helping to get the bride ready. The family would have eaten a hearty cooked breakfast.

The Burchell family travelled about 125 miles in order to attend this wedding, no doubt at least one day beforehand, and staying at a hotel or at friends' homes in the village of Hartshorne.

The family pose for this photo outside Greysich farmhouse during the wedding reception

I can picture the scene in the church. As a boy I had to attend every Sunday in the 1960's with my brother David. The layout inside has not changed. The newspaper on this day mentions Harvest Festivals planned for the coming weekend. With this in mind there would have been an impressive display of flowers. However, there were no bells in this church. The pipe organ was sufficient, located at the right-hand corner in front of where the congregation sat.

As the ceremony began Ernest would have stood at the front with his best man, his brother-in-law, Thomas Jacques. Ernest nervously held his beige Fedora hat as the organ started to play the wedding march. Moments would elapse until the bride, Elizabeth, escorted by her father Daniel Leese, came to stand next to him. The couple would glance at each other, Ernest's heart would be pounding in his chest with pride at the sight of his beautiful bride.

Elizabeth wore a stunning dress of ivory crepe de chine, embroidered with butterflies and lover's knots in pearl, and trimmed with silver tissue. Her veil was the one that her mother Mary had worn at her wedding,

311

and she had an orange blossom headdress. Elizabeth carried a beautiful bouquet of white carnations. The couple exchanged their vows and left the church in procession, followed by their bridesmaids Beryl and Francis Burchell, and Maud Leese, all of whom were nieces of the couple. The procession left the Church to the sound of Mendelssohn's Wedding March.

The wedding reception was held at Greysich Farm. I can imagine a feast fit for a king, given the ample amounts of fresh fruit, vegetables and meat you can expect to have on a working farm, with the ration restrictions circumnavigated!

What would be the odds of Ernest, his brother Walter, and his now brother-in-laws, Daniel (Junior) and Albert Leese, returning home, having survived this horrendous war. The odds would have been massive, but return they did. So many families were not so lucky. I wonder if during this reception, they took a moment together and raised their glasses to their friends that had not returned home. I would like to think they did.

Ernest gave Elizabeth the gift of a piano, and Elizabeth had purchased a silver mounted leather travelling case for Ernest. I guess they would have spent the first night at Greysich farmhouse before travelling the following day to their honeymoon in Llandudno, North Wales.

I can still picture Grandma's piano in the passageway of the old farmhouse in Hartshorne. As a little boy I would occasionally hear Grandma's beautiful singing through the walls of our adjacent farmhouse.

Thanks for coming home, Grandad, you were my Grandad and my hero, I'm a better person for having known you.

The End

EPILOGUE

When I embarked on this project, I had little knowledge of the period between 1888 and 1919, which was essentially the first 31 years of Ernest's life. I have been fascinated by the facts I uncovered.

Never did I realise the sheer scale of how the world developed in inventions and technological, health, welfare and social reform during this period. The Victorian era came to an end soon after Ernest left school. The British Empire was by far the biggest in the world.

It makes you wonder if only this vast wealth that the nation had accrued, had been spent on more worthwhile projects than on the pointless war of 1914–18. What position would we all be in now? A lot better, I'm sure!

It's a sad fact that mankind seems to have this mechanism for self-destruction. It never ceases to amaze me, how whole populations can be brainwashed and manipulated into following the ambitions of just a few individuals.

It's easy to look at the casualty figures and just see lines of noughts on a page. When you visit the cemeteries in France and Belgium, as we did, you get more of an appreciation of the suffering and horror of those years. Yet, as I've stated in the chapters of this book, in every generation there are a small number of individuals whose inventions and endeavours make a massive contribution to the wellbeing of the human race. There were many such individuals who lived through this period, who did make a massive difference, Marie and Pierre Curie, Wilbur and Orville Wright, Henry Ford, Alex Carrol, Louis Pasteur, and Alexander Graham Bell, to name a few.

How many other individuals amongst the millions that died would have also contributed in similar way, had they survived? In other words, these horrendous losses are not just tragic for their families but also a considerable loss in the gene pool of life.

During the period of writing this book, I have had a list of men who were part of B squadron of the Wiltshire Yeomans. Grandad was in number One Section of the Second Troop, Marlborough. This list had been complied by Major R.W. Awdry and is dated August 1917. The list consists of 139 men, and includes the officers and NCOs, all the Privates, transport troops, Army Service Corps, and other attachments. I refer to these in Chapter 2 (see photo). It is likely that this Squadron would have been together when they marched and stayed at Winchester College in 1914. Of the 4 squadrons of the Yeoman's namely A, B, C, and D. We know that C squadron was disbanded, and all the men were divided up and were transferred to the remaining A, B, and D Squadrons. These three remaining squadrons eventually went to France.

It was my hope to try to identify some of these soldiers who fought and died fighting with Ernest Burchell. Sadly, I failed in this task. The enormous losses which the regiments sustained meant that soldiers were frequently transferred to reinforce depleted regiments. There were so many comings and goings. The huge losses meant that many 'composite battalions' were formed from survivors. Also, I was impeded by the fact that a lot of World War 1 records were destroyed in the London Blitz in World War 2.

The nearest I managed in my aim, was identifying three soldiers who together with Ernest were in trouble with the Major, having overstayed their leave in Dunkirk in 1917. As to whether these were close friends, I can't say, but they must have had some fun together in Dunkirk!

I would have loved to have identified some of the ten other soldiers who were with Ernest when they were surrounded at Spanbroekmolen in April 1918. There is one soldier, Sergeant 11881 J.E. Ackland, also of the 6th Wiltshires. His name is also listed in the issue of The London Gazette on 3rd October 1918. Ackland's citation reads that he assumed command of a small number of soldiers at Spanbroekmolen over the same period of two to three days that Ernest was deployed. His group of men were in possession of a Lewis gun. This was effectively used to suppress enemy snipers.

If they were not in the same group of men, they would at least have been very close to one another. Each of their citations implies that they took charge of a small group of men, which clearly cannot be the case if they were together. It is likely, even if they were not together, that Sergeant Ackland witnessed Ernest's bravery and put pen to paper after the event.

Sergeant Ackland appears to have survived the conflict. He is also listed on the same medal certificate as Ernest Burchell, dated the 23rd of June 1918. I have created a special e-mail for this book, in the hope that any likeminded relatives, who have done similar research, can get in touch with me if they wish.

For the period between arriving in France and the regiment being disbanded, we know that the Yeomans were to a large part, in a support role. There was however, a period during the German withdrawal to the Hindenburg Line from February to April 1917, when they engaged elements of the German 'rear guard' and sustained casualties in both men and horses.

Following disbandment in August and September 1917, we know that Ernest and many other Yeomans transferred to the 6th Wiltshire Battalion. Over the period between September 1917 and May 1918, the 6th Wiltshires were involved in heavy fighting in the German Spring Offensive of 1918, when they are nearly wiped out. In July 1918 Ernest, together with other survivors, transferred to the 2nd Wiltshire Battalion, where they are again involved in heavy fighting for the remainder of the war.

I have referred to the 'Roll of Honour' for both of these battalions and can say that approximately 565 men of the 6th Wiltshires were killed or died of their wounds, and that in the 2nd Wiltshires it was approximately 1,366 men. These figures include officers, NCOs and Privates. If my research is correct, I have counted nine men of the original B squadron of the Yeomans who did not make it back home. It is interesting to note that many of these casualties came from all over Britain, such were the comings and goings of the men.

At the Menin Gate Memorial in Ypres, there is a list of over 55,000 soldiers whose bodies are not accounted for, and of these there are a total of 412 men listed from the Wiltshire Regiments (see QR code tribute). The detail of losses sustained by the 6th and 2nd Wiltshires, which I have quoted, may be slightly incomplete, due to the scale of casualties and the enormity of the task in recording them.

I want to pay a particular tribute to these poor men of the Wiltshire Regiments, and to all the other soldiers that didn't make it back home. May they Rest in Peace!

*   *   *   *

So, what happened to Ernest after the war? Upon their return from honeymoon in Llandudno, North Wales, Ernest and Elizabeth returned to Marlborough in Wiltshire in October 1919. My Grandfather sold his share in the greengrocery business to his brother, Walter. With some of the proceeds they moved to a lovely cottage in nearby Savernake Forest. In November of the following year they had their first child, Marion, born on the 24th of November 1920 (see photo below). Shortly after this Ernest bought his first farm at Pewsey in Wiltshire.

The fact that Ernest Burchell survived the war, meant that his and Elizabeth's gene pool has extended to four generations, with eight children born to him and Elizabeth, seven grandchildren, ten great grandchildren, and four great, great, grandchildren. Naturally, this gene pool has been enriched by the partners who married into this family tree. But I for one, am proud to have Ernest's and Elizabeth's DNA!

I ask myself did this dreadful war affect Ernest? I suppose the answer has to be that of course it did. He always insisted that it was necessary, because the Germans had to be stopped. Grandad despised them at the time. He and his fellow soldiers had been brainwashed with accounts of numerous atrocities that they had carried out in Belgium in those early years of the war.

Elizabeth Burchell photographed with Marion

'*We were told of accounts of Germans bayonetting young Belgian babies and parading down the streets, holding them above their heads, showing no remorse whatsoever. At the time we believed these accounts. Years later I have to ask myself if they were really true*'.

Many regarded Ernest as a hard man. Grandad did not suffer fools gladly. He was very strict with his children, in particular his sons. With the passage of time, he did soften, and he adored his grandchildren. He was very thrifty, and only ever borrowed money once in his life, paying the debt off within 12 months. He told me this story so many times.

Ernest suffered 'survivors' guilt syndrome' which explains his reluctance to engage with me during those memorable afternoon teas we shared. However, he did love to advise me on his outlook on life and his opinions and principles. Some of these opinions are outdated, and I for one have certainly had to moderate my own attitudes when I joined the Police Force.

Grandad had a full life. He was a well-respected businessman. During my life I have aspired to have many of his virtues, and I'll never forget those afternoon teas we shared.

Grandad, I grew to love and respect you so much.

Grandad and the author – his roguish Grandson, Paul

*This photo was taken in 1961 and shows the author held by his mother
Pauline Burchell, standing next to her is Grandad Ernest, and Grandma
Elizabeth (Bessie) and the author's eldest Brother David.*

BIBLIOGRAPHY

War Diaries

1/1 Wiltshire Yeomanry Regimental Diaries – courtesy of the National Archives at Kew, this document was handwritten on the Western Front by the NCO's between 1914 and 1917, the NCO's that compiled them were; Lieut Colonel Thynne, Major C S Awdry, Capt Noel Furlong, Major Jeff Stern.

The 58th Brigade War Diary March 21st to September 1918 – courtesy of the National Archives Kew WO-95-2089-2. Author not known.

The 19th Western Division Diary by Everard Wyrall, Published by Naval and Military Press.

Other documents

Cavalry Training 1915 – War office Documents published by The Naval Military Press ltd, Uckfield East Sussex.

Trench orders – official Government Document, War Office, published by Memorabilia Pack Co Forth St, Edinburgh.

Books

Blackbourne, David. The Fontana History of Germany, published in 1997 by Fontana Press of Hammersmith, London.

Broadhead, Richard. The Great War – Calne district soldiers published by O&B Cromwell Press Group Services in 2009 in Hilmarton.

Bull, Stephen. The German Soldier's Pocket Manual 1914–1918 published in 2018 by Osprey Oxford.

Butler, Simon. The War Horses, published in 2011 by Halsgrove companies, Wellington, Somerset.

Chilton, David. The Wiltshire Regiment in First the World War – 2nd Battalion 2nd edition by David Chilton, published by The Rifles Wardrobe and Museum Trust in Salisbury, Wiltshire in 2006.

Chilton, David. The Wiltshire Regiment in the First World War – 6th Battalion 2nd edition, published by the Rifles Wardrobe and Museum Trust in Salisbury, Wiltshire in 2006.

Cove, Ronald. Rifleman, Marksman, Sniper, published by Amazon.co.uk Michael Terence Publishing, 2020.

Eldridge, Jim. My Story in the Trenches, published in 2008 by Scholastic Children's Books, London.

Christine E Hallett, Nurses of Passchendaele: Caring for the Wounded of the Ypres Campaigns 1914–1918, published in 2017 by Pen and Sword History, Barnsley, South Yorkshire.

Hesketh-Prichard, H. Sniping in France, with Notes on the Scientific Training of Scouts, Observers and Snipers, 1920, digital version by Amazon Digital.

Jünger, Ernst. Storm of Steel, first published 1920, published in 2003 by Penguin books, London.

La Vardera, Dee. Calne Living memories, published by Francis Frith in 2004, in Salisbury Wiltshire.

Laws, Felicity Jane. War on Two Wheels, compilation David Winder Small's Diary (Royal Engineers), published by 'C' also original document held at the Imperial War Museum London.

Lloyd, Nick. Passchendaele, published in 2017 by Penguin books, London.

Marsh, A.E.W. The History of the borough and town of Calne, published by Forgotten books Ltd in 2015, Windsor Avenue London.

Mayhew, Emily. Wounded: A New History of the Western Front in World War 1, published in 2013 by The Bodley Head, London.

Martin McIntyre, The Wiltshire Regiment, published in 2006 by The History Press Ltd, Stroud, Gloucestershire.

Oldham, Peter. Messines Ridge, published in 2001, Pen & Sword Books Ltd, Barnsley.

Platt, J.R.I. The Royal Wiltshire Yeomanry 1907–1967 published in 1972 by Carnstone Press Ltd, London.

Robertshaw, Andrew. Feeding Tommy: Battlefield Recipes from the First World War, published in 2013 by Spellmount, Stroud, Gloucestershire.

Shepherd, Walter Scott. The 2nd Battalion Wiltshire Regiment (99th) 1914–18 2nd edition, published in 2011 by The Rifles Museum Trust, Salisbury, Wiltshire.

Sheffield, Gary. The Chief: Douglas Haig and the British Army, by Gary Sheffield, published in 2011 by Aurum Books, London.

Sheldon, Jack. The German Army on the Somme 1914–1916, published in 2005 by Pen and Sword Books Ltd, Barnsley, South Yorkshire.

Shore, C. With British Snipers to the Reich published in 1997 by Greenhill Books, London.

Westerman, Percy. F. The Dispatch-Riders, First Published in 1915 by Blackie and Son Ltd.

Paperback Michael Terence Publishing 2010.

Trench orders – official Government Document, War Office, published by Memorabilia Pack Co Forth St, Edinborough.

Museums

A number of museums have provided valuable information. These include:

The Great War Museum, located at the Cloth Hall, Ypres, Belgium

The Imperial War Museum, London

The Military Museum, Aldershot

The National Museum of Scotland, for their photo of the soldiers in winter (Chapter 4)

The Passchendaele Military Museum and trench display

The Royal Engineers Museum, Kent

The Staffordshire Military Museum, Lichfield

The Tank Museum, Bovington Camp, Dorset

The Thackray Medical Museum, East Leeds

The Wardrobe Military Museum, Salisbury, Wiltshire

The Winchester Military Museum

<u>Libraries and achives</u>

The staff and archivists at a number of libraries and archives throughout the country have been most helpful:

Ashdown Forest Information Centre

East Grinstead Library

Forest Row Library, East Sussex

Kent History and Library Centre

Lewes Library Sussex, Archivist Hayden

The British Press Archives

The 'Keep' West Sussex Library

The National Archives, Kew

The Swindon Archives, Chippenham, Wiltshire

Wrotham Library, Kent

The QR bar code links to a brief video with "The Last Post" which is a tribute to the Wiltshire soldiers who died and whose bodies were never identified. These names appear on the Menin Gate War Memorial at Ypres.

The following pages are a typed list showing the Wiltshire names and badges as they appear on the memorial. This is my tribute to these brave men.

The colour photo of an unknown grave with the famous war poem
"For the fallen" – written by Laurence Binyon

THIS IS A LIST OF PRIVATES AND NCO'S OF THE
WILTSHIRE REGIMENTS WHO APPEAR ON THE
WALLS OF THE MENIN GATE WAR MONUMENT AT
YPRES. IT'S MY SMALL TRIBUTE TO THESE BRAVE
MEN. THEY APPEAR IN ALPHABETICAL ORDER.

ADLAM.A

ALDER.AE

ANDREWS. AE

ANGELL.PH

ARCHER. RF

ASHFORD .W

ATKIN.JT

BAIGENT.A

BAKER.H

BARDEN.HL

BARNES.GWDCM

BARNFIELD.GH

BARRADELL.A

BEAVAN.H

BERRY.W

BIGWOOD.J

BLAKE.B

BLUNSDON.FA

BOULTER.A

BRAIN.WT

BREWER.WA

BRIDGEMAN.M

BROOKFIELD.B

BROWN.G

BROWN.J

BRYANT.HT

BULL.F

BULL.WC

BURGESS.J

BURNES.WJ

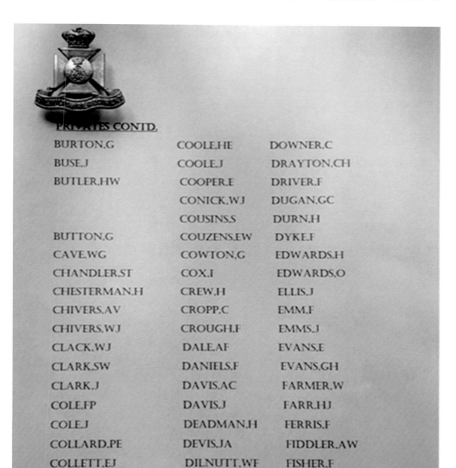

PRIVATES CONTD.

BURTON,G	COOLE,HE	DOWNER,C
BUSE,J	COOLE,J	DRAYTON,CH
BUTLER,HW	COOPER,E	DRIVER,F
	CONICK,WJ	DUGAN,GC
	COUSINS,S	DURN,H
BUTTON,G	COUZENS,EW	DYKE,F
CAVE,WG	COWTON,G	EDWARDS,H
CHANDLER,ST	COX,I	EDWARDS,O
CHESTERMAN,H	CREW,H	ELLIS,J
CHIVERS,AV	CROPP,C	EMM,F
CHIVERS,WJ	CROUGH,F	EMMS,J
CLACK,WJ	DALE,AF	EVANS,E
CLARK,SW	DANIELS,F	EVANS,GH
CLARK,J	DAVIS,AC	FARMER,W
COLE,FP	DAVIS,J	FARR,HJ
COLE,J	DEADMAN,H	FERRIS,F
COLLARD,PE	DEVIS,JA	FIDDLER,AW
COLLETT,EJ	DILNUTT,WF	FISHER,F
COOK,JT	DIMMER,RG	FISHER,HL
COOK,WJ	DOUGHTY,W	FISHER,WJ
COOKSEY,CF	DOWLING,A	FITZGERALD,AW

PRIVATES CONT'D

FORD.J

FREEBURY.E	GREGORY.J	HEWETT.J
FULLWELL.L	GRIMSLEY.WC	HIGGINS.WJ
FURNELL.G	GUEST.EG	HILLIER.J
GARNETT.J	GWILLIM.A	HILLS.L
GAY.JW	HALL.E	HISCOCKS.SA
GIBB.AJ	HALL.H	HOBBS.R
GIFFORD.G	HALL.W	HOCKIN.GH
GIPSON.J	HALL.WH	HOLLIDAY.J
GIRLING.HA	HAND.AJ	HOLLMAN.JW
GOODWIN.WF	HARFORD.WHC	HORTON.H
GOLDSMITH .CF	HARRIS.HW	HOWARD.J
GOOD.H	HARRIS.R	HUDD.A
GOODFIELD.AE	HAWKINS.C	HUNT.J
GOUGH.FG	HEAVANS.AE	ILSTON.EV
GOULDEN.F	HEAVANS.F	JEFFCUTT.S
GREEN.W	HEDGES.CA	JEFFRIES.WH
GREENMAN.FA	HEDGES.H	JENKINS.T
GREENMAN.WM	HEDGES.T	JOHNSON.JS
GREENWOOD.L	HENDERSON.G	JOLIFFE.F

JONES,CL	LEIGHFIELD,IJ	MINSULL,AE
JONES,GW	LEWIS,JH	MINTRAM,AG
JONES,HT	LIDDEN,W	MITCHELL,JE
JUDD,P	LLYOD,A	MOON,AG
KEEL,EA	LONG,T	MOORES,EH
KIMBERLEY,GF	LONGHURST,AA	MORBY,J
KING,CF	MCKAY,HD	MOULAND,W
KING,E	MACKINDON,GW	NASON,W
KIRBY,S	MCKLEANE,J	NEWMAN,F
KNIGHT,AJM	MAILL,AW	NEWTON,SI
KNORR,HF	MANLEY,H	NICKOLSON,W
LANDFEAR,WJ	MARGETT,AJ	OXFORD,BI
LANE,EF	MARKS,FH	PACKER,J
LANG,C	MARSH,H	PAGET,EJ
LANGFORD,L	MARSH,R	PARSON,A
LATHAM,W	MARSHALL,WC	PAYNE,EW
LAWRENCE,LE	MARSHALL,WG	PEARCE,AF
LEAK,ER	MATTHEW,RJ	PEARCE,HG
LEARNER,CL	MATTHEWS,SW	PEDLY,T
LEGG,SH	MEAD,H	PENNY,HW

PERRY,J	ROGERS,A	SMITH,WH
PETT,NM	ROGERS,HC	SNOOK,H
PIKE,C	ROSE,HJ	SPACKMAN,P
PIKE,W	ROSE,R	STEPHENS,F
PLEDGER,H	ROWDEN,SC	STEWART,EG
POTTER,F	ROWLAND,W	STINCHCOMBE,A
POUND,AE	RUSH,RH	STOCK,WT
POUND,J	SCAMMELL,W	STOKES,WF
PRATLEY,R	SEAGER,H	STOODLEY,A
PREWETT,C	SELLICK,JA	STRONG,FWC
PRICE,J	SHARPS,C	STROUD,S
PRINGLE,F	SHERWOOD,T	SULLIVAN,JP
PROVIS,N	SHINER,EF	SWANBOROUGH,
PRYOR,IW	SILVERWOOD,T	TABB,WV
RANDALL,W	SLYFIELD,J	TALBOT,HW
READ,F	SMART,P	TAYLOR,FS
RENYARD,W	SMITH,HJ	THICK,F
RICKETTS,AJ	SMITH,J(6035)	THOMAS,AE
RIVERS,W	SMITH,J	THOMAS,SW
ROBINSON,A	SMITH,WH(1983)	TOMLIN,T

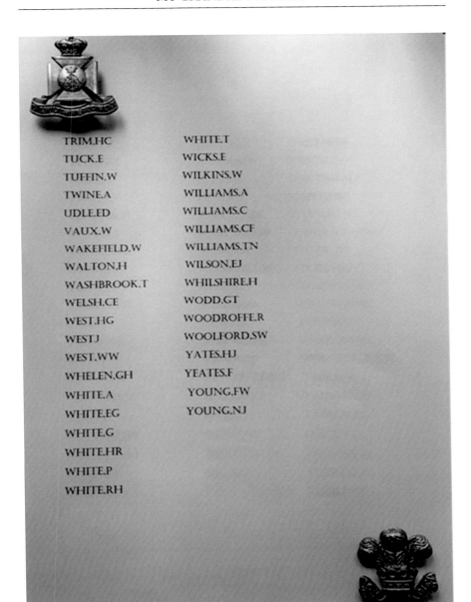

TRIM.HC · WHITE.T
TUCK.E · WICKS.E
TUFFIN.W · WILKINS.W
TWINE.A · WILLIAMS.A
UDLE.ED · WILLIAMS.C
VAUX.W · WILLIAMS.CF
WAKEFIELD.W · WILLIAMS.TN
WALTON.H · WILSON.EJ
WASHBROOK.T · WHILSHIRE.H
WELSH.CE · WODD.GT
WEST.HG · WOODROFFE.R
WEST.J · WOOLFORD.SW
WEST.WW · YATES.HJ
WHELEN.GH · YEATES.F
WHITE.A · YOUNG.FW
WHITE.EG · YOUNG.NJ
WHITE.G
WHITE.HR
WHITE.P
WHITE.RH

NCO'S

CAPT CARTER.CGM

CAPT HARVEY.EG

CAPT MAGOR.AC

CAPT VINER-JOHNSON.PJV

.   .   .   .

LANCE CORP AINSWORTH.TR   LANCE CP HAYWOOD.A

LANCE CORP ALLSOP.JH   LANCE CP HILLIER.A

LANCE CORP AUSTIN.F   LANCE CP HOLDER.W

LANCE CORP BALL.G   LANCE CP JEHAN.W

LANCE CORP BARTHOLOMEW.HG LANCE CP JOYCE.WE

LANCE CORP BERRETT.AJ   LANCE CP KENT.WA

LANCE CORP CLARKE.H   LANCE CP LANGFORD.

LANCE CORP COHEN.J   LANCE CP LAW.JWA

LANCE CORP DAVIDEE.EJ   LANCE CP LEGGETT.EG

LANCE CORP FACKRELL.FJ   LANCE CP LEGGETT.WS

LANCE CORP GAY.WCF   LANCE CP LEWER.ET

LANCE CORP GRAINGER.CEG   LANCE CP MAPLE.J

LANCE CORP HALL.WH   LANCE CP MATTHEWS.

LANCE CORP HARPER.RDT   LANCE CP PALMER.C

LANCE CORP HAYES.AC   LANCE CP PEITZ.FJ

LANCE CORP'S CONTD

LANCE CORP ROWE.PW	LT EMANUEL.O
LANCE CORP SEDGWICK.O	LT KING.NGB
LANCE CORP SHEPPARD.RHP	LT SPENCER.F
LANCE CORP SMITH.PG	2ND LT BURGESS.ELAH
LANCE CORP STOCKHAM.WJ	2ND LT CAIN.EW
LANCE CORP SUMMERS.M	2ND LT CAMBELL.WP
LANCE CORP SUTTON.WM M	2 ND LT CHANDLER.C
LANCE CORP TURNER.HH	2ND LT MC CLENACHAN.A
LANCE CORP WHALE.A	2 ND LT MCLEAN.AN
LANCE CORP WHILTSHIRE.J	2 ND LT WOOD.J
LANCE CORP YEATES.L	

. . . .

COMPANY SGT MAJOR ARTER.BC

COMPANY SGT MAJOR GOULDING.AJ

. . . .

SGT BLENCOWE	SGT KEELEY.FC
SGT GULLEY.PS	SGT MILES.E
SGT HURST.C	SGT MORRIS.FW

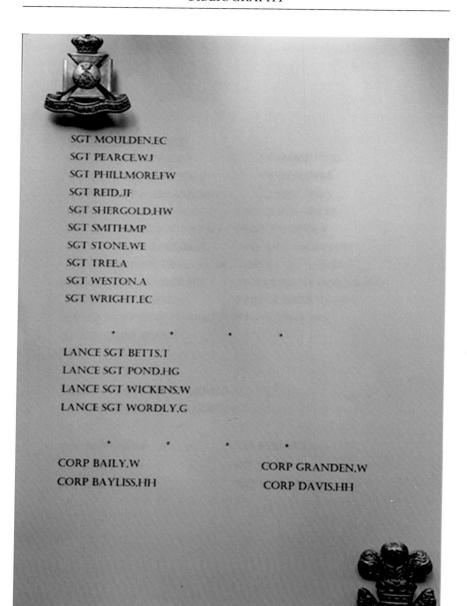

SGT MOULDEN,EC
SGT PEARCE,WJ
SGT PHILLMORE,FW
SGT REID,JF
SGT SHERGOLD,HW
SGT SMITH,MP
SGT STONE,WE
SGT TREE,A
SGT WESTON,A
SGT WRIGHT,EC

LANCE SGT BETTS,T
LANCE SGT POND,HG
LANCE SGT WICKENS,W
LANCE SGT WORDLY,G

CORP BAILY,W   CORP GRANDEN,W
CORP BAYLISS,HH   CORP DAVIS,HH

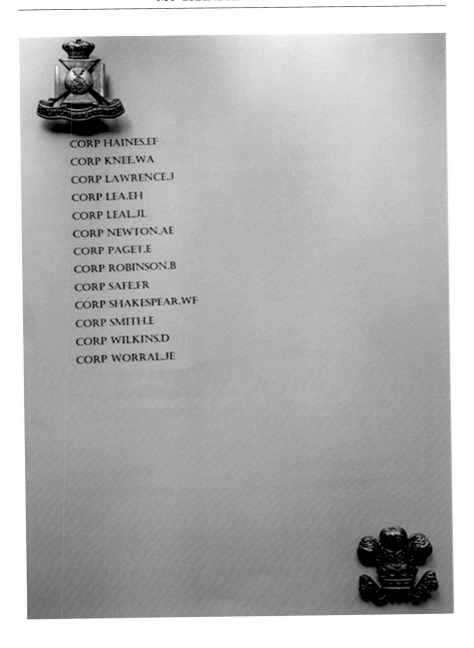

CORP HAINES.EF
CORP KNEE.WA
CORP LAWRENCE.J
CORP LEA.EH
CORP LEAL.JL
CORP NEWTON.AE
CORP PAGET.E
CORP ROBINSON.B
CORP SAFE.FR
CORP SHAKESPEAR.WF
CORP SMITH.E
CORP WILKINS.D
CORP WORRAL.JE

For the fallen – written by Laurence Binyon

They shall not grow old, as we that are left grow old; Age shall not weary them, nor years condemn. At the going down of the sun and in the morning we will remember them.